Longitudinally Speaking: The Best of *Drishti*

About the Editor

Dr. Vinayshil Gautam is an internationally acclaimed management expert, consultant and trainer. He has been a past President of ARTDO International and has been conferred the Honorary Fellowship and International Management and HRD Award (individual category) of this federating organisation.

An institution builder, Dr. Gautam's career has several firsts including : First Head, Management Department, IIT Delhi; First Director, IIM Kozhikode; First Chairman, D.K. International Foundation; First Coordinator, Entrepreneurship Program, First Dalmia Chair Professor, First Coordinator, Research Program on Management in Asia, First A Al_Sagar Chair Professor, First A Al_Sagar Emeritus Chair Professor all at IITD. He has also been the First Editor of *Drishti*.

He has represented India in activities of UNESCO, Asian Productivity Organization and in international bodies such as International Union of Anthropological and Ethnological Sciences etc. He has contributed to Management interventions in Germany, UAE, Saudi Arabia, Malaysia, Singapore and some of the major corporates of India. Besides, being a member of various significant policy level committees of Government of India, Dr. Gautam has served on the Board of various National and International Organizations.

He is the recipient of several honors for his accomplishments which include Fellowship of the Association of Business Executives, UK; All India Management Association, Indian Society for Training & Development, India; G-56 Millennium Award; Hall of Honor Award; Dewang Mehta Life Time Achievement Award. He was awarded a medallion on the completion of 400 years of Merida City of Venezuela. He has addressed a host of International audiences from Merida to Tokyo and Montréal to Melbourne.

A celebrated author himself, he is widely published with many recognitions being bestowed upon him for his writings. Dr. Gautam's contributions to Organization Management, Human Resource Management and Strategy Management have often been quoted and used.

Longitudinally Speaking:

The Best of *Drishti*

A Project of

ARTDO
International

(in collaboration with)

Bahrain Society for
Training and Development
Sponsor

विद्ययाऽमृतमश्नुते
DK International
Foundation

Editor
Vinayshil Gautam, PhD; FRAS (London)

CONCEPT PUBLISHING COMPANY PVT. LTD.
NEW DELHI-110059

ISBN-13: 978-81-8069-983-2

First Published 2013.

Published and Printed by

Concept
Since 1974

Concept Publishing Company Pvt. Ltd.
A/15-16, Commercial Block, Mohan Garden
New Delhi-110059 (India)
T: 25351460, 25351794, *F*: 091-11-25357109
E: publishing@conceptpub.com, W: www.conceptpub.com
Editorial Office: H-13, Bali Nagar, New Delhi-110 015, India.

Cataloging in Publication Data--Courtesy: D.K. Agencies (P) Ltd. <docinfo@dkagencies.com>

Longitudinally speaking : the best of Drishti / editor, Vinayshil Gautam.
p. cm.
Contributed articles.
Includes bibliographical references and index.
ISBN 9788180699832

1. Personnel management. 2. Executives—Training of. 3. Leadership. 4. Human capital. I. Gautam, Vinayshil.

DDC 658.3 23

Preface

21st century has, widely, raised expectations of being an Asian Century. There are good reasons for it, in terms of economic growth, development and otherwise. That is an important matter, but so far as this book is concerned, it is only a contributory feature.

The bald truth is that Asian thought has been in the vanguard of human evolution through millennia. Be it Krishna, Confucius, Buddha Christ, Mohammad or some seer or sage, there are Asian names for which many feel, almost instinctively, reverential. They signify a high evolution of thought and have led a following which subsequently became global. Almost all major religions of the world have originated in Asia.

In terms of civilization, the Arab, the Indian, the Chinese, the Japanese worlds, just to name a few, have held out tremendous intellectual sophistication. Their arts and crafts not to overlook their civilizational refinement are in many ways, still unsurpassed. It is, therefore, natural that there be an 'Asian point of view'.

ARTDO International represents this in the best meaning of the term with utmost respect to thought processes which were born and developed in other parts of the world. In short, ARTDO International is a global federating organization from an Asian perspective. There is a case and space for such institutions.

Early years of ARTDO and its growth years have had one continuing theme. Conferences are important, training efforts are significant. However, in the ultimate analysis it is the contribution to the world of knowledge and in effort to push the boundaries of learning that lies the more enduring contribution. Interestingly, there is belief that to understand, and see global concerns from an Asian perspective, does not have the prerequisite of being an Asian.

Indeed "Asia" and "Asiatic" is a frame of mind. Indeed the concept of 'Orientalism' or 'Asian' gained much clarity to the Western mind from the works of some of their own ilk such as Max Mueller (a German) or George Grierson (a Briton), to name just two of the many.

The Silver Jubilee Convention held in 1998 in Delhi was a watershed in the growth of Asian Region Training & Development Organization as, it was then known. For Asian Region Training and Development Organisation to reinvent itself as ARTDO International meant moving on from a regional frame of reference into a global one. Australia and New Zealand, not to overlook Europe and America, African and the Latin American continents were all to be simultaneously incorporated into the postulated frame, with moorings that had an Asian origin.

Collaboration and cooperation was to be the touchstone and not competitiveness. Religion was recognized as predominantly a matter of personal faith and spirituality was to be the algorithm of collective dealings, emphasizing the ethical frame. Feminity was to have its inexplicable and effective identity with its uniqueness and resilience. All stages of life cycle were to be respected with recognized spaces for contribution. Fetish of youth was not to overtake all thinking. Age and aging got its due, just as much as the youth and the young were to be nurtured. Family as a concept was to move to the centre of the stage and even corporate could look at life long relationships. Governance was for common good and not just aggressive expansion of its various boundaries of influence. Even finance and assets could be seen with a certain Asian perspective. In all things, accumulation and physical indulgence was to be seen in suitable proportion.

At the end of the day who knows all this itself would gradually move forward incorporating elements of other perspectives to make this planet a happier place ! Intellectual engagement is the mother of all things new and in many cases the best preparation for the future. The Asian perspective is known to be a dynamic one.

It is a historical truth of life that many cradles of civilization of this planet have their hoary beginning in the river valleies of Yangtze, Ganga, Tigris, Euphrates, Nile and more. It may be a reality for the future, to account for.

Longitudinal thinking can cause a selection process where the banal component of heritage is eliminated, the positive component is preserved. On this grafting of the new on the old, a live process begets better coping mechanisms for challenges of time, territory and temperament..

It is the merging of the living heritage with the emerging principles, including technology, that could assist the organic socio-economic welding of the globe. The world does not shrink on its own!

The selection contained in volume is from the periodic publication called *Drishti* which was initiated in 2002 as representing the thoughts outlined above.

As the list of contributors show, people from different parts of the world and widely varying professions pooled their talent and effort to present well researched and documented set of texts. They are often focused on concerns which the present and the future generation must address. They come from Asia Pacific Region, South East Asia, South Asia, West Asia, Europe, America and from a good cross-section of the English speaking world.

As a celebration of the 40th Annual World Conference of ARTDO International appropriately, positioned in Melbourne, this book is a tribute to the spirit of seeking, knowing and attempting to arrive.

The papers contained, herein, do not need a testimony or a critique. They do not even need a summary. They speak for themselves.

You are invited to savor them. The future may already be knocking.

New Delhi **Vinayshil Gautam**
Feb. 15, 2013

Acknowledgements

Any effort of the order of this book stands in debt of a large number of institutions and individual. The first name which comes to my mind is of Dato Dr. Thomas Chee Khy Huat, President Emeritus of ARTDO International. A leader *par excellence* he nurtured ARTDO International in days when it was passing through a lean phase, some decades ago. His efforts saw fruition in many ways and one of them was in the institutionalization of publications.

This particular celebratory project 'Longitudinally Thinking: The Best of *Drishti'* has been sponsored by Bahrain Society for Training & Development. The name of Mr. Mohamed Mahmood and Mr. Isa Abdullah Bu-Ali, President and Vice President respectively of BSTD are acknowledged with appreciation, in this regard

Typically Dr. Dipti Tripathi, Secretary General, DK International Foundation, continued to do what DKIF always does, for *Drishti,* namely, amongst other things, looking after the professional logistics, provide editorial support, and find ways of meeting, the gap of resources in bringing out such a number, as and when they occur. This support is appreciated.

The grateful acknowledgement are due to the contributions of Dr. Lyndon Jones of U.K. Mr. Les Pickett is always been available for all items of demand whether logical or illogical !

The grateful appreciation is due to Bernie Ople, Secretary General of ARTDO International who in many ways symbolizes the continuity of the institution in a statesmanly manner. Datin Eleen Cheong, President, Malaysian Society for Training and Development has always helped out, often without even being seen. Cordial complements are due Ms. Jeanne Marshall and Ms. Elizabeth Robinson, President and CEO respectively of Australian Institute of Training and Development.

The authors, the publishers and distributors of this effort, embedded as they are in the context in which the effort is released, are worthy of praise for their selfless team work

To all and to everyone, thank you for helping out in this unique continuing publishing venture, perhaps futuristically, called *Drishti* (Insight).

Contents

Preface v

Acknowledgements ix

Contributors xv

1. Leaping Forward with Cutting Edge Practices 1
   Sora-at Klinpratoom

2. Selecting Performance Improvement Interventions That Produce Results 5
   Arthur Luis P. Florentin

3. Running to Catch Up... Or...Collaborating to Triumph: The Action Power Consulting Model 13
   Graham Arnold and *Rod Oxenberry*

4. Competitiveness from a Different Perspective and Implications for Business Strategic Planning 39
   Kriengsak Chareonwongsak

5. Transforming Institutional Knowledge into Organizational Effectiveness: The Challenges of Becoming a Learning Organization 53
   Crispin Garden-Webster

6. The Impact of Training on the Economic Development of Mauritius 62
   R. Dubois

7. Leadership in Knowledge Management Domain 75
Rosclina A. Saufi

8. Human Capital: Its Valuation and Management 83
Lyndon Jones

9. Uncertainty, Work and the Individual 94
Gillian Stamp

10. Building a Bridge between Academia, Industry and Graduates of the Future 102
Said Irandoust

11. Applied Longitudinal Thinking: An Exploration 117
Meenakshi Khemka and *Vinayshil Gautam*

12. Psychological Types and Trainer Styles 127
John Cullen

13. Leadership and Change Management 135
Annabel Beerel

14. Adopting Competition Policy in Appointments for Top Management Positions in Government Bodies in the Republic of Yemen Pilot Experiment at the Ministry of Civil Service 155
Nabil Shamsan

15. Addressing Tomorrow's Need of Human Capital Competency Based Continuing Education for the Knowledge Society 174
Bambang Supriyanto and *Anton S. Wahjosoedibjo*

16. Upgrading Small and Medium-Sized Enterprises (SMEs) in the GCC Region 184
Rudy Yaksick

17. Strategies of Establishing E-learning System for Public Sector: A Case of Regional Civil Service Development Institute, Central Personnel Administration, Executive Yuan, Taiwan — 204
Chen Chung-Chih

18. Managing Talent in a Borderless World: Challenges and Opportunities — 214
Tanvi Gautam

19. Strategic Human Resource Development: An Empirical Study in Taiwan — 226
Irving Yi-Feng Huang

20. Global and Cultural Human Resources Management — 235
Michael A. Potter

21. The Political Economy of Human Capital Outflow: A Case Study of Malaysia — 244
Toh Kin Woon

Annexures

1. Annual ARTDO International Conferences and their theme — 258
2. Name of Presidents of ARTDO International and photographs from ARTDO International; Bahrain Society for Training and Development — 261
3. A Brief on ARTDO International — 264

Index — 268

Contributors*

Sora-at Klinpratoom, Minister of Labour, Government Thailand, Bangkok, Thailand.

Arthur Luis P. Florentin, Assistant Vice President and Head, Human Resources Development, MERALCO, Philippines.

Graham Arnold, West Beach, South Australia, Australia.

Kriengsak Chareonwongsak, President, Social Science Association of Thailand, and Member of Parliament, Bangkok,Thailand.

Saufi Rosclina, Associate Professor, University of Malaysia, Sabah, Malaysia.

Garden-Webster Crispin, Asian Development Bank, Manila, Philippines.

Dubois R, International Labour Organisation, Delhi, India.

Jones Lyndon, Former President, Association of Business Executives, London, U.K.

Gillain Stamp, Brunel Institute of Organization and Social Studies, University of West Brunel, London, U.K.

Said Irandoust, President, Asian Institute of Technology, Bangkok, Thailand.

Meenakshi Khemka, Senior Lecturer, Globsyn Business School, Kolkata, India.

Vinayshil Gautam, A Al-sagar Chair Professor, Department of Management Studies, IIT, Delhi, India.

John Cullen, President, International Association for Managerial and Organizational Psychosynthesis, California U.S.A.; Gulf Institute of Management, Abu Dhabi, United Arab Emirates.

Annabel Beerel, Christos and Mary Papoutsy Distinguished Chair in Ethics; Southern New Hampshire University, Manchester, U.S.A.

---

*designations, as at the time of initial contribution.

Nabil Shamsan, Vice-Minister, Ministry of Civil Service, Yemen.

Bambang Supriyanto, Human Resource Professional Program Advisor, Majaya University, Indonesia.

Anton S. Wahjosoedibjo, Faculty of Law, Majaya University, Indonesia.

Rudy Yaksick, Founding Partner, Concord Capital Partner, LLC, Concord, Massachusetts, USA.

Chen Chung-Chih, General-Director, Regional Civil Service Development Institute, Taiwan, China.

Tanvi Gautam, Researcher, Virginia Commonwealth University, Virginia, USA.

Irving Yi-Feng Huang, Associate Professor and Head, Department of Public Administration, Tamkang University; Secretary General, Chinese Society for Training and Development, Taiwan, China

Michael A. Potter, CEO, MPA Consulting Ltd. And Michael A. Potter International, Manchester, UK.

Toh Kin Woon, Former State Executive Councilor for Education, Economic Planning, Human Resource Development, Science, Technology and Innovation, Penang, Malaysia.

1

Leaping Forward with Cutting Edge Practices

Sora-at Klinpratoom

Thailand has come a long way since the Asian Financial Crisis in 1997, which affected the whole ASEAN region. The crisis has highlighted the importance of sound financial management, good governance and sensible leadership.

Leadership is about having the courage to make tough decisions and have a willingness to accept responsibility for the actions taken. Leadership is about anticipating the future. The leaders need to anticipate possible scenarios and events shaping the future. Their decisions eventually shape the destiny of country.

The leaders are also human and are not absolutely perfect. History is full of examples of great leaders who were great for a moment and fell from grace the next moment. More importantly, great leaders are also fast learners who can bounce back quickly from the mistakes made. Nevertheless, mistakes give experiences and wisdom. However, in today's fast changing and competitive environment, leaders are not given many chances to make mistakes. They are sitting in the hot seat. Their decisions may make them a hero or a villain. For that, history will always be the final judge.

Effective leaders usually come with a proven track record in making sound decisions that brought about significant benefits. But where can we find such effective leaders? Are leaders born or can they be groom? Instead of giving you the answer, I am sure the conference will provide a great platform for the speakers and participants to enlighten the delegates on the finer points.

The third Millennium has only started and new scientific and technological knowledge are now challenging our conventional wisdom. Most assumptions we once hold true are no longer fit the reality at the present. Increasingly for nations, corporations and individuals alike, the ability to compete in a world where barriers are falling will make the difference between survival and extinction.

According to a management expert, Peter Drucker, the reason such changes are taking place is attributed to the coming of knowledge society along with the knowledge workers. This has resulted in a knowledge-based economy. This new concept of KBE has imposed its own set of rules and regulations, hence changing the economic landscape and the manner of competition. With Internet access, market information that links potential buyers with potential sellers becomes readily available. And vice-versa, the world has now become borderless.

With the dawn of a borderless world, driven by technological advances, there is an urgent need to position our countries and our corporations strategically. I the continuously and fast changing world we are living in., new leadership with new strategies is required. Leaders who can inspire people to achieve greatness are essential. New methodologies and tools in human performance are needed to enhance the human capital in the workplace. We need to facilitate a closer alignment with technology and processes.

An American historian, James MacGregor Burns, has differentiated between transactional and transformational leaders. According to Burns, good managers are transactional leaders. However, the true great leaders are those who raised inspiring visions before their people that produced bold and transformational change. Through such leaders, they are able to transform their countries and organizations to compete with the best on a global basis. The world is changing and leadership is no exception.

Leadership is critical and plays an active role in providing vision, mission and direction for others to follow. The old heroes have come and gone. The new ones are taking their places. What has worked in the past may not work in today's environment. With globalization, businesses are required to operate in many different cultural settings, with each culture possessing different value and belief system. Leaders have to deal with such diversities of culture and adopt different strategies to arrange the businesses towards the uncharted territories.

The paradox of staying with the tried and proven may no longer proved to be relevant in today's context.

Therefore, the scientific management theory proposed by Frederick Taylor, which was popular during the industrial era is fast becoming obsolete. The premise that workers are mere instruments to the production process no longer holds true: that theory was premised on a stable operating environment. Under such conditions, a high degree of certainty and autocratic style of leadership was appropriately adopted; one which dehumanizes the workforce.

So what type of leaders are we talking about now? What are the characteristics of today's leaders? What kind of strategies is required to make countries more effective and to compete against others with low cost productions, like China or India? Is there a different leadership style for different situations?

Questions like these are needed to fire up the mind, and to stir the imagination of leaders-those who are responsible to develop strategies and improve human performance.

So what would make a good leader?

In today's competitive world, leaders must possess strategic capacity. Strategic leadership is anticipating the future. They learn all the possibilities. And it is the determination to shape events, rather than allowing events to shape the country or the corporation.

Nowadays, leaders can no longer run things through a top-down approach. A good leader needs the confidence and trust of his or her followers. Power sharing and participative leadership is more commonplace of today's leadership style.

Good leaders have the ability to foresee the trends. They possess a strong intuition of what is happening around them. They are able to see the big picture as well the small picture. They are able to identify factors that will sustain the competitive advantages and devise strategies to match with the situation. More importantly, they are able to implement and execute the strategies developed.

Gary Hamel, a business strategist and an author of "Leading the Revolution", remarked that there is a need for organizations to develop their "internal capabilities" towards finding their own solutions to the new challenges faced. Towards this end, it is important that leaders look within their own organization to develop their internal capabilities in generating new perspectives, new strategies to meet with the new challenges.

Towards this end, the concept of learning organizations, made popular by Peter Seng, requires leaders to engage the collective learning of its people in generative learning that can transform the way corporations operate and cope with changes in the environment.

In a highly competitive environment, learning organizations will seek to capitalize on the available knowledge and convert it to actionable knowledge to increase productivity and effectiveness of its human capital. Governments and corporations must seek out the best minds and talents to provide them with cutting edge practices.

Leadership is a critical factor in today's business. Right strategy without right leadership is not enough and vice-versa. However, right leadership with right strategy can inspire greatness in others and bring real success to their organizations. Great things happen when leaders are able to inspire their people to work together towards achieving the organization's vision and mission. Great leaders draw out the potential that exists within their people. They get their people to work, think and act collectively to achieve high performance and real progress.

2

Selecting Performance Improvement Interventions That Produce Results

Arthur Luis P. Florentin

Selecting performance improvement interventions can be a very tricky business. The tendency is to select interventions that one is already familiar with. On the other hand, how can we select an intervention that we are not yet familiar with? And so, this is quite similar to the proverbial carpenter with a hammer in hand. Every problem he sees is a nail that needs to be hammered down.

Even if we hire consultants, the tendency will be for the consultant to recommend their specialization as the intervention. It is not that this happens all the time but there will be a greater possibility for a Training Specialist to recommend learning interventions, an OD Specialist to recommend Organization Development or a Compensation Specialist to recommend reward and recognition interventions to improve performance.

Perhaps, what will facilitate selection of appropriate interventions is an exposure to a wide range of interventions that will serve as a toolbox from where the Human Performance Improvement practitioner can select. A look can be taken at the broad range of performance improvement interventions that can be used in conjunction with HPI and then be able to systematically select the most appropriate to specific situations.

One can refer to ASTD's HPI Model (Rothwell, p. 7) and a reference can be made to the Cause Analysis and Intervention Selection. To be able to systematically select the appropriate intervention, there is a need to link it with the root causes that have already been determined.

There is a whole universe of performance improvement interventions. Many of them care known. It is also possible to customize or develop hybrids of the existing interventions to suit the specific performance improvement needs of an organization. It is even possible for you to adapt specific actions or combinations of actions to design your own intervention. But my objective at the moment is to systematically select the most appropriate one that will surely produce results.

According to Robinson and Robinson in their book "Performance Consulting: Moving Beyond Training", 5 to 10% of your workforce are exemplary performers and their practices, which are not being practiced by the typical performers can be the source of performance improvement. Just imagine for example that you have an organization of 100 sales personnel. Performance being variable, their sales figures will definitely vary. But we will observe that around 5 to 10 of them will be delivering sales significantly higher than the others. They are the exemplary performers. Just for the sake of discussion, imagine that these exemplary performers are hitting sales beyond a million Baht, while the others are averaging only 800,000 Baht, then the potential value of improving performance will be the difference times the total number of typical performers. For an organization of 100 sales personnel, the value can be estimated at 18 million, which the product of the difference in sales of the exemplary performers and the typical performers, 200,000 Baht and the total number of typical performers, 90.

Given this example, performance improvement is increasing the performance of the typical performers to the level of the level of the exemplary performers. Studying the practices of both the exemplary and typical performers, we will realize some differences in practices. The question is, what caused the difference. At this point we hypothesize on the possible causes. But if we want to be able to select the performance improvement interventions that will produce results, we also need to validate through data our hypotheses to determine the true root causes. Then, we focus our attention to addressing them.

As we search for interventions that will address the root causes we have already determined, how do we ensure that we do not fall into the trap of the proverbial carpenter with a hammer in hand? I would like to present a framework of factors that influence performance in the workplace. I simplified it into three major factors, policies, processes and people. As illustrated in this framework, the more that we align policies, processes and people to each other, the greater will be the area of intersection, which represents performance.

For simplicity and to aid recall, notice that the factors all start with P's, I labeled the first group of factors as "Policies". But what I included here are all documentations that can govern performance in the workplace such as policies, guidelines, procedures, work instructions, standards and all other important expectations.

The second group of factors is labeled "Processes" and includes the methods and procedures, technology, and materials, equipment and facilities used.

The last group is labeled "People" and this includes organizational structures, culture, leadership and the competencies and attitudes of the workers themselves.

POLICIES

Making use of this framework, we start with "Policies". Standardization and consistency are hallmarks of quality. Without these we cannot ensure quality will always be within acceptable level. The first step to performance improvement therefore is to check if performance is standardized and consistently delivered by articulating and documenting the necessary policies, guidelines, procedures, work instructions, and standards. Even with a good process, if it is not documented and disseminated, there will be a tendency for people to make do with what they are not aware of. If performance is not properly governed by appropriate documentations, then the immediate intervention is simply to document the relevant policies and guidelines.

Notice that in the table shown, two types of interventions, are recommended, the immediate and the long term. If the performance gap or deficiency is an isolated case pertaining only to a specific process or part of a process, then simply documenting that part will suffice. However, if the problem is systemic and recurring, then a more long term intervention will be to introduce a Quality Management System such as ISO 9001, which will ensure that the organization focuses on its Quality Policy and has a system of documentations that will govern its business process towards the attainment of said Quality Policy. The system also ensures that the documented process are adhered to and systematically updated towards continual process improvement.

Another area for performance improvement is making expectations known to the performers. Not all organizations have written objectives. Not all companies with written objectives have published their objectives to all concerned. An opportunity for performance improvement is having written objectives that are properly aligned at various organizational levels cascaded throughout the organization. One approach is the Balanced Score Card which provides a framework for balancing performance of key interdependent variables by looking at the organization's financial results, customer satisfaction, operational efficiency and learning and growth aspects. This may entail major review of key result areas and therefore I consider this as one of the long-term interventions.

On the other hand, it is possible there is only a need to consciously discuss performance expectations and commitments between levels. In our company, we have what we call the Covenant Signing which consists of the process of informing direct reports of current directions and requiring them to commit to objectives that will support those directions. The Covenant Signing also involves a ritual that makes performers more aware of performance expectations and commitments.

Management by Objectives is already an old approach but is still handy in harnessing the power of Goal Setting Theory by clarifying objectives, setting them at sufficiently challenging levels and establishing ownership by involving the participation of the performers.

PROCESSES

From "Policies", we now go to "Processes". It is possible that some parts of the processes need enhancements. For isolated problems it may only need specific Corrective Actions. But it is also possible to institutionalize continual improvement by involving the performers themselves to identify areas for improvement and recommend the necessary improvements. This can be done through Quality Control Circles. There is no better way than to allow and empower those performing work to improve the way they are doing it. People are dynamic and they will also find better ways of doing things.

Although processes may already have been "perfectly" streamlined, our environment is in continuous flux such that sooner or later, there will be new technologies or major innovations that can dramatically enhance our operations. If the technology is not a major one then there is simply the need to introduce the technology. But if it will entail major changes and if it cuts through several processes, then the Business Process Reengineering approach will be more appropriate.

There will be occasions when the process output is highly variable such that some of the times quality is met but at other times unmet. For example, with respect to processing time, experience show us that sometimes we are able to meet the standard processing time while at other instances we go beyond the acceptable period. Or, for example, our products at times have no defects but at other times they sustain unacceptable defects. Then our process outputs are considered highly variable. By discovering the factors that influence such variability and controlling them, we improve performance to the level that output will always meet established quality levels. This approach is the Six Sigma approach.

Another opportunity for performance improvement within the "Processes" factor is the quality of materials used. For certain processes, the quality of materials, even the equipment and facilities used, can significantly affect the quality of our output. In this case the specifying the characteristics, or even to the point of specifying the brand and/or the supplier, will ensure performance improvement through consistency. For a long-term intervention, the Materials Requirement Planning will come in handy.

Ready access to information also facilitates process implementation. Job Aids such as templates, correctly filled forms, checklists, worksheets, photo diagrams, task lists, and conversation tables immensely reduce man-hours by providing guides to implementation (Piskurich, pp.78-79, 178-179). On a larger scale, Knowledge Management provides a database of information that can facilitate decision and actions. Just imagine, with a database of common documents, one will not need to compose from scratch but can readily assemble new documents based on available templates and patterns. For training professionals, creating and maintaining their own database of powerpoint presentations will enable them to readily produce new presentations by cutting and pasting old ones and adding new slides..

PEOPLE

The third and last group of performance factors is "People". It is possible that the organizational structure or the culture of the organization itself is not supportive of performance by inhibiting coordination or nurturing the wrong values. Publishing the desired Corporate Values and living them are two different things. In case this is isolated to a small sub-organization, then reviewing and redesigning the organizational structure of the affected area will suffice. However, if this is systemic and prevalent in the entire organization then the Organization Development approach will be very appropriate as a long term intervention.

Part of the "People" factor is leadership. Although the performance of the workers are the ones being improved, it is possible that intervention is needed not by the workers themselves but by the leaders the supervisors and managers that greatly influence workers' behavior that will need intervention. Leaders may have risen from the ranks without the benefit of training, education and development. If so, leaders may have assumed certain responsibilities without being prepared to properly plan, communicate, delegate, and motivate. This will definitely affect performance. If performance deficiencies vary between individual leaders, then sending them to the appropriate training intervention for their specific leadership competency needs is appropriate.

On the other hand, if the organization realizes that it has a very narrow leadership bench and it needs to develop future managers and executives, then, the Succession Planning Process should be considered. By the way, the Quality Control Circles is also a very good opportunity to expose workers to leadership responsibilities and therefore prepare them for higher responsibilities through learning by doing.

At this point, we now consider the workers themselves. Are workers technically competent? Note that we consider technical competencies only at this point in time. Even if workers are already competent but the workplace is not conducive to performance, then competence will not be maximized. Besides, it is safe to assume that to a certain extent the workers are competent because we hired them according to the qualifications that we ourselves established. The need to develop technical competencies may be isolated to specific competencies, jobs or individuals. Then providing technical training is in order. However, if there is a need to systematically develop and recognize technical competencies then developing a Competency Framework will be necessary. Through Competency Frameworks,

Technical Competencies are established and standardized, and processes for assessing, certifying and recognizing them through promotions are put in place. In this manner, the Competency Framework also provides the motivation for self development through upward mobility.

If competencies are not consistently applied, coaching and counseling can be considered. If lack of performance consistency is due to health or other non-work related concerns then Corporate Wellness or Work-Life balance may be looked into.

If workers are competent but are not supportive of performance objectives, they may not be properly motivated. Behavioral Training or Team building may be in order. If we want to entire workforce to focus on contributing to the organization's business objectives then Performance Related Pay may provide the appropriate motivation.

It is obvious that the selection of the performance improvement intervention is not based on its own merits alone but in relation to the validated root causes that we have identified.

It may be best to customize or design our own interventions or even derive hybrids.

It seems important to repeat that the important consideration is its appropriateness with respect to the root causes identified. Results can only be attained and sustained if the interventions directly addressed the root cause of the problem.

The costs of these interventions vary greatly. There can be one time interventions with very minimal costs and there are interventions that will entail large-scale projects entailing very prohibitive costs. The selection of the intervention should not be based primarily on its cost but on its appropriateness. Appropriateness maximizes probability of results. Results translate to tangible and intangible benefits. The primary basis for selecting performance improvement interventions should be the value it creates in terms of potential cost-benefit ratio.

REFERENCES

Chadha, Gaurav and S. M. Nafay Kumail (2002). *E-Learning: An Expression of the Knowledge Economy*. India: Tata McGraw-Hill Publishing Company Limited.

Hammer, Michael and James Champy (1993). *Reengineering the Corporation*. USA: HarperCollins Publishers, Inc.

Kaplan, Robert S. and David P. Norton (2001). *The Strategy-Focused Organization: How Balanced Scorecard Companies Thrive in the New Business Environment*. USA: Harvard Business School Press.

Piskurich, George M. (2000). *Rapid Instructional Design*. USA: Jossey-Bass Pfeiffer.

Robinson, Dana Gaines and James C. Robinson (1996). *Performance Consulting: Moving Beyond Training*. USA: Berret-Koehler Publishers, Inc.

Robinson, Dana Gaines and James C. Robinson (1998). *Moving From Training To Performance: A Practical Guidebook*. USA: Berret-Koehler Publishers, Inc.

Rossett, Allison (2002). *The ASTD E-Learning Handbook: Best Practices, Strategies and Case Studies for an Emerging Field*. USA: McGraw-Hill Companies, Inc.

Rossett, Allison and Kendra Sheldon (2001). *Beyond The Podium: Delivering Training and Performance To A Digital World*. USA: Jossey-Bass/Pfeiffer.

3

Running to Catch Up...
Or...Collaborating to Triumph

The Action Power Consulting Model

Graham Arnold and *Rod Oxenberry*

INTRODUCTION

In 1871, the mathematician Charles Lutwidge Dodgson wrote: "Now, here, you see, it takes all the running you can do, to keep in the same place. If you want to get somewhere else, you must run at least as twice as fast as thaf\ The fact that the words were attributed to a white rabbit and spoken in a book called "Through the Looking Glass', and were published under another name, namely, Lewis Carroll, perhaps meant that their significance was lost for a couple of centuries. But if anyone asks managers today how fast do they have to run, the words of the white rabbit are likely to find resonance with their direct experience.

Whilst it is the pace of change that tends to be most talked about, if it was as simple as that, coping with it would be reasonably straight forward. Rather it is the complex nature of change that gives rise to uncertainty that determines the problematic circumstances in which managers frequently find themselves; circumstances that often lead them to seek help. We empathies with those in those circumstances.

We do not intend for this paper to be academic in either purpose or style although it is built upon solid theoretical concepts. Our purpose is to stimulate thinking, reflection and discussion amongst practicing managers, consultants and "would be' consultants about the area of management consulting in contemporary and emerging environments. In it we summaries the development of management consulting; define the uncertainty context of the environments in which organizations and today's managers are situated; highlight our concerns about matters that impinge on management consulting; declare our position and advocate approaches for addressing complexity; and outline, in very broad terms, the particular approach we take to management consulting.

MANAGEMENT CONSULTING

What is it?

Consultation is the process of seeking or giving professional help. And, like love or leadership, consulting is the general label for a variety of relationships.

The general definition of consultation used in this paper assumes that:

1. the consultation is a voluntary relationship between
2. a professional helper (consultant) and help-needing system (client)
3. in which the consultant is attempting to provide help to the client in solving some current or potential difficulties or challenges, and
4. the relationship is perceived as temporary by both parties.

Also, the consultant is an "outsider", i.e., he or she is not a part of any hierarchical power system in which the client is located.

Whilst there is some benefit in exploring different areas of consulting, we are specifically focusing on management consulting; more particularly, on what is generally understood as general management consulting rather than specialist consulting, such as IT. Also, it is convenient to keep to the general case of external consultants although the concepts discussed are, in the main, equally applicable to internal consultants.

The International Labour Office's guide to the profession of management consulting suggests that there are five generic consulting purposes:

- Achieving organizational purposes and objectives
- Solving management and business problems
- Identifying and seizing new opportunities
- Enhancing learning
- Implementing changes (Kubr, 2002, p. 10).

We believe that these general guides to what consulting is about are sufficiently robust for the reader to mentally translate our messages into a personal experience context.

Management Consulting: An Historical Perspective

Historically, management consultancy has been largely an Anglo-Saxon activity. Recall the names of prominent pioneering management consulting firms 4ike Arthur Little, A.T. Keamey, Booz-Allen, McKinsey, Arthur Anderson founded in the early part of the 20th century. Around that time too, of course, was Frederick Taylor, the acknowledged father of management science, who in many ways might be seen as the forerunner of people like Peter Drucker, Tom Peters, Peter Senge. Some have suggested that management consultants might be traced back to the 1870s (Ransom in Sadler, 2000) as the modernization of the industrial economies gave rise to the emergence of the corporation, with all its power bringing together the interplay of investment, ownership, the exploitation of resources whether they be physical, financial or human, and delivering product by the most efficient and effective means.

Business organizations turned to these firms and individuals when they were dissatisfied with aspects of the way their businesses were going, or with their organizational performance. There were problems, real or perceived, and it was felt that there was unlikely to be resolution of them internally, or at least, resolution within the time frames wanted. They turned to outside intervention. The management consultant then focused upon the problems, locating them, defining them, identifying the means toward greater productivity and efficiency, and devising recommendations for solutions and change. All of this activity centred upon the external consultant looking from "the outside in", applying the consultant's external, objective view to the problem situation.

Management consulting activity grew and grew throughout the 20th century. Czerniaswka (1999) suggests that the growth was fairly steady until the 1990s when it exploded! Until then, she suggested that the growth in consultancy was largely organic as consultants made particular contributions to organizations and then, more structural-functional as the consulting firms established their practices and linked to various businesses. She argues that things changed in the 1990s, and we might argue that this situation has continued unabated in 2000-2005. The example she provides is the dramatic increase in consultants and consultancy firms in the UK. It appears that this is mirrored in Europe as a whole. North America, Australia and a number of countries in Asia. At this point, we might be tempted to postulate that this has been brought about by demography, and the numbers of experienced managers changing to part-time work into which management consultancy can fit quite nicely! Others might be tempted to suggest that this was a product of the down-sizing drives of the late 80s and early 90s, with numbers of mangers finding themselves without corporate positions. But this is trite. Czerniaswka and others have pointed to the dramatic changes of corporate life in the 90s and to the increasing professionalisation of the management consultancy field as possible factors in its growth.

THE HERE AND NOW

There is no doubt that we have seen an explosion in management consulting activity with a greater number of people involved in it. There also appears to be less concentration in the big consulting firms and a greater proliferation of individual and small consulting businesses. Moreover, the phenomenon is quite widespread. The growth for instance, throughout Asia replicates that in the traditional centres. Whatever the reasons, be it ease of entry or other factors, from a pragmatic viewpoint, it would seem that there is the demand.

But rather than concentrating on the industry, let us first focus upon the environment in which managers and organizations find themselves.

The Organizational/Management Environment

We adhere to the viewpoint that suggests that the task of managing human organizations is becoming more difficult; increasingly complex. We believe that the task of management is more perplexing than it has ever been. Managers face increasingly:

- New areas which lack adequate historical precedent and

historical information.

- Areas which involve judgments about the impacts of many converging factors.
- Situations where technological innovation, indeed innovation of all kinds, is dependent on the activities of highly diverse and differentiated societal groups.
- Situations whose evaluation requires subjective inputs as the dominating parameters.

Today's managers are operating not just in situations of rapid change, as is commonly suggested, but in situations of high uncertainty characterized by complex interdependencies and novel features. Managers today are having to cope with kinds of changes which are outside contemporary experience and for which traditional coping strategies are ill-suited.

A relatively recent feature that pervades the environment of all organizations and contributes to their uncertainty context is that of globalisation. Whether or not an organization engages in global operations it will nonetheless be affected by its impacts. All must be internationally savvy and must internationalise to some extent. Clearly then, the managements of all organizations have to cope with globalisation. It impacts upon what managers need to do and how we need to develop our management skills and knowledge. This becomes a concern for the area of management education and for management consultants.

OUR CONCERNS

We have concerns about various approaches to problem solving, packaged solutions and strategy recipes that influence managers and consultants, and the practices of management consultants. They range from the philosophical to the pragmatic. In our view, they give rise to many of the dissatisfactions associated with consultancy outcomes and they also constitute underlying reasons for the different approach we take and advocate.

Philosophical Concerns

As previously asserted, in today's environment organizations and their managers are characteristically confronted with complex, confused situations. An appreciation of this would thus seem to be fundamental to any worthwhile approach to dealing effectively with such situations. Yet, this is far from the case. Our concern is that in both consulting and research the conventional "scientific approach" continues to flourish despite its inappropriateness in many situations. The scientific approach to dealing with complexity is to "split" it up into parts and tackle "problems of the parts" one by one. Thus we have concerns about the uncritical and inappropriate use of positivistic research in the management, about reductionism and "management science', and other manifestations of the "scientific approach" in management consultancy.

1. Reductionism

Reductionism consists of the belief that everything in the world and every experience of it can be reduced, decomposed, or disassembled down to ultimately simple elements, indivisible parts. Understanding of the world is therefore taken to be the sum or resultant of the understanding of its parts.

Consistent with reductionism all relationships between parts, and between parts and the whole are believed to be explainable by one ultimately simple relationship-cause and effect. One thing or event is taken to be the cause of another, its effect if it was both necessary and sufficient for the other. Because a cause was taken to be sufficient for its effect, nothing other than the cause was required to explain the effect. This of course makes little sense in the context of multicausality-the general rather than the particular in real-life complex situations.

2. Management Science

Traditional management science approaches are closely related to reductionism. Taking up the line put forward by Checkland (1981), the approach most typical in management science is founded on the assumption that problems recur. Thus problems are classified and techniques for dealing with these 'model problems' (often in the form of mathematical models) are worked out. The approach is then to recognise one of the model problems in a real-life situation, apply the appropriate technique and thus solve the problem.

It seems probable that the reason management science has made such a small impact on real managers is that these are inadequate models for real-life problems. The "problem" is identified and the techniques used to solve it, but in the end the real problem is still intact. The methods pass the problems by.

How relatively easy it is, working at a desk, to construct return-on-investment models; how difficult it is, working with the management situation itself, to engineer systems within which return-on-investment models can be fruitfully used.

3. The Rational Comprehensive Approach

The rational comprehensive approach to problem solving, policy formulation, planning which goes under a variety of names and guises comprises that approach that has as its start point definition of the problem or statement of objectives. But in human activity systems you cannot always do that. Often the situation will be pluralistic, there will be different value positions, or it will be conflictual.

Questions that are always relevant are:

- Whose problem is being tackled?
- Whose objectives are being taken into account?

To Sir Geoffrey Vickers the more fundamental issues were not how goals were achieved, but how they were set; not how problems were solved but why some situations were classified as "problems" and others were not.

Pragmatic Concerns

4. Management Fads

Management fads have been with us for a long time but especially over the last several decades. They come in and out of favour. Michael Jackson (1993) in his paper "Beyond the Fads: Systems Thinking for Managers" cites several illustrative ones, namely: Guru Theory, Total Quality Management (TQM), Business Process Re-engineering and The Learning Organization.

Jackson gives an analytical critique of these but our focus here is somewhat different. Our intention is not necessarily to run down fads completely nor to suggest that there is anything wrong with popularizing ideas, rather to sound warnings about them in the context of management consultancy and the circumstances in which today's managers find themselves.

Huczynski (1993) identifies three types of guru-academic gurus like Rosabeth Moss Kanter; consultancy gurus like Tom Peters, perhaps the best known management guru; and hero managers (take your pick from the plethora of those who write or are written about.)

Thus we see in the Havard Business Review a plethora of prescription type "management-problem-solution" contributions. We see the phenomenon of Peters' in the Peters and Waterman launch book "In Search of Excellence" that sold 1,160,491 copies in one year and thereafter enabled Peters to command $50,000 a presentation. By 1989 Peters had discounted his erstwhile eight characteristics of excellence and was providing 45 prescriptions for 'thriving on chaos'. Again this was short-lived because by 1992 his (although it is unclear whether he actually wrote it) 834 page tome, "Liberation Management" became a "fashion accessory" on managers bookshelves.

Total quality management swept the industrialized world, yet in its flourishing period, as reported by Jackson, surveys in the United States in 1991 revealed that 80% of CEOs regarded their TQM results as disappointing and an Arthur D Little survey in 1992 indicated that while some 93% of US firms had TQM programs, only 36% of the executives polled regarded these as having any significant effect upon their competitive position.

Business process re-engineering (see the book by four consultants from Coopers and Lybrand advocating BPR (Johansson et al, 1993)) is said to go far beyond TQM and JIT (Just in time philosophy). It places the emphasis on core business process, but the measures are external so you are looking for improvement in terms of your market share. You think in terms of the processes involved in delivering products to the market, so you defunctionalise completely, you improve processes, you get rid of bureaucracy and the old organizational charts, and you need a flatter, less hierarchical organization with lots of teamwork in it. But there is no clear idea of what model really is underpinning BPR.

We applaud Peter Senge's best seller "The Fifth Discipline" in that it promotes systems as the fifth and most important discipline and because it promotes and reinforces the important, but not new, concept of the organization as a learning organization. On the down side it provides tends to be focused on the "fix" for organizations and management and has been used in a way that has promoted management faddism in the extreme.

- We generally share the general criticisms that Jackson has of management fads, namely that:
- The advocates of fads seem to know the answers before the event.
- The people propagating management fads tend to have a partial view of what makes an organization successful.
- The necessary theoretical ideas are missing from fads, they don't explore the theories underlying their recommendations, they don't ask what they are taking for granted in organizations and intervening in them. They don't know the theory on which their recommendations are based so how can they relate their experiences back to theory and leam why something has succeeded or why something has failed?
- The fads tend to recommend solutions for all circumstances.

We particularly though have concerns about the "consulting industries" that have grown up around these and other fads and the practice of those consultants using them.

5. Misleading Consulting Practices

We have real concerns with consultants who purport to be taking a systems approach when they are not;

consultants who purport to taking a participative approach when they are not; consultants who purport to be using action learning when they are not.

These practices have coincided with the emergence of the popularity of the terms-'systems' (especially following Peter Senge's framing of it as the 'fifth discipline'), 'participation' but the mere involvement of people does not imply real participation), 'action learning' (use of the term does not imply that the fundamentals of action learning are being exercised)

6. Traditional Management Consulting

We are concerned that the traditional "diagnostic" management consulting approach is not relevant in these times. That is where the consultants) enters the situation, spends time in observation and some discussion, makes a diagnosis of the problem and prescribes some remedy. Arguably the implementation of relevant change is amongst the most challenging of tasks that the consultant needs to help with.

Problems

An issue that deserves special attention is the question of defining problems.

In complex situations, and these are the norm in human activity systems, it is difficult to identify or define what is a problem. Indeed it may not even be productive to do so, at least not in conventional ways.

Many writers have tackled this issue. We draw on a few.

Peter Checkland (1981) uses the term (unstructured problems' and in reference to them makes the following points:

- 'it is not possible to take for granted the concept of "a problem" and the activity of trying to solve it'
- "What is "a problem"? itself [becomes] a part of the [inquiry]'
- 'unstructured problems... are manifest in a feeling of unease but which cannot be explicitly stated without this appearing to oversimplify the situation'
- We are 4... concerned not with problems as such but with problem situations in which there are felt to be unstructured problems, ones in which the designation of objectives is itself problematic.'

He goes on:

The language of conventional approaches implies time-independent situations in which the sequence of events is: recognition of problem; definition of problem; action to solve problem; problem solved. Whilst this may be useful for tackling many structured problems but it is inadequate for unstructured problems for two reasons.

"Firstly, such problems, though 'recognizable', cannot be "defined". Secondly, in problems in human activity systems history always changes the agenda! The contents of such systems are so multivarious, and the influences to which they are subject so numerous that the passage of time always mollifies the perception of the problem.... Such perceptions of problems are always subjective and they change with time.'

"A problem relating to real-world manifestations of human activity systems is a condition characterized by a sense of mis-match, which eludes precise definition, between what is perceived to be actuality and what is perceived might become actuality."

Russell Ackoff (1999) uses the term 'messes'. He argues that:

'Problems exist only as abstract subjective constructs, not as concrete objective states.'
"Problems are extracted from unstructured states of confusion."-messes.
'a mess is a system of external conditions that produces dissatisfaction.'

and maintains that

"Decision makers deal with messes, not problems."

We Empathise with Managers

Now let us focus for a bit on the lot of today's managers.

Fred Emery (1978, p. 39) tells us that if we put anyone into a situation of high uncertainty and we can pretty much predict possible behaviours. It is apt to be marked by its being:

- exploratory, tentative. Even the most innocent proposal is treated as if it might turn into something too hot to handle;
- trial-and-error. "Suck-it-and-see"-no commitment if it can in anyway be avoided;
- vacillation. Today's hot-bake bread is tomorrow's stale loaf;
- contradictory. An order to managers to introduce participatory schemes goes out on the same day as an instruction to HR to recruit extra supervisors.

This sort of behaviour might lead us to doubt the mental stability of a normal person in a normal environment. In turbulent environments however, a person has insufficient knowledge of what leads to what, of what is connected to and could be influenced by what.

We are most certainly of the view that today's managers operate in turbulent environments. And we empathise with them their circumstances.

We also see managers taking action that would appear to be quite rational, namely turning for help. Thus we empathise with managers who seek answers in management fads. In particular we empathise with managers who turn to management consultants as the process of going down that road is problematic in itself. Choosing a management consultant is not a clear cut process. How often do we see organizations, more or less out of frustration, engage a big consulting firm in the hope that there might be some security in "bigness". Whilst technology and the world of the internet and web pages makes it much easier than ever for individuals to promote themselves, professional accreditation becomes more and more important.

OUR POSITION

We have somewhat unusual and diverse backgrounds and perhaps this has contributed to our particular worldview. We have both occupied senior positions as practicing leaders and managers, albeit in different fields; we have held leadership positions in academe-specifically in the area of management education and research; and we have significant real-world consulting experience both as professional consultants and as university management professors. Over the last 12 years or so we have been intimately involved in international management education-principally throughout Asia, but also in Europe, the Middle East, South Africa, and North America. We are presently freelance educators, researchers and consultants.

Our consulting approach and consulting advocacy encompasses a number of principles.

We are systems proponents. This fundamentally means that we look at problematic situations holistically, as wholes, as distinct from just looking at parts of them and reducing the situation to its parts. It means that we use systems ideas and concepts, employ systems thinking and systems modeling and use a systems methodology and systems techniques. The term "systems thinking" has been around for along time now. The great Australian thinker, Fred Emery edited a book "Systems Thinking" back in 1969. In 1981 Peter Checkland introduced his seminal work on soft systems methodology in his book titled "Systems Thinking, Systems Practice" while Peter Senge popularised a systems approach in his 1990 best seller book, "The Fifth Discipline".

We maintain the importance of research as an essential precursor to taking effective action. We are not talking about esoteric notions of academic research but about research that organizational members, with a modicum of learning and guidance, are quite capable of undertaking. Some readers may feel more comfortable in using terms like inquiry or investigation as substitutes for research. We do though stipulate that such activity must be valid, reliable and ethical. We, in particular, use and are strong advocates of "Action Research' for the principal method of inquiry within organizations.

We believe that it is important to establish conceptual frameworks to guide action and as an evaluative reference.

We are adamant that the consulting process be participative with key players in the organization being directly and intimately involved.

We uphold the necessity of the consulting process proceeding within an explicit learning environment. Indeed we ensure, for instance, that the methodology is transferred to participants.

ACTION POWER CONSULTING

Action Power Consulting is the name we give to our consulting approach. Action power consulting is intended to imply that it is an action-based, as distinct from passive, approach and that it is an approach that empowers people through learning and participation.

Although it is an over simplification, the methodological approach of action power consulting is based upon an amalgamation of two widely known methodologies: Soft Systems Methodology and Action Research. We give a brief account of these below.

Soft Systems Methodology (SSM)

SSM was developed out of a research program at Lancaster University in the UK by Peter Checkland and his colleagues with the first full account of the methodology appearing in 1976 (Checkland, 1976). It has continually evolved within an action research environment under Checkland since then (Checkland, 1981;

Checkland and Scholes, 1990; Checkland and Holwell, 1998) with inputs from a wide range of users from around the world.

"The Checkland methodology grew out of the frustration experienced by consultants trying to use hard systems methodologies in soft problem situations. It was recognized that hard systems methodologies were simply not appropriate as tools for dealing with the complexity and ambiguity of social reality."

(*Jackson*, 1982, p. 22)

Although there are significant methodological departures from Checkland's original seven stage construct, the latter is still the most relevant start point for gaining an understanding of SSM. We give just a brief overview of it here.

In the first and second stages a problem situation is analysed and a "rich picture" of the situation is built up. This activity is not undertaken in systems terms, rather the inquiry uses conventional techniques such as interviewing and the like. Uses of the methodology often use diagrams to enhance understanding of the situation. A plurality of views can be readily accommodated in this investigation with account being taken of the various perceptions of the situation by various actors.

The third activity involves the preparation of "root definitions" of some of the systems which appear relevant to the problem situation. A root definition should be a condensed representation of a system in its most fundamental form: its aim is to capture insight. Each root definition reflects a different way of looking at the problem situation: it embodies one particular Wellanschauung or worldview. Since this activity is part of systems thinking rather than real-world thinking, a root definition is not meant to be a definition of a real-world system under study, but of a notional system which may be usefully compared with the real-world system.

Stage 4 involves the construction of "conceptual models" of the systems defined in the root definitions. In the conceptual models are compiled and structured those minimal activities which are necessary to produce the systems enshrined in the root definitions. Some help in building conceptual models may come from formal systems concepts and other systems thinking. The formal system concepts are a set of characteristics which all soft systems must posses. They are:

- The system has an objective or on-going purpose.
- The system has measure(s) of performance.

- The system is complex-a change in one component may affect many others.
- The system has components which are themselves systems.
- The system interacts with wider systems and environments.
- The system has resources, physical and human.
- The system has a decision maker or decision-making body, and has a decision-making process.
- The system has a guarantee of continuity and will recover stability after disturbances.

Other systems thinking may also be useful for building conceptual models. This can derive from such contributions as cybernetics, open systems theory and the like.

Stage 5 of the methodology involves a comparison of the conceptual models developed with the real world problem situation. The purpose of this is to generate debate about changes which can bring about improvements in the problem situation. This is Stage 6 of the methodology. Finally, Stage 7 of the methodology involves taking action to implement the agreed changes. Stages 5 to 7 require the involvement of people from within the problem situation, as it is they who must decide which changes, if any, to implement. There should not be too wide a gap between the conceptual model and the real world, as this is likely to suggest changes which, although desirable, are not politically feasible and therefore cannot be implemented. The soft systems methodology is not concerned with generating optimal solutions to problems, although it is quite capable of doing so if the meaning of "optimal" can be defined. More often than not with soft systems, there is no realistic way of defining an optimum or knowing when it has been reached, and the implementation of feasible changes which represent an improvement on the previous system is the best that can be hoped for.

When conceptual models are compared with the real-world, questions normally arise, such as: Is this activity being done? How is it done? How well is it being done?

The conceptual models are used to structure a debate about change among the actors in the problem situation. The various Wehanschammgen or appreciative systems which have been elucidated in conceptual models are compared and contrasted. The actors become aware of their own world views and of the existence of other, possibly conflicting world views. Thus the methodology facilitates a social process in which appreciative systems-the judgements of fact and value-are held up for examination and possibly changed.

In this way it is a quite common occurrence that the comparison stage of SSM generates a fresh understanding in the minds of managers who thought they understood their system. It frequently suggests better ways of doing familiar things. Quite often organizations, or departments within organizations, have not defined their objectives very well, nor considered how achievement of these objectives can be measured.

Although the description of SSM or diagrammatic representations of it appear to be a series of sequential steps, in practice it is not applied this way. SSM is more a philosophy than a technique, and the consultant/analyst can start at just about any of the stages and iterate around the loop as understanding is enriched.

SSM has been used in hundreds of applications throughout the world and is a robust methodology. Watson (1987, p.25) identifies some of the ways in which SSM can bring about improvements to problem situations as:

(a) to identify desirable and feasible organisational or procedural changes:
(b) to effect desirable changes in the values and attitudes of participants;
(c) to provide a logical framework for the design and development of management information and control systems;
(d) to explain the structure and interrelationships of a complex system so that the different groups affected by it can work together; and
(e) to identify problems amenable to quantitative modeling.

Action Research

Whilst the exact origins of action research are unclear, Kurt Lewin (1890-1947), a Prussian psychologist who emigrated to America in 1933 to escape Nazi persecution, is generally regarded as the father of action research. From his pioneering work in the 1940s, action research has moved to further developments in organizational change, in teacher education, community development, and the health arena. It has made a strong impact in each of these fields and its applications continue to grow.

Kemmis and *Mc Taggart* (1988, p.8) comment that Lewin described action research as

> 'proceeding in a spiral of steps, each of which is composed of planning, action, and the evaluation of the result of action. In practice, the process begins with the general idea that some kind of improvement or change is desirable. In deciding just where to begin in making improvements, a group identifies an area where members perceive a cluster of problems of mutual concern and consequence. The group decides to work together on a thematic concern.'

They go on to say that

> "The general idea prompts a reconnaissance of the circumstances of the field, and fact-finding about them. Having decided on the field and made a preliminary reconnaissance, the action research group decides on a general plan of action."

Lewin did not publish a definition of action research but the one provided by Rapport (1970, p.89) is widely quoted in the literature, viz.:

> "Action research aims to contribute both to the practical concerns of people in an immediate problematic situation and to the goals of social science by joint collaboration within a mutually acceptable ethical framework."

In the U.K. there was in the 1950s and 60s an almost independent growth of Action Research centred in the Tavistock Institute-the prestigious British Institute that contributed much to the understanding of management and organizational practice. Although they did not use the term "action research" the work of people from the Institute had the characteristics of being problem-centred, based on a long term involvement with clients and centred on the needs of those clients, involved with following through and monitoring changes in the organizations in which they were working. Interestingly, Tavistock researchers referred to themselves not as researchers but as consultants.

Over time the label of action research has become identified with the familiar spiral of steps: planning, action, observing and reflecting (Mc Taggart, 1991, p.170). A fuller understanding of Action Research may be gleaned by reference to a summary of twelve general characteristics of Action Research provided by Abraham (1996).

Table 3.1: General Characteristics of Action Research

	Characteristic	*Summary Description*
1	Problem Focus Characteristic	The action research method is problem focused in the context of real life situations and the solving of such problems in a research sense would contribute to the practice and the development of social science knowledge.
2	Action Orientation Characteristic	The diagnosis of a problem and the development of a plan can only be considered to be action oriented if it becomes part of a process to implement the plan. This brings an action element to the solving of an immediate problem of the organisation which has strategic change implications for the organisation.
3	Cyclical Process: Spiral of Steps	The action research method involves cycles of planning, action observation, and reflection (evaluation). Also the cycles of the action research method allow the group members to develop a plan, to act, to observe and to reflect on this plan and to modify this plan based on the needs of the group members and the requirements of the organisation and situation. A record of the processes of each cycle enables its strengths and weaknesses to be reviewed so that modifications and strategies can be developed for future cycles.
4	Collaborative Characteristic	Collaboration is a fundamental ingredient of the action research method, because without this team effort to solve problems in an environment of participation, action research cannot exist. Collaboration on group problem using the action research method can be viewed as a continuum from total dependence on the facilitator, who acts as a leader directing the group problem solving process, through to the total management of the problem by the group members with the facilitator acting as a resource person. The position of the facilitator and the group on this continuum depends on the situation and the needs of the group.

(*Contd.*)

Table 3.1 (*Contd.*)

	Characteristic	*Summary Description*
5	Ethical Basis Characteristic	Community interests, improvements in the lives of the group members, justice, rationality, democracy and equality are some of the themes of "ethical' behaviour. The ethical basis of action research is an important characteristic to consider, because the action research method involves, to a large extent, groups of people with limited power who are open to exploitation. It behoves the researcher to compromise his/her personal needs so that the needs of the group are given the highest priority.
6	Experimental Characteristic	Experimental action research involves the rigorous testing of hypotheses and can thus contribute to knowledge in social science. Nevertheless, the quality of the action research may be affected by the control group which can lead to other problems and complications.
7	Scientific Characteristic	Since the action research method does have a scientific basis and can provide an alternative to the positivistic view of science, it is essentially that the research be conducted in such a way as to defend itself against criticisms of lack of scientific rigour.
8	Re-educative Characteristic	Action research can be viewed as re-educative, since it contributes to a change in the knowledge base of the client organisation, a change in the skills, attitudes and knowledge of the individual group members and a change in the skills and knowledge of the researcher. It also makes a contribution to several of the social sciences.
9	Emancipatory Characteristic	The action research method includes an emancipatory characteristic which will result in some improvements in the lives of the people involved in the action research project, and may also lead to wider social action and reform.
10	Naturalistic Characteristic	If one accepts that action research should be scientific but that there are problems in adopting a positivistic model of science and applying it to social science settings, then it follows that a naturalistic approach is appropriate for the action research method. The approach involves qualitative descriptions recorded as case studies rather than laws of cause and effect tested experimentally with statistical analysis of data.

(*Contd.*)

Table 3.1 (*Contd.*)

	Characteristic	*Summary Description*
11	Normative Characteristic	The normative characteristic of action research implies that the social 'norms' of the group are not only considered during the research, but, in order to bring about change in the group, they are modified during the action research process.
12	Group Dynamics Characteristic	The success of the action research method will depend on how well the group can operate as an effective team. An understanding of group dynamics therefore seems essential in facilitating this process and dealing with problems that arise during the action research cycles.

Within the management arena Action Research is invariably concerned with significant or strategic change. This is the case whether it is applied within an academic research study or in a strategic change exercise.

The Action Power Consulting Model

As with both Action Research and SSM, mere descriptions are insufficient other than to gain a superficial level of understanding. So too it is with the Action Power Consulting Model (APCM); familiarity only comes by engaging with it. Notwithstanding this, the rudimentary knowledge of AR and SSM provided should be helpful in gaining an appreciation of the APCM.

Think in terms of the APCM as a guiding framework with explicit philosophical underpinnings rather than a step-by-step procedure. The philosophical principles which are collectively embedded in AR and SSM both govern the overall approach and provide guidance about what techniques may be usefully employed and what ones would unduly distort things. Thus, the guiding principles of Action Power Consulting are:

- the participative principle;
- the holistic principle;
- the action principle; and
- the principle of learning.

While, systems thinking is the conceptual glue that binds these principles together.

We present this brief overview of the process of the APCM in terms of phases to emphasise that it is not a set of sequential steps. Also phases are a useful device for regulating the consulting contract.

Preliminary: Project Negotiation

Negotiate the project and conditions with the Decision Maker(s). Setting aside any commercial elements, this entails, inter alia, providing a presentation of the approach and ensuring the necessary discretionary authority is in place to enable the project to proceed.

Phase One: Project Organization

Determining the initial Participatory Group and inducting the members. This entails a learning process wherein the methodology is transferred to the participants.

Where necessary, establishing a Referral or Decision-Making Group. This is needed unless the principal leaders of the organization are in the Participatory Group. Progressive key findings and/or decisions are referred to this group. This provides another level where legitimate debate about issues can beneficially occur.

Elaborating roles. This will be an activity that will occur continuously throughout. These roles relate to the project and may not necessarily coincide with work roles or positions.

Phase Two: Appreciation of the Situation

This involves gaining an appreciation of the situation wherein there are believed to be unstructured problems, about which there is some sense of unease, and which is problematic. Activities entailed in this include:

- Inquiry (research) and the generation of data. This is done employing the framework of Action Research within which conventional techniques such as interviewing, surveying and participant observation may be used.
- Building rich pictures of the situation including diagrammatic representations that borrow from techniques developed in

SSM experience. These rich pictures include the cultural environments (social and political); structural environments; and task or work flow environments. Also included is an appreciation about the impact of the consultation intervention itself. Both the Participant Group and the Referral Group are involved in this process in which the principles of participation (AR); holism (systems; SSM); critical reflection (AR); and learning (AR) are upheld. The learning aspect is given explicit attention and involves learning about the methodology and learning about the situation.

Phase Three: Application of Soft Systems

In this phase we draw on the third and fourth stages of SSM-defining root definitions and building conceptual models.

Root Definitions. Definitions of relevant systems (root definitions) that encompass problematic issues and which take account of various perceptions (see notes below) are developed, but herein, unlike in SSM, within an Action Research framework. Root definitions are examined to identify the existence of different and/or conflicting values and activity engaged in where appropriate to resolve or reconcile these. Conceptual Models. Conceptual models of these systems are constructed, again within an AR framework, and activity undertaken to resolve or reconcile different values where such are revealed.

Phase Four: Reporting and Evaluation

Conceptual models are compared to the real-world situation and the differences highlighted. These differences are identified as candidates for potential change. All of the findings of the inquiry are collated and overall changes summarized in terms of their desirability and feasibility over relevant time horizons. A process, which is essentially one of debate, is engaged in to determine prioritised changes. This may be assisted by reference to developed future scenarios covering appropriate time horizons (we use Subjective Information Modelling-a participative process developed by John Tydeman and Bob Mitchell). An important activity is to establish measures of performance (e.g. efficacy, efficiency, effectiveness, ethicality, aesthetic) so that monitoring and control can be exercised.

Intermission

At this point in a live consulting episode and with a fully documented report it is often convenient for the parties to review and re-negotiate the consultancy, the next phase being implementation. Notwithstanding the fact that participants have gained a significant learning experience with some first hand knowledge of action research, we are strong advocates for the consul tanl(s) to continue the engagement through implementation phase. In many respects this is the most difficult and contentious activity and one where the experience and expertise of the consultant is critical to effectiveness.

In our experience, the continuity of consultant involvement is something that the client invariably wants.

Phase Five: Implementation

This phase is addressed using the action research spiral of: planning, acting, observing, critically reflecting

(On the planning, the action and the observation), evaluating and re-planning...

This activity is typically decentralized with participant groups engaged in those areas that they are intimately concerned with.

The planning activity is guided by the 'Interactive Planning" approach of Ackoff (1999) with its participative, holistic and continuity principles and which sits comfortably within systems thinking and action research principles.

Phase Six: Disengagement

The consultants exit from the organization leaving:

- a learning legacy that permits the process to be ongoing as the "way of doing things"-as a self-discovering learning organization; and
- a relationship that is long-term and which permits the periodic reviewr and learning re-vitalisation either on a time basis or as stimulated by particular events or changes in key staff.

It should be noted that at various points in the process it is important to identify and establish other relevant Participatory Groups that can provide relevant perspectives and insights and whose members comprise people who are involved in the areas of concern and who may be impacted by change. The formation of these is analogous to the establishment of quality circles. Thus inquiring/learning groups are cascaded as appropriate throughout the organization. And, as with SSM, the APCM is a philosophy with a process that is iterative rather than a strict set of sequential steps.

CONCLUDING MESSAGE

The demand for management consulting is great and we see no signs of this abating as we see turbulent environments and states of uncertainty being the norm for organizations and their leaders in a globalised world.

Yet we do not see that there will be an accompanying growth in large consulting firms. They too are subject to uncertainty and we posit their most likely response is to contract into specialisations in order to contain personnel costs.

Today's technology makes it easier than ever for individuals to market themselves and their services-even academics can do this without reliance on institutional membership. The net and web pages are ready made for the individual.

However, in an unregulated industry like management consulting, and given that a particular consultant actually does have something worthwhile to offer, differentiating oneself from others such as to appeal to clients is extremely challenging. Your creative message today becomes someone elses overnight. This, of course, has nothing to do with real capability.

This difficulty is part of the reason that fads propagate. The "topic" becomes common ground for the consultant and client.

Having a robust consulting model replete with philosophy and process and underpinned by theory goes a long way along the effectiveness continuum, but this is not easy to get across in marketing messages. And in any event, the ab initio development of such a model takes a very very long time. Just gaining sufficient mastery to effectively apply an extremely well documented model such as Soft Systems Methodology by oneself takes a long time and is difficult. Naturally the process is much more efficient under tutelage if that prospect feasibly exists.

We see the emergence of accredited professional consultant

credentials as a legitimate response to this challenge; increasingly important to both consultant practitioners and clients.

Whilst a number of management consultant bodies exist, they tend to be associations with rather loosely defined membership and credential criteria. One of better known is the Institute of Management consultants USA which offers its Certified Management Consultant (CMC) designation. Notwithstanding the marketing gloss associated with this Institute and its CMC, entry criteria are very general and do not, for instance have any formal assessed course component unlike the requirements of the accounting profession's CPA credential.

We believe a professional approach analogous to the CPA qualification is a necessary step for management consultants. Admittedly, management consulting covers a much broader field than accounting and so the challenge is somewhat greater, but it is nonetheless possible. Indeed we are working with ARTDO (Asian Regional Training and Development Organization International) and the Institute of Training and Development (ITD) to develop a qualification program to serve this purpose from a regional perspective.

REFERENCES

Abraham, S. (1996) *Advanced Seminar for University of South Australia's PhD candidates in Hong Kong*, May 1996 and reproduced in Abraham, S., Arnold, G.R., and Oxenberry, R. (1996) The Self-Discovering Organisation: Fusing Action Research to the Learning Organisation', paper presented to conference on Building a Learning Organisation through Action Learning and Action Research, Singapore Institute of Management 25/26 October 1996

Ackoff, R.L. (1999) *Ackoffs Best*, John Wiley & Sons, NY

Boog, B., Coeneu, H., and Keune, L. (2001) *Action Research: Empowerment and Reflection*, Dutch University Press.

Checkland, P.B. (1972) "Towards a systems-based methodology for real-world problem-solving": *Journal of Systems Engineering*, Vol. 3 No. 2, Winter 1972.

Checkland, P.B. (1981) *Systems Thinking, Systems Practice*. Wiley, Chichester

Checkland, P.B., and Holweil, S. (1998) *Information, Systems and Information Systems*, Wiley, Chichester

Checkland, P.B., and Scholes, J. (1990) *Soft Systems Methodology in Action*. Wiley, Chichester

Czemiawska, F. (1999) *Management Consulting in the 21st Century*, Macmillan Business, London

Czerniawska, F. (2002) *Management Consultancy: What Next?* Palgrave Macmillan, London.

Emery, F. (1969) *Systems Thinking*, Penguin.

Emery, F. (1978) *Limits To Choice, Centre for Continuing Education*, The Australian National University.

Flood, R. (1999) *Rethinking the Fifth Discipline*, Routledge, NY.

Hart, E., and Bond, M. (1995) *Action Research for Health and Social Care*, Open University Press, Buckingham, UK.

Huczynski, A.A. (1993) *Management Gurus*. Routledge, London.

Jackson, M.C. (1982) The nature of soft systems thinking: the work of Churchman, Ackoff and Checkland, *J. Appl. Sys. Anal.* 9:9.

Jackson, M.C. (1993) *Beyond The Fads: Systems Thinking for Managers*, Working Paper No. 3, The Centre for Systems Studies, The University of Hull, December 1993.

Jackson, M.C. (2003) *Systems Thinking: Creative HoOlism for Managers*, John Wiley & Sons, Chichester.

Johansson, H.J., McHugh, P., Pendlebury, A.J., and Wheeler, W.A. (1993) *Business Process Re-engineering*, Wiley, Chichester.

Kemmis, S., and McTaggart, R. Editors (1988) *The Action Research Planner*, 3rd ed. Deakin University Kubr, M. (ed) (2002) Management Consulting 4th edition. Int. Lab. Office, Geneva.

McTaggart, R. (1991) "Principles for Participatory Action Research, Adult Education Quarterly, Vol 41, No 3, *Spring*, 168-182.

Peters, T.J., and Waterman, R.H. (1982) *In Search of Excellence*. Harper and Row, New York.

Peters, T.J. (1989) *Thriving on Chaos*. MacMillan, London.

Peters, T. J. (1992) *Liberation Management*. MacMillan, London.

Ransom, C. (2001) "The Management Consultancy Industry" in *Management Consultancy* 2nd edition, edited by Sadler, P., Reason, P., and Bradbury, H. (2001) *Handbook of Action Research*, Sage, London.

Rapoport, R. (1970) "Three Dilemmas in Action Research", *Human Relations*, 23, 448-513.

Senge, P.M. (1990) *The Fifth Discipline*. Random House, London.

Stringer, E. (1999) *Action Research* 2nd Edition, Sage, London.

Stroh, P. (2000) "Leveraging Change: The Power of Systems Thinking in Action", *Reflections*, Winter, Vol. 2 Issue 2. pp. 51-65.

Tydeman, J., and Mitchell R. (1977) *Subjective futures for decision making*. Research monograph series No. 3, The Australian National University

Vickers, G. (1983) *The Art of Judgement*, Harper and Row.

Vickers, G. (1968) *Value Systems and Social Process*, Tavistock.

Vickers, G. (1972) *Freedom in a Rocking Boat*, Pelican Books.

Vickers, G. (1984) *The Vickers Papers*, Harper and Row.

Walker, B., and Haslett, T. (2002) *Action Research and Systemic Thinking*, Monash Working Paper Series 15/02 March 2002.

Watson, R.B. (1987) *The Lancaster Soft Systems Methodology*, ASOR Bulletin, June, pp. 24-31.

4

Competitiveness from a Different Perspective and Implications for Business Strategic Planning

Kriengsak Chareonwongsak

INTRODUCTION

"Individual interest always contrasts with social interest,
but individual and society inevitably depend on each other."

Many countries try to choose their strategic industries so that they can position themselves to compete in the world market. These industries are given priority for development or promotion, due to resource constraints that prevent all industries from being promoted. Thailand is one such country that has chosen its strategic industries. A question arises as to which industries should be Thailand's strategic industries.

I have conducted research to answer this question. The findings contradict the result of Porter's study (Porter, 2003), which was initiated by the Thai government. The result of Porter's study is now being implemented in Thailand.

Porter's study was made on the basis of a business analogy, comparing a nation to a company, which is a view that studies each industry separately. I argue with his study on the grounds that it is not proper to make such an analogy due to the inter-relationships that exist between many economic agents in a nation. When there is activity or a change at one point in the economy, the impacts are spread throughout the economy and can even finally be fed back to the original point. Therefore, the total impact on the economy may not be limited to only a specific sector.

In Figure 4.1, a comparison of strategic industries obtained from my study is presented alongside the government's export strategy. The government policy shows three different strategic industries out of a total of five industries.

Chareonwongsak (2004)	Government Policy	
1. Food	1. Food	✓
2. Non-metal products	2. Fashion	✗
3. Electrical machinery and appliances	3. Motor Vehicles	✗
4. Rubber and plastic products	4. Software	✗
5. Tourism	5. Tourism	✓
6. Wood		

Fig. 1: Comparison of strategic industries from Chareonwongsak's study, and Government policy

When raising the competitiveness of a nation is mentioned, many recognize this as enabling a country to receive as much revenue as possible from exports. This view is based on the notion of competitiveness being equivalent to export capability.

However, nothing is gained without incurred costs, either direct or indirect costs. This is also true in the case of exports. Exports incur costs, even with foreign income gain. These costs involve an increase in the price of goods and services in a country, the decrease of employment, the restructuring of industries, worse income distribution, and other costs.

As a matter of fact, the target of competitiveness development should not be viewed as equivalent to export revenue, but the target of competitiveness is to increase the living standards of people. Export revenue is not the final target in itself, but it is only an instrument used to achieve the target that should be used properly. Therefore, the economy-wide impact of export policy should be studied carefully.

I used an applied general equilibrium model as a tool to assess the impact of export on the economy. The model gave the answers for many variables in the economy, both micro and macro, which then enabled us to determine the strategic export industries of Thailand by comparing the impact on the economy of the export of each industry. The strategic industries should be those giving the most desirable impacts.

Export, even though generating income to the country may decrease people's standard of living or worsen macroeconomic conditions. The living standard of people, if it decreases, will cause the nation to, for example, lack quality labour, and other effects. Eventually, the nation will be unable to compete, as much evidence proves that a competitive nation results from its quality of labour.

Based on my previous study (Chareonwongsak, 2004), this paper aims to outline factors that should concern companies in the export'sector and raise their competitiveness. It will help companies increase in capability so that they can act responsibly for the sake of society. It can also be applied to companies in other sectors that contribute to the sustainable development of the country.

The paper is separated into seven sections. Following this section, both the definition of competitiveness, and the target of national competitiveness development, will be discussed. The fourth section will deal the impact of export on economic development. The fifth section presents strategies for Thailand's export industries, followed by a discussion on why companies should be concerned for the social welfare. A conclusion is presented in the final section.

THE DEFINITION OF COMPETITIVENESS

The definition of competitiveness can be classified at company level and national level.

At company level, competitiveness refers to the ability of a company to produce goods or services that can compete with other companies due to such advantages as low costs, superior technology, and other advantages. Indicators of a company's competitiveness could be the company's long-term ability to produce and sell certain goods, or the market value of the company's shares together with its market share and profitability (Reiljan et. al., 2000).

The concept of competitiveness is based on the idea of a zero-sum game, that is, one's success prevents others from achieving their success. The result of one's activities depends greatly on the performance of other entities. The main principle of competition is the conflict of interests between entities.

However, at national level, there is no consensus on the definition of competitiveness. There are some definitions of national competitiveness, such as:

"The ability of a country to achieve sustained high rates of growth in GDP per capita" (*World Economic Forum*, 1996),

"The ability of a country to produce goods and services that meet the requirement of foreign markets, while the country is still able to maintain the increase of real income of population"

(*U.S. Competitiveness Policy Council*, 1992),

"The ability of a country to create added value and thus increase national wealth by managing assets and processes, attractiveness and aggressiveness, globality and proximity, and by integrating these relationships into an economic and social model".

(*International Management and Development-IMD*, 1996).

The popular definition of national competitiveness is the definition of Tyson (Krugman 1994), that is, "the ability to produce goods and services that can compete internationally causing the living standard of population to increase sustainably".

From the definition of competitiveness above, it is shown that the target of increasing competitiveness is not to increase export revenue or increase market share on the world market, as many businessmen understand. In that case, the target of increasing competitiveness may be achieved by decreasing currency value, wages, etc. Even though these measures may enable a country to export more, the well being of people may deteriorate. To increase national competitiveness is indeed to export so that the living standard of the population increases, which may be measured by real GDP per capita or by social welfare.

From Porter's viewpoint, the competitiveness of a nation is measured by the productivity of its economy. Productivity is therefore the target of competitiveness development. This view is based on a microeconomic foundation. However, competitiveness development also needs proper management from a macroeconomic point of view, due to the inter-relationships that exist between economic agents in the economy, as already mentioned. Proper microeconomic conditions do not guarantee proper macroeconomic conditions. The competitiveness of a company, being always to gain the most export revenue or market share, is therefore not consistent with the competitiveness of a country.

THE TARGET OF NATIONAL COMPETITIVENESS DEVELOPMENT

It could be said that the target of competitiveness development is the same as the target of general economic development, that is, to raise the living standard of the population or the standard of social welfare. A rise in social welfare can be represented by a rise of income deflated by a rise in the price of goods and services, which can determine a population's well being.

Furthermore, the target of economic development can be viewed as good macroeconomic conditions, which can be classified into 5 sub-targets.

1. *Growth*: Economic growth determines the income of the nation, of which the increase can imply the well being of the population. Economic growth is always represented by GDP (Gross Domestic Products) growth, or GDP per capita growth.
2. *Stability*: Stability can be classified both as internal stability and external stability. Internal stability involves, for example, inflation. External stability involves balance of payments, exchange rate stability, and other factors.
3. *Income distribution*: There are two viewpoints on income distribution; the absolute view and the relative view. From the absolute viewpoint, income distribution is the measurement of poverty, which is the proportion or the number of the poor in the country. From the relative viewpoint, income distribution is measured as the income gap among people. The popular index is the Gini coefficient.
4. *Full employment*: Full employment can represent the well being of a population because it ensures people's earning capability.
5. *Sustainability*: This is the state of an economy being able to grow constantly in the long run. The main issue of this target is always the issue of environmental or natural resource preservation.

Since there is a cost to industry restructuring, another aspect of economic development, from a microeconomic viewpoint, is to minimize the adjustment of industrial costs. Apart from these targets, there are social and political targets that should be discussed further than this paper allows.

THE IMPACT OF EXPORT ON ECONOMIC DEVELOPMENT

To study the impact of export, we should first understand the relationships between economic agents. The relationships among economic agents involving export are shown in Figure 4.2.

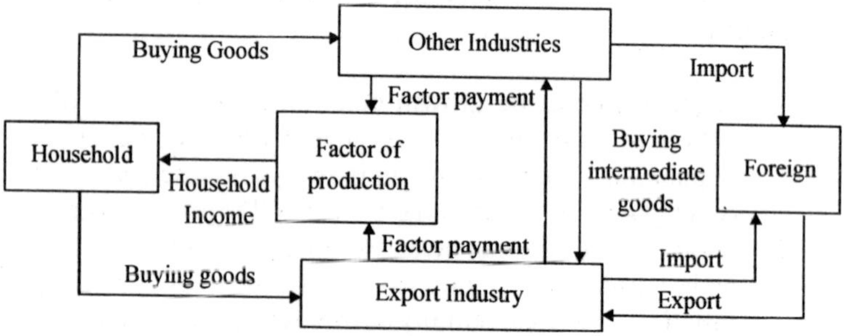

Fig. 4.2: Flows of revenue among economic agents

From Figure 4.2, the export industry receives revenue from export while paying for intermediate goods (raw materials) and factors of production, which are labour, capital, land, and natural resources. Furthermore, the export industry may import intermediate goods to use in production. Production factors are partly household owned, therefore, households receive return from them as household income. Households pay to buy goods and services that become the revenue of the industry. Other industries also have the same activities as the export industry.

The impact of export on some important macro variables can be described as follows.

IMPACT ON SOCIAL WELFARE

Social welfare is defined as the well being of a population. It is always measured by the level of the overall population's utility in society. The export of goods and services may cause social welfare to be increased, unchanged, or decreased, depending on the total income from the return of factors of production, and the rise of price level, or inflation. If the total income grows more than the price level, social welfare will be higher, but if the total income grows less than the price level, social welfare will be lower.

IMPACT ON REAL GDP

Export may influence real GDP to be increased, unchanged, or decreased. We can analyze the change of GDP by considering the quantity of total product domestically produced. Generally, upstream industries of the export industry always expand while downstream industries always contract. The total product will be the summation of expansion and contraction of all industries. However, export generally causes a positive total impact on GDP because the expansions of upstream industries are usually more than the contraction of downstream industries. The exceptional case is when the export industry is an upstream industry of many industries, for example, when the export industry is an agricultural industry. In this case, export can cause GDP to be decreased.

IMPACT ON INFLATION

When there is a higher export demand in an industry, the consumer price index will generally increase due to the increased price of products, both in upstream industries and downstream industries. The magnitude of the increase depends on the following factors.

1. The type of the export product, upstream-industry products, and downstream-industry products
   This is whether they are consumer products or not. The more they are consumer products, the more inflation there is, and vice versa.
2. The price elasticity of consumption demand on export products
   If the price elasticity of demand is low, when the price of product goes up due to export, the consumption quantity of that product will not decrease much, causing the consumer price index to increase by much.
3. The elasticity of substitution between domestic products and imported products

The less the elasticity of substitution is, the higher the products' price and the consumer price index will increase, due to the inability to use other products for substitution.

Nonetheless, the consumer price index can be decreased where there is a great contraction of downstream industries, causing their upstream industries (excluding the export industry) to be contracted with decreased prices. However, this is a rare case.

IMPACT ON CURRENT ACCOUNT BALANCE

The increase of export demand can cause the current account balance to be more or less surplus, unchanged, or more or less in deficit. However, export generally causes the current account balance to be more in surplus or less deficit, due to the greater degree of export revenue increase compared to import expense increase.

Factors determining the magnitude of change of the current account balance are the proportion of import content used to produce export product, and the elasticity of substitution between domestic products and import products.

IMPACT ON EMPLOYMENT

In the short run, wages will not adjust, and the total employment will adjust itself to clear the labour market. Employment can increase or decrease depending on characteristic of the industries being expanded or contracted. If expanded industries are labor-intensive, employment will likely be increased. If contracted industries are labor-intensive, employment will likely be decreased. Furthermore, the change of total employment also depends on the price change of other factors of production. If prices of other production factors are higher, demand for labour will increase, causing employment to increase, and vice versa. The increase or decrease of total employment will depend on the overall impacts of these factors.

In the long run, wages will adjust so that equilibrium is at full employment. The size of change depends on the elasticity of substitution between labour and other factors of production, particularly those of export industry. If the elasticity of substitution is high, the wage change will be small, and vice versa. This is because elasticity of substitution represents the ability to use other factors to substitute labour when wages are higher.

IMPACT ON OTHER INDUSTRIES

Upstream Industries

The direct impacts of export on upstream industries are the higher price and the expansion of upstream industries. However, the overall impact on upstream industries may differ from the direct impact, depending on the total sum of direct and indirect impacts. The general case is that upstream industries will be higher in their price and in the expansion of their output.

Downstream Industries

The direct impacts of export on downstream industries are in the higher price but contraction of downstream industries. However, the overall impact on downstream industries may differ due to the indirect impacts. The general case for the overall impact is the same as for the direct impact.

Figure 4.3 shows the impact of export on social welfare in terms of the industry of Thailand. It shows that the export of different products contributes different social welfare or macroeconomic conditions (not shown here). The export of some industries can even decrease social welfare while the export of some industries significantly contributes more social welfare than other industries contribute.

Strategies for Thailand's Export Industries

From my previous study, the strategies for export industries that will help to maximize social welfare can be summarized as in Table 4.1.

The detail of each strategy in Table 4.1 can be specified as follows.

Active export promotion both in the short and long term. This includes market expansion, trade negotiations, and defining competitors' strategies, as well as investment promotion. These measures are appropriate for non-metal products, electrical machinery and appliances, processed food, rubber and plastic products, and wood products, because Thailand is competitive in this group in the world market. The export expansion of this group of sectors will bring about a significant rise in social welfare. The share growth of these products in the world market are high.

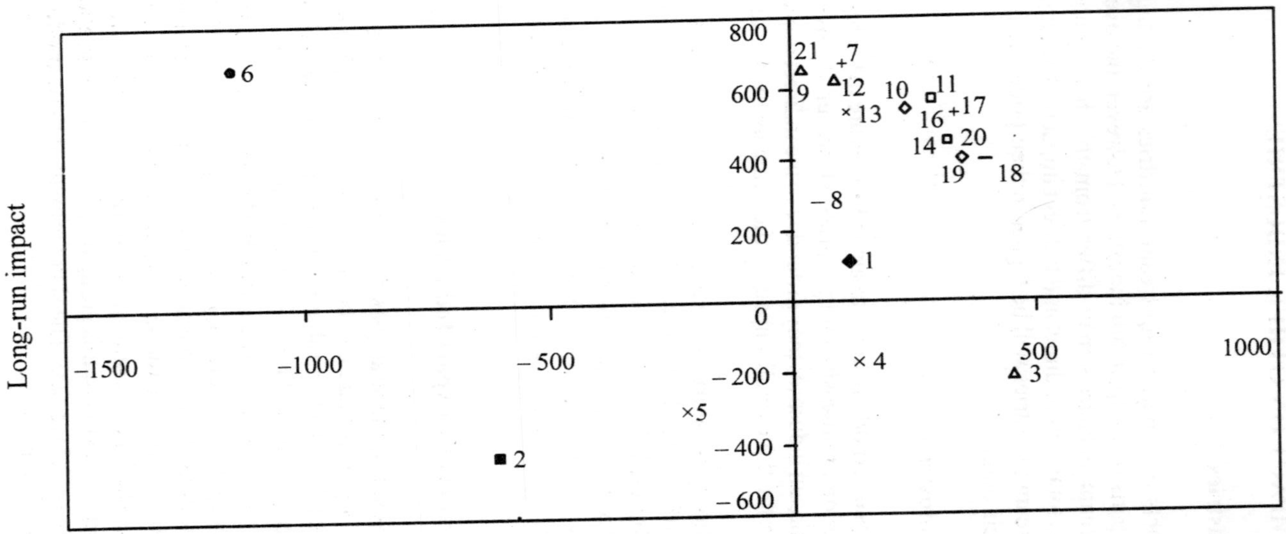

Fig. 3: Impact of Export by Industry on Social Welfare

Note: 1 = Cereals. 2 = Fruits and nuts, 3 = Rubber. 4 = Other crops. 5 = Livestock, 6 = Forestry and fisheries, 7 = Mining, 8 = Processed foods, 9 = Beverages and tobacco. 10 = Textiles and leather goods, 11 = Wood products. 12 = Paper production and printing, 13 = Chemical and petroleum products. 14 = Rubber and plastic products. 15 = Non-metal products. 16 = Metal products, 17 = Machinery and equipment, 18 = Electrical machinery and appliances. 19 = Motor vehicles and parts. 20 = Other manufacturing products, 21 = Utilities

Table 1: Strategies for each group of industries to maximize social welfare

1.	Active export promotion both in the short run and long run:	2.	Short-term protection but development for long-run competitiveness:
	Non-metal products, electrical machinery and appliances, processed food, rubber and plastic products, wood products		Chemical and petroleum products, motor vehicles and parts, beverages and tobacco, mining, utilities
3.	Export promotion in the short run, but not promoting large investment in the long run: Textiles and leather goods, other manufacturing products	4.	The maintenance of market share in the short run and moving labour to other sectors in the long run: Machinery and equipment, metal products, cereals, and paper production and printing
5.	A focus on domestic consumption, while encouraging link-ups with other related sectors: Vegetables, fruits and nuts, rubber	6.	Production restructuring: Other crops, livestock, forestry and fisheries

Source: Chareonwongsak, 2004.

Short-term protection but development for long-term competitiveness. This measure is appropriate for chemical and petroleum products, motor vehicles and parts, beverages and tobacco, mining, and utilities, as they are sectors in which an expansion of exports results in a significant increase in social welfare. The world market growth of these products is high while Thailand's level of competitiveness remains moderate. Among these sectors, chemical and petroleum products should be given the first priority due to their significant exports for the country.

The promotion of exports in the short run but in the long run we should not encourage or promote investment that needs large amount of capital. This measure is appropriate for textiles and leather goods, and other manufacturing products. Despite the fact that their export value is high, their competitiveness is also high; and an increase in their export renders an increase in social welfare, yet the world market growth is low. Therefore, these sectors tend to be in decline all over the world.

The maintenance of market share in the short run and measures taken to shift some labor from these sectors to other sectors in the long run. This measure is appropriate for machinery and equipment, metal products, cereals, and paper production and printing. This is due to the fact that the expansion of world markets is low while Thailand has a moderate level of competitiveness. Furthermore, the short-run measure to emphasize should be that of increasing the elasticity of the production factor's usage of cereals because this will help to increase social welfare.

A focus on domestic consumption, while encouraging link-ups with other related sectors. This is appropriate for vegetable, fruits and nuts, and rubber due to the fact that the expansion in their export will cause a decline in the social welfare and the world market growth is low or even decreasing.

Production restructuring. By having measures to shift some labour from these sectors to other sectors in the long run, focusing on domestic consumption, and encouraging link-ups with other related sectors. This measure is appropriate for other crops, livestock, forestry and fisheries because their export expansion causes social welfare to decrease, the world market growth is also low or even decreasing, and Thailand has a low level of competitiveness in these sectors.

WHY SHOULD COMPANIES BE CONCERNED FOR SOCIAL WELFARE?

Generally, a company's objective is to maximize its own profit, not to maximize social welfare. Why would companies consider this issue? Furthermore, to maximize company profit often contrasts with maximizing social welfare, for example, companies always minimize their costs by letting society bear some costs from their activities. For example, they generate pollution without payment. This is what we called externality.

Nevertheless, companies should take into account the impacts of their activities on the society or even help to develop better social welfare by the following reasons.

1. *Companies use resources from the country as factors of production:* The quality of resources in the country will affect the performance of companies. For example, a society that owns a high quality of labour will enable companies to be more productive. Therefore, the benefit provided by the country will affect the companies' performance in the long term.
2. *Companies should be socially responsible:* Companies should

be socially responsible because their activities have economic and social impacts on the society. Furthermore, some studies support that Corporate Social Responsibility (CSR) has a significant positive impact on a company's competitiveness. For example that of Pearce (2003), it was found that a business with a strong sense of corporate social responsibility will often be more successful in generating Economic Value Added, for reasons rooted in business strategy.

CONCLUSION

This paper has shown that competitiveness should not be viewed as the ability to generate the highest revenue from export, but rather to raise the highest population's standard of living. This is due to the fact that the export of different products contributes different living standards to a population, or different macroeconomic conditions. Furthermore, the export of some industries can even decrease the standard of living, while the export of some industries significantly contributes to the standard of living more than the export of other industries contribute. Concerning social responsibility, companies should therefore consider the impact of their export on the country's social welfare, or on its macroeconomic conditions.

Furthermore, companies should be able to adjust themselves to suit for the economic condition or current macroeconomic target of the country, because in different period of time, the country may have to focus on different target.

REFERENCES

Chareonwongsak, Kriengsak. (2004). *Strategies for Enhancing Competitiveness of the Thai Production Sector (in Thai)*. A thesis submitted to National Defense College.

International Institute for Management Development (IMD). *The World Competitiveness Yearbook*. 2003.

Janno Reiljan, Maria Hinrikus, and Anneli Ivanov. (2000). *Key Issues in Defining and Analysing the Competitiveness of a Country*. Working Paper, No. 561, Faculty of Economics and Business Administration, University of Tartu.

Krugman, Paul. "Competitiveness: A Dangerous Obsession," *Foreign Affairs*. Vol. 73, No. 2, March/April 1994, pp. 28-44.

Krugman, Paul. "Making Sense of the Competitiveness Debate," *Oxford Review of Economic Policy*. Vol. 12, No. 3, 1996, p. 17-25.

Learner, Edward E. and Stem, Robert M. *Quantitative International Economics.* Allyn & Bacon, 1970.

Pearce, Brian. (2003). *Sustainability and Business Competitiveness.*

Porter, Michael E. *"Thailand's Compctitiveness:. Creating the Foundations for Higher Productivity."* A paper presented in Bangkok, Thailand, 2003.

US Competitiveness Policy Council. "The first Report to the President and Congress, 1992." *World Economic Forum.* The Global Competitiveness Report. 1996.

5

Transforming Institutional Knowledge Into Organizational Effectiveness

The Challenges of Becoming a Learning Organization

Crispin Garden-Webster

INTRODUCTION

Throughout history knowledge has been the most important asset for development of economies and societies in general. This is because efficiently generating and distributing knowledge is a prerequisite for doing more with less and thus generating value and wealth. In recent decades this process has undergone exponential change with advances in information and communications technology. This has happened very quickly. Most of us here would find it hard to imagine working without email and yet as little as 15 years ago many of us did not have e-mail, many may not have had a PC or Mac on their desk. We have witnessed a dramatic increase in the flow of information and a change in work processes to accommodate the fact that the issue now is not so much one of possession of knowledge but of access to it. There are now unprecedented opportunities to collaborate, innovate and share what we know with others for our mutual benefit.

KNOWLEDGE AND THE ORGANIZATION

A major challenge facing most of us is how to tap into the wealth of talent and knowledge that courses through the veins of our organizations. This capability exists in three forms; there is (i) our human capital; the result of hiring, managing, developing and accessing talented people, while providing an enabling environment within which they may learn, work, and collaborate; (ii) secondly, there is structural capital or what remains in the organization when everyone goes home; this is the core capabilities, processes, databases, and systems that guide and document action and outcomes; and (iii) thirdly, stakeholder capital—the 'value' of the relationships we have with our staff, clients, investors and partners in terms of intelligence about our environment, trends and networks.

Models and frameworks on sustainable growth tend to follow a line of inquiry that involves value chain analysis of stakeholders, internal processes, human capital and the channels that deliver value to clients. The frontier of thinking around supporting strategy and vision is the exercise of evaluating the strength and relative quality of internal processes, and the "capabilities" necessary to support growth plans. This is the domain of knowledge management and harnessing the learning of the organization.

WHAT IS A LEARNING ORGANIZATION?

Being a learning organization is about management behavior, business processes and the commitment of senior leaders in setting priorities, removing barriers and directing the activity that allows the organization to be more sensitive to its stakeholders needs. Successful learning organizations are knowledge based. They understand that knowledge moves through networks rather than through structure, and they ensure that they:

- Translate learning into improvement of their operations, building the capacity to respond proactively to the challenges in their sphere of operations.
- Make themselves trans-parent, responsive and adaptable to the needs of their stakeholders.
- Establish an understanding that culture lives in the business processes and rules of the organization. Culture is experienced in such things as how hard or easy it is to get things done or how status is managed. Business processes drive management behavior, which sets the example for staff—this is where culture is created.
- Hold senior leaders accountable for valuing, actively channelling and seeking optimal utilization of the organization's human resources.

- Enable a mature and open acceptance of the fact that mistakes and unexpected outcomes are not embarrassments to be feared or hidden, but valued as opportunities to learn and improve.

Knowledge management is the capture, storage, analysis and dissemination of unstructured data within and outside the organization. Unstructured knowledge can account for up to 90 per cent of the organization's documented information and also includes extensive undocumented knowledge held by individual staff.

Managing knowledge can be pursued through one of two strategies. *Codification*—explicit knowledge and information coded and stored in databases, enabling people from across the organization to systematically access the information; and *Personalization,* where knowledge that is intangible or tacit, residing in individual experience and capability is shared. Personalization is often where the organization's greatest learning opportunities exist. In this environment, the role of technology is to connect and facilitate person-to-person dialogue. The critical exchange is via people's shared interactions, relationships and networks. Learning is a profoundly social activity and as noted earlier, knowledge moves through networks not structures.

The pursuit of *codification* fits with:

- an economic model of re-use that generates increasing value per transaction;
- information technology that captures and disseminates knowledge;
- people who are implementers of solutions (not generators of solutions) and are technology capable;
- e-Learning via the desktop/intranet;
- encouraging and recognizing contributions to a knowledge database.

The pursuit of *personalization* fits with:

- an economic model of customized solutions that have the potential to create some form of comparative advantage;
- information technology that facilitates contact and dialogue between people;
- people with superior interpersonal, communication, thinking skills and learning ability who are generators solutions;

- a learning and development framework that advocates one-to-one coaching rather than collective training;
- recognizing and encouraging those who share their knowledge.

OUR KNOWLEDGE ENVIRONMENT—GLOBAL AND REGIONAL TRENDS

After two decades of restructuring and re-engineering many organisations coming out of the days of planned economies face the challenge of organizing what they know and channelling their expertise in ways that make them resilient to the discontinuous change that characterizes operations in both private and public sector environments. There is also a growing recognition on this 'frontier' that the capabilities that will create value in the future are typically found in formal and informal networks of people and communities of practice working together across organisational boundaries. The response to recent SARS and Avian flu crises exemplifies this latter point. People will innovate, adapt and overcome if they are allowed to and if compelled to by a common threat. For ADB where I work this issue is critical as our work relies heavily on networks and relationships of people at regional and local level.

In the Asia Pacific region, local and global trends converge to create complex and diverse issues for leaders. It is important that those of us charged with leading organizations have an understanding of the trends that influence government and commerce at a macro level. These trends shape our experience of work and they both facilitate and frustrate our efforts to learn from unexpected outcomes and encourage people to share what they know. The key trends that provide context for the Asia Pacific region are:

(a) **Megamergers:** Global mergers create giant multinational organizations that are larger, richer and more powerful than small to medium size countries. Of the 100 largest economics in the world, 51 are corporations and 49 are countries. Globalization of companies and brands also makes it increasingly difficult to determine the home country or culture of many corporations.

(b) **Regional Economic Power:** Strong regional trade associations such as the EU, NAFTA, ASEAN, APEC etc.

are shaping economic bases in supranational geographic terms around the world.

(c) **Economic Interdepen-dence:** Global monetary and regulatory agencies will be required to handle severe volatility in the international financial system and thus create economic interdependence on the one hand and threaten independence on the other.

(d) **Privatising Power:** The privatisation of state owned enterprises and the associated diminishing economic decision-making power of nation states changes the landscape of ownership and therefore the value structures of economies.

(e) **Identity Problems:** In an increasingly interconnected world, people will have choices between being global cosmopolitans, regional traders, national cheerleaders, ethnic personalities and local citizens.

(f) **American Backlash:** Defensiveness against ubiquitous American culture, democracy, military might and free market capitalism will counter the continuing strength of the US as the primary world power.

(g) **European Integration:** The EU and the Euro with the seemingly inevitable political integration to follow will further solidify Europe's influence on the world stage.

(h) **Asian Potential:** The hardworking nature of Asian communities, the speed of economic growth in the region, the intangible value of their extended social and family networks, combined with their commitment to education, will fuel a level of growth unmatched in the west. China and India have the potential to become the largest and most important markets in the world. The expatriate Chinese, Indian and Philippine communities around the world are a substantial global network.

(i) **Poverty Reduction:** The gap between 'haves' and 'have-nots' both within and among countries will continue to widen unless more developed countries make a stronger commitment to wealth creation and wealth distri-bution in less developed nations.

(j) **Ethnic Conflicts:** The number and intensity of ethnic conflicts are increasing worldwide as is terrorism driven by ethnic, political and religious differences. The rise of weapon states presents significant challenges to world order.

(k) **Economics *vs.* Environ-mentalism:** As economic development expands globally; shortages of natural resources, pollution and environmental harm will accelerate, creating political and economic conflicts in all countries with all parties culpable.

(l) **Demographic Dilemmas:** The swelling population of young people in the developing world and the need to create jobs for them-combined with the growth of the elderly population in the develo-ped world and the need to care for them-will create economic and political challenges for all.

HOW IS THE EMPLOYMENT RELATIONSHIP CHANGING?

We are witnessing the beginnings of a change in the dynamics of the employment relationship that is characterized by:

- a readiness to challenge the accepted wisdom;
- a shift from a labor economy to a knowledge economy;
- a casualization of the labor market as individuals begin to manage their personal value and take accountability for determining the kind of employment relationship that they have and how they work. This is reflected in the rise of free agents, independent contractors and amongst employees a push for more flexible work hours to meet work life balance interests.

Today people are equally likely to describe what they do as much as who they work for; they are more likely to manage their employability and seek to be involved in successful ventures. Herein lies something of a paradox and a key challenge for organizations in the immediate future—maintaining a coherent organizational brand in terms of employer value propositions while accommodating the emergence of 'personal brand' amongst educated, talented and marketable people. This reflects a fundamental shift in the power from the employer to the individual worker, particularly in high demand, strategically imperative capability areas. People are swapping the old values of *status and stability* for the new values of *personal growth and opportunity*. This is particularly the case with so called knowledge workers who will be the engines of economic growth in the future.

WHAT IS A KNOWLEDGE WORKER AND HOW MUST THEY BE MANAGED?

A knowledge worker is someone who produces value from ideas and their intellect. Their products are improvements in ideas, designs, processes or service levels. It may be simply more knowledge. In November 2001 *The Economist* published an article by Peter Drucker (**The Next Society**. *The Economist*, Edition 3-9 November 2001) entitles 'The Next Society'. The article is about the knowledge economy in which Drucker proposes that this new knowledge economy will rely heavily on knowledge workers. At present, this term is widely used to describe people with considerable theoretical knowledge and learning: doctors, lawyers, teachers, accountants, chemical engineers. But the most striking growth, Drucker believes, will be in "knowledge technologists': computer technicians, software designers, analysts in clinical labs, manufacturing technologists, and paralegals.

These people, it is suggested, are as much manual workers as they are knowledge workers; in fact, they usually spend far more time working with their hands than with their brains. But their manual work is based on a substantial amount of theoretical knowledge, which can be acquired only through formal education, not through an apprenticeship. They are not, as a rule, better paid than traditional skilled workers, but they see themselves as "professionals". In the article Drucker reminds us of the old saying, 'you cannot hire a hand: the whole person always comes with it'. But you cannot hire a person either; the spouse almost always comes with it. Duel careers are now a feature of the new economy and must be accommodated, in our thinking about careers.

So how do we manage these knowledge workers? Drucker suggests that while knowledge workers need to be satisfied with their pay, because dissatisfaction with income and benefits is a powerful disincentive. The incentives, he believes are different. The management of knowledge workers should be based on the assumption that the organization needs them more than they need the organization. They know they can leave—they are volunteers with both mobility and self-confidence in the same way as volunteers who work for not-for-profit organizations.

The first thing such people want to know is what the organization is trying to do and where it is going. Next, they are interested in personal achievement and personal responsibility—which means they have to be put in the right job. Knowledge workers expect continuous learning and continuous training. Above all, they want respect, not so much for themselves but for their area of knowledge. In that regard, they have moved several steps beyond traditional workers, who used to expect to be told what to do, although later they were increasingly expected to "participate". Knowledge workers, by contrast, expect to make the decisions in their own area.

THE ADB EXPERIENCE

At ADB our long-term strategic framework that looks out to 2015 identifies the need for the Bank to become a learning organization. To respond to evolving challenges, we must maximize the use of our vast knowledge resources and draw upon resources, skills, and expertise both inside and outside the organization. We must not only develop the capacity to learn quickly from our operational experiences and those of our development partners, but also develop the capacity to disseminate such experience in the form of "best practices" among our development member countries, our staff, and our development partners.

To do this we will develop the capacity to stimulate, test and adopt new ideas. Practical examples of some of the things we have embarked on are:

1. We are developing an HR strategy that will provide incentives and investment in skill-development;
2. We are developing a diversity framework that acknowledges the importance of encouraging people who think differently; and in our processes we will look for opportunities to encourage constructive dissent, disagreement and debate.
3. We are looking for ways to adapt the culture to assess appropriate risks and be open to learning from well intentioned but unintended outcomes.
4. We will train managers and supervisors to offer timely, accurate feedback and proactively share knowledge and reward collaboration.
5. We have developed a comprehensive knowledge management strategy that identifies priorities and processes for sharing and disseminating what we know and aims to foster a knowledge supportive environment by improving our KM

monitoring system, improving our business processes and IT solutions for knowledge capture, enrichment, storage and retrieval, enabling com-munities of practice and expanding our collaborative capacity through external networks.

6. We have created a business unit focused on developing our capacity for measuring development results. This is a critical element of our internal reform agenda and to this end our management have endorsed a results based management frame-work that emphasizes the need to focus on poverty results. This means being clear about outputs, indicators and measuring outcomes. It is an outward focus rather than an internal processing focus.

Internally these initiatives require robust change management and incentive systems. Externally as noted earlier we operate in a rapidly changing, knowledge based labor market and we work with organizations with strong visions and diffuse boundaries who also recognize the need to develop their institutional learning capacity. This presents HR management challenges.

Becoming a valued business partner is about being part of the value creation process in terms of development solutions. An HR Group that develops and maintains an organization's strategic infrastructure will be considered a critical investment.

SUMMARY

So in conclusion we are embarking on a journey that marks the departure from the assumptions and understandings of the industrial and information age that were about technology and access to this technology. Looking forward the knowledge economy is about grasping the opportunities that this access provides. This is not an obscure world of ideas and intentions; it is a world where practical development solutions are fuelled by the compelling proposition that 'none of us are as smart as all of us'. Through the effective brokering of knowledge, we can make changes faster with greater levels of engagement. For ADB as a development institution this means putting people with questions in touch with people with answers and harnessing the collective knowledge of our development community to develop sustainable solutions to poverty reduction across the region.

6

The Impact of Training on the Economic Development of Mauritius

R. Dubois

BACKGROUND

When Mauritius became independent in 1968, it had a mono-crop economy with fast population growth rate, high unemployment and low per capita income. Agriculture alone contributed to 24 per cent of its GDP. Nowadays, it has a diversified economic base comprising Agriculture, Manu-facturing, Tourism, Financial Services and Information and Communication Technology (ICT). And it is already planning to diversify further with two additional economic pillars, namely knowledge and seafood.

Today it stands amongst the upper middle income countries with a GNP per capita of USD 4000. It has had an average GDP growth rate of 5.6 per cent for the last decade. Mauritius tops the list of the Sub-Saharan African countries on the international Human Development Index. In addition it was ranked second, only next to Tunisia in the 2000 Africa Competitiveness report after being first in 1998 report. It is often cited as a success story and a model for many small island economies.

Different factors have been identified to have contributed in the success of Mauritius. According to the World Bank (2002), the key ingredients of this success have been the stability of the democratic order, ethnic tolerance, macro-economic stability and a focused strategy aimed at being globally competitive for labour-intensive activities. This presentation purports to demonstrate the part played by a sound human resource development in the economic development of Mauritius.

THE ECONOMIC OVERVIEW

The Mauritian economy has undergone significant changes since its independence in 1968. It was basically a mono-crop agricultural economy in the early 1970s with agriculture contributing to 24 per cent of its GDP and employing over 70,000 people.

Together with the rising tourist trade and favourable international sugar prices, the country experienced an economic boom during the period 1971 to 1977. Despite this initial boom the economy experienced a decline at the end of the 1970s, due to rising oil prices and decreased sugar prices, forcing the government to tighten spending

The country was faced with increasing unemployment and underwent a prolonged programme of structural adjustment, through World Bank and IMF support to fiscal stability. The government focused its energies around boosting exports, restructuring the sugar industry, diversifying agriculture and enhancing the tourism industry. This lead to the creation of the Export Processing Zone within the manufacturing sector focusing mainly on textiles and clothing as the second economic pillar. The sector developed rapidly in the early 80s benefiting from the Hong Kong syndrome. Investors were moving away from Hong Kong in search of another location and Mauritius offered the alternative with a range of tax incentives, cheap labour and the quota factor. By the mid-1980s, the manufacturing sector was the major employer in the country with up to 90000 people at its peak.

Manufacturing industry has been a key driving force behind economic growth. In 2000 it contributed 25 per cent of GDP, half of which was accounted for by the EPZ. The EPZ also began diversifying from a strong reliance on clothing and textiles to more sophisticated industries, such as information technology and light engineering and financial services.

Mauritius is classified by the World Bank as an "upper middle income country" with a GNP per capita of USD 4000. It has had an average GDP growth of 5.6 per cent from 1990 to 2001 and GDP per capita growth of 4.4 per cent annually.

As of end 2001, the Mauritian population was estimated at 1,205,665, with annual growth of 1 per cent. The total estimated labour force of the island in 2002 was 541,100, comprising 353,700 males and

187,400 females. Employment in 2002 stood at 490,000 (90%), with 10 per cent unemployment. This figure has now been revised to 8.7 per cent.

Probably the most important source for international comparison is the Human Development Index, which provides the rankings of Mauritius with respect to the other countries. The 2003 index as shown in Table 6.1 shows a generally favourable performance. In addition, Mauritius ranks 17th on the UNDP Human Poverty Index, which places it substantially higher than other Sub-Saharan African countries. It was also ranked second after Tunisia in the 2000 Africa Competitiveness report, after being first in the 1998 report.

The clothing and textile industries still accounted for more than half the industries in the EPZ in 2000. However, significant challenges emerged in the textile industry in the late1990s due to heightened labour costs and increased competition. The increased cost of labour coupled with the phasing out of the MFA in January 2005, the entry of China in the WTO etc. has made it that Mauritius is no more competitive in the range of basic garment where some big companies are pitched. Hence companies have started to retrench employees.

So Mauritius had to revisit its development strategy. Textile Sector is being restructured in order to concentrate more on the production of a higher level of quality products. The tourism industry, given our geographical location, is seen more as a high class destination. The financial services sector requires greater transparency and professionalism. Hence the reason for the high importance given to well qualified and trained people. In addition, globalization resulting from the deregulation and liberalization and rapid changes in the field of ICT has called for higher skilled type of human resources.

PEOPLE: OUR PRINCIPAL ASSET

Mauritius has no other asset but its people. And people can only be

Table 1: Mauritius and the 2003 HDI

HDI Rank	*Life expectancy at birth (years) 2001*	*Adult literacy rate (%age 15+) 2001*	*Gross enrollment ratio (%) 2000/1*	*GNP pc (US$) 2003*	*Life Expectancy Index*	*Education Index*	*GDP Index*	*HDI*
62	72.6	84.8	69	4,000	0.78	0.80	0.77	0.779

assets if they are adequately qualified and competent. The past economic development of Mauritius is a vivid example of how human resources can be harnessed for the betterment of standards of living in a country with virtually limited resources. It must, however, be mentioned that the abundance of labour and the low level of technology required were very conducive to the initial industrialization process.

With the shift from labour intensive operations to higher-value added activities, the demand for high-calibre technicians has increased considerably. Furthermore, to compete successfully in this era of globalization characterized by trade liberalization and rapidly changing technology, it is widely recognized and accepted that significant improvements in productivity, quality and delivery need to be made. Unsurprisingly, human capital is being seen as a determinant factor in meeting these challenges. More specifically, we would require a competent, productive and flexible human resource capable of acquiring new skills for new jobs.

A comprehensive human resource development strategy becomes central to the success of Mauritius. It must be pointed out that human resource development has always been high on the agenda of all the successive governments of Mauritius. The figure shows that the expenditure on education as a percentage of the total government expenditure. This is why the education and training system arena has always drawn attention of the stakeholders and has continuously been under a change process.

THE SCHOOLING SYSTEM

The education system is vested in the Ministry of Education and Scientific Research. Education is free at pre-primary level, at primary level, at secondary level to age of 20 years, and at the University of Mauritius. Prior to 1976, education was free only at the primary level. In 1976 in an attempt to provide maximum access to the Mauritian youths, the Government declared universal free education right through to the University of Mauritius. As of 1991, education was compulsory from ages 5 to 12. From January 2005, eleven year schooling will be introduced which will make it compulsory to attend school for eleven years or up to the age of 16. This would assist in raising the level of general education and better preparing learners to enter the TVET system or continuing with the academic stream.

All scholars who successfully complete six years of primary

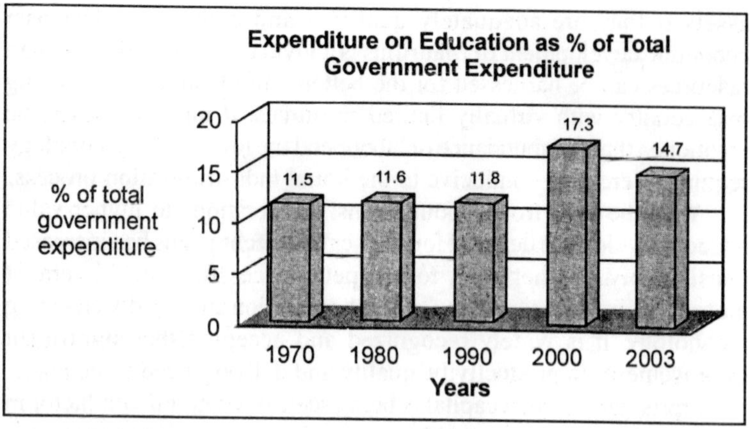

schooling receive the Certificate of Primary Education (CPE). These scholars can then go on to do the Cambridge School Certificate, which ends at Form V. Those who pass Form V and wish to follow the formal academic route, can continue to the Higher School Certificate, which requires the completion of "A" levels. Those who fail the CPE twice are able to access pre-vocational courses.

At the post-secondary, there are three Polytechnics, offering advanced skills in Management and Technical Trades and five Higher Education Institutions, including one distance education institution.

In addition, the Industrial and Vocational Training Board (IVTB) provides training for those who have dropped out of the mainstream as well as those who, after completion of their Higher School Certificate, wish to pursue studies in a vocational stream.

Table 6.2 shows the Human development index trends from 1975 to 2000.

Table 6.2: Human Development Index Trends, 1975-2000

	1975	*1980*	*1985*	*1990*	*1995*	*2001*
Mauritius		0.654	0.683	0.720	0.744	0.779

Source: UNDP 2003.

Figure 6.2 below shows the prevailing Mauritian structure of the formal education and training system. The private training institutions who contribute significantly to the development of the Mauritian human resource development is not shown here. Presently there are

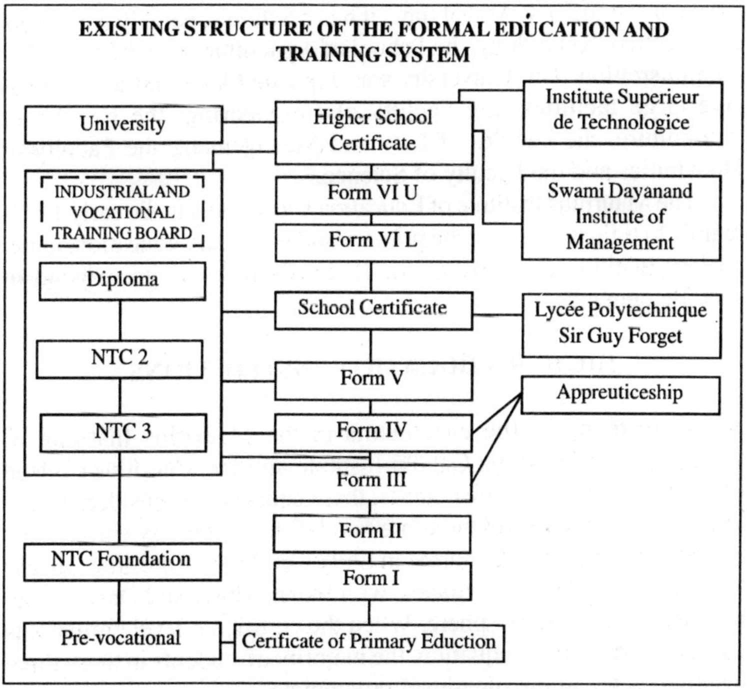

Fig. 2: Structure of the Formal Education and Training System

about 300 of them offering training at different levels up to university level.

MILESTONES IN THE EVOLUTION OF EDUCATION

When Mauritius was a predomi-nantly agricultural based economy, a College of Agriculture saw the light in the early 1900s. The COA which later became the School of Agriculture at the creation of the University of Mauritius has helped to form most of the Agronomists, sugar chemists, agricultural engineers etc. practising in the agricultural sector in Mauritius. Its impact on this sector cannot be emphasised enough. Today it has changed in the Faculty of Agriculture of the University of Mauritius and is also providing training in other areas such as horticulture, biotechnology etc. to respond to the demand of the country.

The University of Mauritius was created as a Developmental University in the late 1960s again to respond to the developmental needs of the country. At that time, it has 3 Schools, namely the School of Industrial Technology, the School of Agriculture and the School of Administration. The University was expanded later and today it has five large faculties: the Faculty of Engineering, the Faculty of Agriculture, the Faculty of Law and Management, the Faculty of Humanities and the Faculty of Science.

The Mauritius Institute of Education was created in the early 1970s mainly to train teachers of the primary and secondary education. Other tertiary institutions as shown in Table 6.3 followed to respond to specific demands.

HIGHER EDUCATION INSTITUTIONS

Although many of the enrolments in the Mauritius Institute of Education, the Mahatma Gandhi Institute and the Mauritius College of the Air are in certificate courses, these courses are considered to be vocational in nature and therefore not defined as tertiary enrolments. As expected, certificate courses in Early Childhood Education appear to be most popular with females, with Indian Music and Dance being popular in the cultural sphere. When the certificate-level enrolments are removed from the equation, the majority of students in these three institutions are in diploma-level programmes.

The University of Mauritius provides the large majority of enrolment in degree qualifications, with these being primarily in the Faculties of Engineering, and Law and Management. In 2001/2, the University produced 766 degree-level graduates, but only 3 graduates from post-graduate programmes.

Different departments were set up in the different faculties as and when the need arose. For instance, a department of textile of textile was set up to meet the needs of the textile industry while the department of computer was set up to prepare IT technicians and graduates to work in the IT and IT enabled services sector.

THE VET SYSTEM RESPONDING TO THE NEEDS OF THE ECONOMY

It is generally recognized today, that training is a prerequisite for exploiting the potential of a growing economy. To ensure its success, an education and training system needs to be demand-led, flexible and responsive to the economic and social needs of the economy. In

Table 6.3: Post-secondary (Higher Education) Statistics for 2002

Institution	*Total Student Popu-lation*	*Non-formal*	*Certificate Advanced Certificate*	*Diploma/ Advanced Diploma*	*Degree*	*Post-Grad-uate*	*Male Student Popu-lation*	*Female student Popu-lation*
University of Mauritius	5,310		46	254	4,359	526	2,849	2,461
Mauritius Institute of Education	5,212		3,397	1,297	257	261	1,830	3,382
Mahatma Gandhi Institute	2,527		2,038	248	199	32	786	1,741
University of Technology	733			151	515	67	412	321
Mauritius College of the Air	1,935	247	1,156	25	9	14	484	1,451
Total	15,717	247	6,637	1,975	5,339	900	6361	9,356

Source: Central Statistics Office: Digest of Educational Statistics.

Mauritius, with the on-going structural transformation of the economy, we are constantly witnessing a major change in the type of manpower demanded by industry.

Provision of vocational training is mainly taken care of by:

(i) the Industrial and Vocational Training Board (IVTB)
(ii) the Technical School Management Trust Fund (TSMTF)
(iii) Private registered training providers-about 300

The type of training to be delivered and the consequential investment in training facilities have always been tributary to the needs and demand of the market. In order to support the tourism industry which was in its nascent state in the early 1970s, the first hotel and catering school was created under the then Ministry of Economic Planning and Development. The school was later absorbed within the IVTB at its creation and is today one of the centres of excellence of the IVTB.

In 1988, the IVTB which was to become the lead body responsible for all training in Mauritius, was created in order to respond to the needs of the manufacturing sector which was expanding rapidly and was in dire needs of skilled labour to sustain its growth. The IVTB, a joint partnership of the public and private sectors, was given as main roles to regulate, facilitate and provide training. Immediately, regulations were developed to ensure quality and relevance of training provided by private training providers; various training schemes were put in place to encourage employers to invest in the training and development of their employees in order to upgrade their skills and enhance productivity. In parallel, the IVTB started offering training in a few basic trades identified by industry. It expanded further its training breadth with time and as the needs arose in other trades. Inevitably, as the IVTB grew and as the labour market also changed, it had to review its strategy. The training schemes had to be revisited a few times in order to make it more responsive to the demands of industry and more strategic in its objectives.

Figure 6.2 shows the number of people who have benefited from training under the levy grant scheme administered then by the IVTB. The numbers have been increasing over the years.

As the economy grew, it became more and more evident that there was a need for high caliber technicians and middle managers. The IVTB responded by initiating a series of high level Diploma training programmes.

Today through its 12 training centres, it offers training at the basic level in 22 trades ranging from agriculture to wood trade; training at the intermediary level in 12 trades ranging from communication electronics to tourism and training at the Diploma level in 9 trades spreading from Graphics design and multimedia to Clothing production.

Figure 6.3 shows the number of students that have been trained within the IVTB training centres ever since its inception. Training delivered is for pre-employment either through structured class based delivery or through the apprenticeship system introduced in 1996. Training is also being provided to in-service personnel in order to upgrade their skills and to facilitate lifelong learning. As a matter of fact, the population of in-service training is roughly 65 per cent of the total population of the people being trained. As at date, it can be said that the IVTB has provided training to some 44 per cent of the labour force in Mauritius either directly or indirectly through a training levy that was introduced in 1989.

Consequently, It can be advocated without doubt that the IVTB through its training has contributed significantly to the economic development of Mauritius.

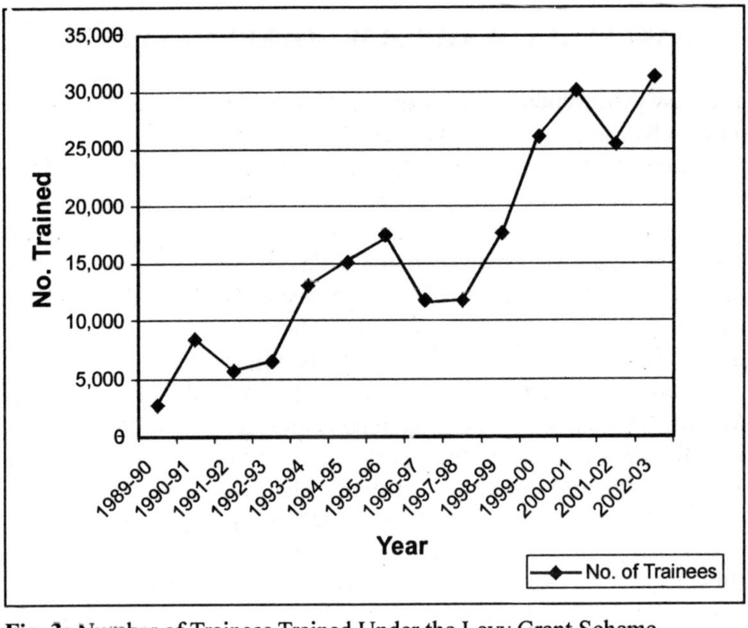

Fig. 3: Number of Trainees Trained Under the Levy Grant Scheme

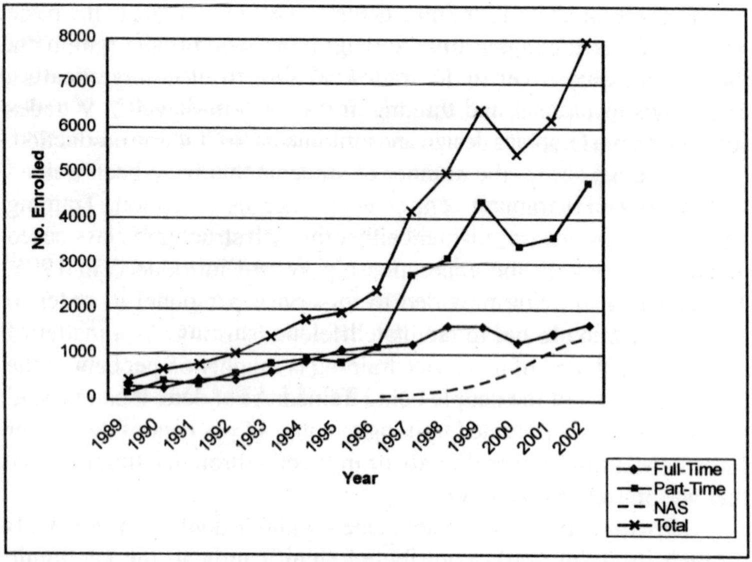

Fig. 6.4: No of People Enrolled on IVTB Training Programmes Over the Years

CHALLENGES OF THE NEW GOVERNMENT IN 2000

The new government which came to power in 2000 was faced with major challenges of ensuring economic growth whilst ensuring a reduction of unemployment and alleviation of poverty. Some of the economic indicators were an unemployment rate of 8 per cent.

The new government took the challenge of launching ICT as the fifth pillar of the Mauritian economy. Software development engineers then ITE enabled services were seen as sectors where Mauritius may have comparative advantage given the higher literacy rate of Mauritius, the political stability of the nation and its bilinguism.

However, no economic growth can be sustained in a country like Mauritius which has only human resources as its asset unless the right investment is effected in the development of human capital to drive productivity and economic growth. The new government fully conscious of this decided to make HRD the cornerstone of the development of Mauritius. This was reflected in the speech of the President of the Republic of Mauritius at the opening of the First Session of the Third National Assembly in October 2000:-

"Human Resource Development remains one of the cornerstones of our development strategy. Government is adopting an integrated approach to Skills Development, Training and Productivity with the creation of a new Ministry. A National Training Strategy will be formulated with a view to upgrading the knowledge and skills of our labour force and to promote employ ability"

Government created a new Ministry devoted to Training, Skills Development, Employment and Productivity and leaving the Ministry of Education to concentrate on the academic stream.

THE VET SYSTEM REFORMED

Immediately on coming into being the Ministry initiated a range of reforms aimed at consolidating the training system.

Hence the IVTB was streamlined and two other organisations were established. The Ministry now incorporates

- the Industrial and Vocational Training Board (IVTB) which is now an enhanced provider of training;
- the Mauritius Qualifications Authority (MQA)—formed in May 2002, which is the regulatory body;
- the National Productivity and Competitiveness Council (NPCC), which is responsible for the development of a culture of productivity in enterprise; and

Ministry of Education & Scientific Research

↓

- Eliminate rat race by pulling up more secondary schools
- Compulsory education up to age of 16 or 11 years of schooling
- PV stream for those who fail CPE twice
- ZEP school for vulnerable region

Ministry of Training, Skills & Developments Productivity

↓

NITS

↓

- the Human Resource Development Council (HRDC)—Act passed in July 2003 promote human resource development in line with national economic and social objectives.

The intention of the government was confirmed in the first budget speech in 2001-2002

> "To attain this objective, Government will invest massively in education, training and Information and Communication Technology (ICT) as well as in infrastructure and environment to transform Mauritius into a diversified, hi-tech, high income services and knowledge economy fully integrated in the new global economic environment".

Many new measures have been announced and implemented since then that directly impact on the economy. Just to mention a few, namely:

- Setting up of a School of IT within the IVTB
- Free training to SC and HSC in IT, Call centre operations and BPO
- Skills development programme for fresh diplomats and graduates in order to provide them with the necessary experience to facilitate their being employed
- Additional training facilities in hotel and tourism in order to support the new hotels coming up and the growing tourist industry
- National Trade Certificate foundation course mounted for those who fail the certificate of primary education twice and followed a prevocational route in order to allow them to join the vocational training courses
- Special training programme for the unemployed and retrenched

CONCLUSION

The economic success of Mauritius has been based on many factors, one of the main ones being, the quality of its human resource. The wisdom of the successive governments of Mauritius in investing massively in its human resource, its only asset, has been determinant in sustaining the growth of its different sectors of activities.

7

Leadership in Knowledge Management Domain

Rosclina A. Saufi

INTRODUCTION

Knowledge management (KM) has been seen as the heart of the organization as to facilitate the flow of knowledge into and within the company. Scholars have regard KM as movement of tacit knowledge (Birkinshaw & Julian, 2001), as a process that deals with the development, storage, retrieval, and dissemination of information and expertise within an organization (Gupta *et al.*, 2000), and as multi-faceted as it involves information, technology and culture (Alavi & Leidner, 2002). Wiig (1993) defines KM as the management of corporate knowledge that can improve a range of organizational performance characteristics by enabling the enterprise to be more "intelligent acting".

The development of ICT is expected to assist managers and professionals to create focus from organizing information to providing systems for decision-making. As such, the importance of developing leaders and managers that are capable and able in managing information as to what it requires within the organization is essential. The essence of leadership process in knowledge management includes motivation, knowledge, wisdom, influencing and communicating, as well as to reduce problem-solving time.

PERSPECTIVES ON KNOWLEDGE MANAGEMENT

Evidence in the past indicates that KM can be ascribed as an information-based, technology-based, and culture-based (Alavi & Leidner, 2002; Harris, 1996). From the information-based perspective, studies by Alavi and Leidner indicate that KM is about characteristics of information such as that it should be accessible, real-time and actionable. It also acts as corporate yellow pages for employee reference not only on gathering information but who holds the knowledge and how to locate them.

Vehicles to gather and store information are referred to technological-based perspective. The need for data mining, search engines, IT infrastructure and others often to be associated with KM. In terms of culture-based perspective, Alavi and Leidner describe KM as cultivating learning organization, com-munication process and intellectual property. The third perspective involves the culture dimension. It is believed that the teamwork spirit is very much needed to encourage innovation and dynamism in the organization. Teamwork environ-ment would develop the sense of responsibility to be shared and belongings to the company. Teamwork based-structure thus necessitates information and management to be shared. While encouraging the team environment, clear guidelines and understanding of the knowledge impart in the company is essential. As KMS is about integration of management function, therefore, the culture of learning and sharing must be also cultivated.

Thus, the core issues in KMS include:

Infrastructure for KM
- Information
  - Client, market, competitive
  - Activity, financial, product, services
- Technology
  - Integrated databases
  - Global IT infrastructure
  - Larger bandwidth
- Culture
  - Teamwork
  - Practical guidelines
  - Knowledge-sharing
- Human Capital Issues
  - Management
  - Leadership
  - Training and development
  - Reward

The human capital aspect is the critical element where lies the 'machines' that drive the KMS. This includes issue of developing an integration management system, leadership dynamism, training and development and compatible reward system.

The three distinct perspectives together with the dimension of human capital implies the type of leaders required to manage the organization information and to cultivate learning culture, which the author believes to be one of the fundamental issues in KMS. Based on these perspectives, this paper attempts to discuss the characteristics of leader and its process in the context of KMS.

THE CHARACTERISTICS OF K-LEADERS

"The aim of leadership is not merely to find and record failures of men, but to remove the causes of failures: to help people to do a better job with less effort".

—Dr. Edwards Deming

Since knowledge management provides a platform for intellectual thinking (Fuller, 2002) for management and development of "knowledge" in the company thus the requirement for "knowledge-leaders" is essential. The development of knowledge management thus requires knowledge-leaders who have distinct characteristics that able to emulate a knowledgeable environment which in turn cultivating knowledge-workers. Several characteristics are expected to include:

KNOWLEDGE ORIENTED

For a leader to inspire and manage a knowledge system thus he or she must be somewhat knowledgeable. Knowledge here refers to any information that able to assist the leader to lead and manage the organization through facts and evidence. Facts and evidence are those supporting documents that support leaders' decision-making process. Areas that may be relevant to a leader include strategic management, leadership skill, human capital manage-ment, economics and political environment, entrepreneurialship, decision-making tools, marketing, financial market and well-informed about company core and/or related businesses.

VISION

Visionary leaders are necessitating in directing organisation. Establishing a clear vision may imply leader's inspirational statement of where he takes the company in the future. "When a man does not know what harbour he is making for, no wind is the right wind." Thus, the ability to develop a clear focus is needed to assure the strategic choices are made correctly. It is about providing direction and managing information. The ingredients include:

- the need to have a clear vision
- the need to be challenging
- the need to be inspiring
- the need to be shared
- the need to unify
- the need to point to the way

TECHNOLOGY ORIENTED

The next challenge is to have a leader that emphasizes on technology such as development of IT infrastructure which is essential for data mining, storing, retrieving, searching, and disseminating. Creative and innovative characteristics may add values to leadership development in KMS. The leader himself must understand and shared the importance of technology with his employees as the key element for managing day-to-day operations.

FACILITATOR, COACH AND TEAM PLAYER

These three roles are particularly requires to necessitate the process of empowerment. Facilitator is a function that requires managers to do more and more (Kinlaw, 1995). They are expected to demonstrate how they aid, support, expedite, help, assist, encourage, coordinate, integrate, stimulate and do other things to ensure organization achieves superior levels of performance.

Coaching refers to serving as tutor or mentor to facilitate employees in acquiring new knowledge or skills and employees' success.

Team player is a functioning that requires leaders to develop team environment in order to cultivate sense of membership among employees to share responsibility. Leaders in this context serve as conduit of information, manage multiple interfaces among work processes and work units, provide core values and send new ideas into the organization.

EMPOWERING

The ability to empower and delegate jobs to employees is essential in cultivating team work. Leaders need to encourage an open communication system, set goals and strategies, and train for empowerment by giving people the knowledge and skills to be full and competent players in the improvement of total quality.

INNOVATIVE

A leader is a person who inspires his followers to take a journey to its destination. The innovative leader includes the ability to design and manage processes that are efficient and effective, to focus on the customers' needs, to provide avenues for managing information, to have knowledge of and manage change appropriately, to develop new ideas and suggestions, to continuously improve everything, and to spend time to identify and remove obstacles.

ENTREPRENEURIALSHIP

This characteristic includes a leader being able to lake challenge and risk and be accountable for his activities. In the context of managing information the ability of a leader to control the flow of knowledge and information within and outside the organization plays a critical role to the success of managing information effectively.

THE LEADERSHIP PROCESS: THE SUCCESSFUL FRAMEWORK

The process of leadership development in managing knowledge can be described to integrate seven major dimensions: the leadership qualities, the skills, the human capital management, the process management, the strategic planning and direction, the ICT infrastructure and the culture. This can be subdivided to include the following:

Situation analysis
Developing vision
Developing focus
Building the management system
  Input-IT infrastructure, data base
  Process
  Output

Cultivating Culture of learning

The idea is to integrate the dimensions in order to build the synergy for efficient and effective ways in managing knowledge. The framework can be described in Figure 7.1.

For organization to successfully implement its knowledge management system may not only having a good and quality management and process system but also requires a leader to initiate and encourage the development of KMS. The qualities and skills described earlier are predicted to have strong influence in setting direction for the process management, strategic planning, human capital management, ICT infrastructure and culture. These five variables can be labeled as knowledge management environ-ment, which then affect the business performances.

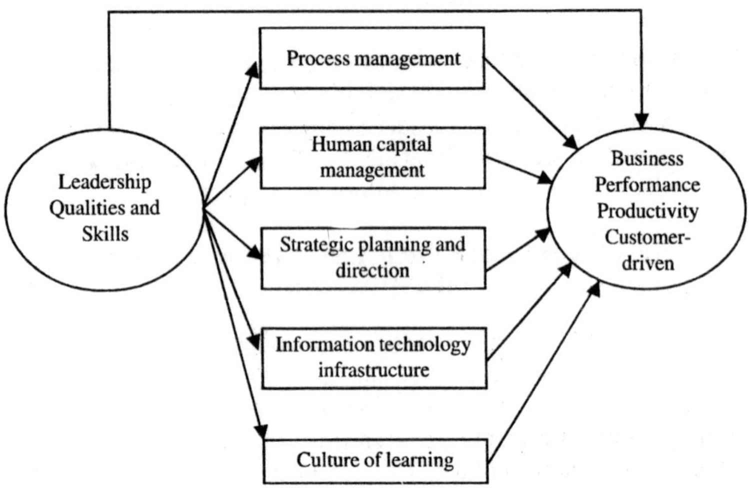

Fig. 7.1: Framework for Knowledge Management Leader

CONCLUSION

Businesses require information to make decision. Businesses thus require effective ways of gathering, storing, and disseminating knowledge. Businesses therefore require full and competent workers to organize information and to run its operation. As such, businesses require an innovative, a technology oriented and a visionary leader to inspire and motivate these processes of knowledge management system. The requirement for today's leader in fostering learning and managing information in organization necessitates avoiding work pitfalls. The leader should facilitate and coach rather than a boss. The leader must be able to capitalize on each employee's skills, abilities, and differences (Smith, 1997). The leader should then set the direction for a right ICT infrastructure and culture that assist the knowledge management system to take place. The efficiency and effectiveness of KMS is then to be measured based on business performance and customer satisfaction. The major challenge of managing knowledge is less its creation and more its capture and integration (Grant, 1996). The ability to integrate and apply specialized knowledge of is fundamental to firm's ability to sustain competitive advantage.

REFERENCES

Alavi, M. and Leidner, D.E. (2002). In Barnes, S. (ed). *Knowledge Management System: Theory and Practice.* Thomson Learning. Oxford.

Birkinshaw, J. (2001). Why is Knowledge Management so Difficult? *Business Strategy Review,* Spring, Vol. 12, Issue 1.

Charles Despres, Jean-Marie Hiltrop. (1995). Human resource management in the knowledge age current practice and perspectives on the future. *Employee Relations,* Volume 17. Number 1. pp. 9-23.

Fuller, S. (2002). *Knowledge Management Foundations.* Butterworth Heinemann. Boston.

Grant, R.M. (1996). Prospering in dynamically-competitive environments: organizational capability as knowledge integration. *Organization Science. 7* (4). 375-87.

Gupta, Babita, Iyer, Lakshmi S., Aronson, Jay E., (2000). Knowledge Management: Practices and Challenges. *Industrial Management & Data Systems.* Vol. 100, Issue ½.

Kinlaw, D.C. (1995). The Practice of Empowerment: Making the most of Human competence. Gower Publishing. England.

Pieiersen, W. (2002). *Reinventing Strategy.* John Wiley. New York.

Smith, G.P. (1997). *The New Leader: Bringing Creativity and Innovation to the Workplace.* First Agency Publishing: Kuala Lumpur.

Swan, J., Scarbrough, H. (2001) Knowledge Management: Concepts and Controversies, *Journal of Management Studies.* Nov., Vol. 38, Issue 7.

8

Human Capital: Its Valuation and Management

Lyndon Jones

In the early 1930s I lived in a town where cotton spinning was the dominant industry. As a child when walking to school, I recall passing factories which would have vacancies for employees. Outside a factory there would be a notice saying "Hands Wanted". This rather confused me for I wondered what happened to the rest of the person. But those were the days when a manager or foreman would tell a worker "You are not paid to think; you are paid to work".

In those days, capital was the scarce resource. In the post-industrial economy, this is no longer the case. The market value of a company depends less on tangible resources than on intangible ones, particularly human resources. For example, in a service based economy, where employee costs can account for almost half of corporate expenses, knowledge is the key differentiator. Similarly, knowledge is also increasingly important in high-value added manufacturing, such as pharmaceuticals. Meanwhile, heads of organisations still pay lip service to "our people are our greatest asset", often accompanied by pictures of two or three of them in the annual report. But their value is not quantified.

An analogy may be drawn with agriculture in respect of the difference between financial accounting and human asset accounting. The job of the chief financial officer who focuses on the profit and loss account, is that of harvesting. But we must have regard for the roots of the organisation, the feeding and nurturing necessary to maintain healthy future growth.

We also have the paradoxical situation that many organisations pay large sums of money to get rid of their assets, whilst others allow them to walk out of the door. Witness the following example.

Some years ago, writing in the Shell Annual Report, the then Chairman, stated:

> "The competence and commitment of Shell people working in over 100 countries all over the world remain one of the cornerstones of future success."

In juxtaposition to this, he wrote:

> "Cost reduction programmes have inevitably resulted in significant job losses, the majority of which are achieved through natural attrition, early retirement or voluntary redundancies. Where non-voluntary redundancies have to take place, the greatest efforts are made to support those affected in finding alternative employment."

There have been a number of reasons why organisations have not produced useful information about their human capital, including:

1. The current financial reporting system makes few demands on them to do so and measurement is not the first priority. Other tasks can absorb the Human Resources department's resources.
2. There is the question of property rights. With inanimate assets, these can be readily transferred, whereas human capital is embedded in the individual. Companies do not own any individual's human capital. Such ownership ended with the abolition of slavery. If an employee elects to quit, then the past investment by the employer to upgrade the employee's skills is lost to the employer.

   Relevant to this there is an additional consideration today. Whereas at one time, there were strong bonds in many organisations between employer and employee, this is markedly less so today. Firms are engaged in talent warfare. Witness how the need to retain staff has been the driving force behind the growth of talent manage-ment.

   There is an exception and that is in the case of some soccer clubs. The introduction of FRS10, Goodwill and Other Intangible Assets, requires soccer clubs to capitalise purchased players at their transfer price. The players are subsequently treated like other fixed assets and amortised over the term of their playing contracts.

3. Some companies are not interested in the subject, while others fear that putting such sensitive information in the public domain may be helping their competitors.
4. There has been no great demand from analysts and investors for such infor-mation, although there is evidence of growing interest from the investment community. For example, some pension funds and social responsibility investors are paying more attention to social, environmental and ethical criteria (SEE). In the UK, there is now a social responsibility index—the FTSE for good.

   Further, in 2000, the UK Government introduced legislation requiring all pension funds to declare whether they consider SEE matters in making their investment decisions. According to a survey of the 500 largest UK pension funds, 59 per cent of funds are incorporating socially responsible investment (SRI) principles into their investment process.
5. Some see it as an intrinsically soft issue on which to report and certainly there has been lack of clear guidance and an absence of universal practice. Benchmarks and indicators vary across industry sectors. Employee turnover, for example, can have higher rates in some sectors than others. So some measures are more appropriate for some sectors than others.
6. Some companies are a group of holding or multinationals. They may not have an HR function in their headquarters and HR is left to each subsidiary, in which case, issues can arise where integrating the information is concerned.

   But change is in the air.

In January 2003, the British Trade and Industry Secretary, Patricia Hewitt, appointed the Accountancy for People Task Force, chaired by Denise Kingsmill, to develop best practice guidance for companies on the external reporting of human capital. This included producing practical guidance.

When announcing the new task force, Patricia Hewitt said:

"In today's fiercely competitive and knowledge driven economy, business success depends on attracting the best qualified people, equipping them with the best skills and training and then keeping them.

'Accounting for People' will share the best ideas for companies to make the most of their people's talents, which in turn will boost profits."

Speaking at the launch of the Task Force, Denise Kingsmill, said:

"Unlocking human assets is one of the keys to higher competitiveness.

There is increasing research evidence that good people management gives companies an edge when it comes to profitability. We want to get away from simply paying lip service to the idea of 'people being our finest asset' or simply accounting for people as a cost.

At the heart of this project is the desire to provide solid performance benchmarks for stakeholders, particularly investors. Our task is to show how this information can be presented meaningfully in Annual Reports."

Meanwhile, investors are beginning to demand such information. For example, the Association of British Insurers whose members own one-fifth of the shares in the London stock market, applauded a recent declaration by Henderson Global Investors that, in future, it would be looking for corporate information beyond that included on the balance sheet. It said "companies with inadequate disclosure on social, ethical and environmental factors are denying their investors the right to make informed investment decisions".

Whilst in the US, according to a study published last year by Mercer Human Resource Consulting and CFO Research Services, chief finance officers are under pressure to know more about 'human capital'. Some 49 per cent say investors are asking for more information, while 23 per cent say their boards are talking about human capital issues to a "considerable or great extent".

The Task Force recommendations have been submitted to Ministers as proposed changes to the Operating Financial Review (OFR) rules. Currently, these are voluntary, but scheduled to become compulsory this year, with implementation expected in 2005.

Meanwhile, it is anticipated that further pressure will result from the European Commission (EU). The EU launched an EU Multi-Stakeholder Forum with a remit which included the need to identify and explore where additional action by businesses in relation to employees and people policies is needed in Europe. The Forum is due to report this year.

Kingsmill opted for an evolutionary approach suggesting a broad framework companies could use in drawing up reports. Some broad categories of information are proposed, such as size and profile of the workforce, training and development, remuneration, career opportunities and fair employment practices. Additionally, it was suggested that initiatives might cover employee motivation, staff turnover and absenteeism. Whilst to ensure rigour, it suggests the report be capable of review by auditors.

In so doing, it accepted investor arguments for a set of standards and comparisons enabling a company's human capital strength to be assessed alongside those of its competitors. At the same time, it also accepted arguments that measures relevant to one sector may be less relevant to another.

As regards the link between human capital and organisational performance, this is based on two theoretical strands:

- first, a resource based view, in which the human capital of an organisation is a key invisible asset alongside its physical and financial capital;
- secondly, a theory of motivation, which links performance to the rewards, not necessarily financial, available to individuals attaining a certain level of performance and their belief that they can achieve at that level.

Recent studies have focused on two main ways in which HCM practice might enhance performance:

- through raising the skills base of employees, for example appropriate recruitment and retention, comprehensive training and broad-based departmental activity; and
- through embracing employee motivation and ability to use their skills through measures such as design of reward systems, participative problem solving and teamwork.

A major study by the UK Work Foundation has been exploring the link between high performance workplaces and productivity. This has led Professor David Guest of the City of London University to propose the following model:

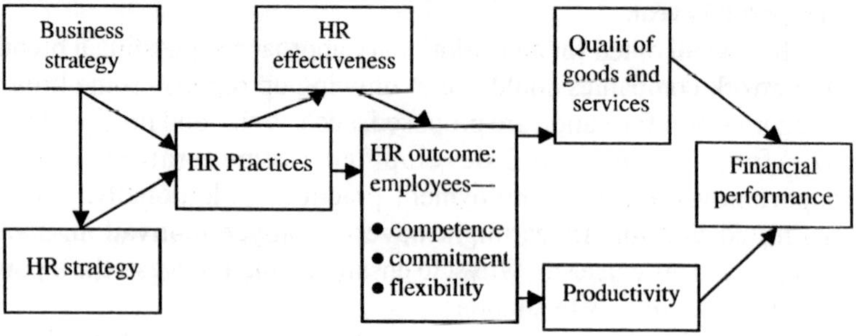

But What is Human Capital?

One definition is that human capital consists of the individuals:

- capabilities;
- knowledge;
- skills;
- experience of the organisation's, employees' and managers' capacity to add to their knowledge, skills and experience.

Currently, outlay on employees is measured as a cost whilst their value is ignored.

One way to measure human capital was proposed in "The HR Scorecard Linking People, Strategy and Performance" by Becker, Huselid and Ulrich. May I also refer you to an article published in Harvard Business Review September-October 2000 by Kaplan and Norton "Having Trouble with Your Strategy? Then Map It".

Seven steps are proposed to making HR a strategic asset, namely:

Step 1

Clearly Define Business Strategy. Our focus on implementation that a consensus strategy exists and that it can be clearly described and communicated to the entire organisation.

Step 2

Build a Business Case for Why and How HR Matters for Strategy Implementation. HR will only become a strategic asset when both line managers and HR professionals assume a shared responsibility for implementing strategy. For this to happen, both parties need to have a common understanding that HR's strategic value is linked to the extent to which it directly contributes to better strategy execution.

Step 3

Build a Strategy Map Describing the Casual Flow of Strategy Implementation. A strategy map takes what tends to be an externally focused vision in Step 1 and links it to an internal roadmap that 'show(s) how an organisation plans to convert various assets into desired outcomes'. It is an essential part of managing HR as a strategic asset because it provides the basis of aligning the HR Architecture with the firm's strategic drivers. It provides the organisational logic that transforms HR from a transaction and operationally oriented function to an organisational asset with strategic impact.

Step 4

Link HR Architecture to Strategy Map. This may be the most important step in transforming HR to a strategic asset. The term HR Deliverable is just a shorthand term for the outcomes of the HR Architecture that directly drive successful strategy implementation. The question is where is the HR Architecture to locate the HR Deliverables? Should we focus on employee performance and behaviours, or the drivers of those behaviours? We believe those HR Deliverables should focus on employee performance behaviours because they most directly influence the strategic goals of line managers.

Step 5

Design HR System in Alignment with HR Deliverables. The strategic behaviours in the Organisation (HR Deliverables) are driven by competencies, motivation, work, structure, strategic focus, etc.

Therefore, the HR system (recruiting, selection, compensation, rewards, career development, etc.) must be focused on those behavioural drivers. The result is an HR system that is both externally aligned with the requirements of the strategy map, and internally aligned among the various elements of the system.

Step 6

Design HR Strategic Measurement System (The HR Scorecard). Steps 1-5 lay the foundation for managing HR as a strategic asset. Next the organisation will need a measurement system that will not only guide that management process, but also validate HP's contribution to firm performance. We use the term HR Scorecard because it is designed to extend the concepts of the Balanced Scorecard to an organisational asset, in this case the HR Architecture. In other words, based on Steps 1-4 above, there is a very clear logic that links the strategic results for the HR Architecture with the ultimate financial success of the organisation.

Step 7

Implement Management by Measurement. Managing HR as a strategic asset will be a significant change initiative for most organisations. It will require a new perspective on HR, as well as acceptance of this new role, by both line managers and HR professionals, Senior line managers need to understand that if the organisation is going to reap the benefits making people 'our most important asset', implementation of the HR Scorecard needs to be approached as a major change initiative. Ultimately, the success of this initiative will turn on whether the people in the organisation who are charged with implementing the firm's strategy, understand the logic of the strategy's execution, and their role in that logic.

In short, the accumulation of exceptionally talented individuals is not enough. The individuals' skills and expertise must be effectively utilised in the organisation. Human Capital Management requires the right people:

- with the right skills and provision for development;
- doing the right jobs;
- in the right environment;

- given the right rewards.

In the words of Jack Welch, the former CEO of General Electric who was the symbol of corporate transformation: "If you're not thinking all the time about making every person more valuable, you don't have a chance".

In addition to human capital, there must also be:

- social capital, based on sociability and trustworthiness. This involves:
    1. structural dimension: network ties, network configuration, and relational dimensions (trust, norms, obligations and identifications);
    2. cognitive dimension (shared codes and languages, shared narratives);
    3. relational dimension (trust, norms, obligations and identifications).

And in addition to social capital, there must be:

- organisational capital which links the resources of the organisations. This includes:
    1. organisational and reporting structures;
    2. operating systems, processes, procedures and task designs;
    3. information and infrastructures;
    4. resource acquisition, development and allocation systems;
    5. decision processes and information flows;
    6. incentives, controls and performance measure-ment systems;
    7. organisational culture, values and leadership.

The interactions between these dimensions are important if employees are to have the motivation to develop and use their skills and knowledge.

The connection between human capital, social capital and organisational capital produces intellectual capital which, in time, affects the management of the knowledge within the organisation. In short, given the importance of knowledge in the organisation, it is crucial that the employees who are the source of knowledge are managed well.

A recent analysis of more than 100 German companies by Linda Bilmes, Konrad Wetzker and Pascal Xhonneux, the latter two work for the Boston Consulting Group, revealed a strong link between investing in employees and stock market performance. Companies which place workers at the core of their strategies produce higher long-term returns to shareholders than their industry peers.

The research examined companies in 10 industrial sectors and 'employee focus' was divided into two components:

— traditional human-resource policies
— opportunities for 'intrapreneurship' within the company

The traditional type of employee focus was measured in four ways:

— Expenditure per employee on training, and continuing levels of training.
— Number of lay-offs relative to the industry average and efforts to help relocate redundant employees.
— Extent to which the corporate philosophy recognises the contribution of employees as reflected in mission statements and publications.
— General human resource policies, including recruit-ment performance evaluation and feedback and promotion opportunities.
— 'Intrapreneurship' means giving an employee the freedom to take decisions and maximise the scope for individual initiative within a given job. Four criteria were used to measure the extent to which companies encouraged intraprenerurship, namely:
  - Flexible working hours.
  - Project organisation, including the prevalence of teams, number of levels of hierarchy, and independence of working units.
  - Opportunities for employees to learn skills in new areas and speed with which a firm can transfer staff to new fields.
  - Extent to which employees share in company

performance through profit-sharing, performance pay and bonuses.

In every industry, those companies which scored most highly on these criteria produced a greater 'total shareholder return' than their competitors. TSR is the sum of share price increases and dividends over a given period. The companies receiving the lowest scores also produced the lowest TSR in their sector.

Further, employee-focused com-panies not only delivered the best shareholder value; they also created the most jobs.

Today, creative employees are the new alchemists—they can make gold out of nothing. Hence, it is becoming vital to know the value of such assets. So, if human capital is at the centre of competitive advantage, investors can be expected to wish to see more disclosure in the future in the annual accounts.

9

Uncertainty, Work and the Individual

Gillian Stamp

INTRODUCTION

My starting point is the challenges of the 21st century and on how individuals and organisations can be supported as they make the most of those challenges which can be summed up in what has now become a clichi—the only certainty is uncertainty, the only permanence, impermanence. The experience of living and working in uncertainty is not new. In Asia there are wisdom traditions about it that are more than two and a half thousand years old. But uncertainty still seems to come fresh and unexpected to each of us and to the organisations of which we are a part. Following the poet Keats, I am going to talk about how 'axioms' about uncertainty are tested on the pulses of peoples' lives.

My comments arise from the experience of my working life which has been spent listening to people talk about their working lives. These people have lived and worked in different cultures and traditions, in economies at different stages of development, in the public and the private sector, at all levels in global and local enterprises. From the richness of their stories it has become clear to me that, although each of us is on many journeys, it is helpful to think about four nays, the ways they weave in and out of each other, and how each is affected by change and uncertainty. Until recently people responsible for training and development would have focused on just one of the journeys—the one at work. Continuous change has the effect of making it less and less effective of deal with only one aspect of anything. One of the reasons for telling you about the four journeys is that it provides a framework for focusing development resource.

A telling image of what it is like to work in multiple interacting uncertainties—is of rafting in the turbulence of permanent white water—surrounded by "surprising, novel, obtrusive events with unknown causes, unknown remedies, unknown urgencies, unknown times to completion and unknown compounding factors that will create additional complexity at later points in the process; Vaill, 1998.

Against this 'white water' background I give a brief description of the four journeys, before looking more closely at how each is touched by uncertainty and at how scarce training and development resources can be focused within this framework.

THE FOUR JOURNEYS IN OUTLINE

The underlying journey is the journey of the self, who we are and who we feel ourselves to be, the thread of movement through which our lives unfold. One important element of this journey is our deep need to use our own judgement in our working lives, our anxiety when we are overwhelmed by the challenges of our work, our frustration and alienation when the challenges are not there. Using our own judgement is about drawing on an inner resource to bring something of ourselves to bear—our experience, the expertise that we feel but cannot put into words; engaging inner resource and outer world in a process through which there is a flow that energises both. As we grow older, our capability to exercise judgement grows and we seek wider challenges so that we can 'go with the grain' of that growth, find challenges that stretch but do not overwhelm us, that provide opportunities to be 'in flow' (Csikszentmihalyi, 1988).

We all have a very finely-tuned sense of being in out of flow. There are times when we choose or have to live and work with conditions that do not challenge us. But people tell me again and again of how they can tolerate that for only so long before something within them compels a renewed search for the chance to bring something of themselves to bear, to use their judgement.

This "judgement reservoir" is a powerful source of latent energy for organisations making the most of uncertainty and I will come back to that in a moment.

It is in the second journey—our public journey at work—that we have the opportunity o express our capacity to make judgements in the light of the responsibilities we carry. On this journey, there are times when our capability is affirmed, times when we may be under or overwhelmed by what we are being asked to do.

In their public journeys more and more people now carry some responsibility for the conditions in which other people work and I will return to this too.

The third journey is the private journey rooted in our 'habitat'—the place we leave and return to each day. This journey may be shared with close friends, neighbours, a spouse, children and they are all on their own journeys, each living in his or her own way with uncertainty—at minimum, the sense that things never turn out quite the way we expect, that we do not always get what we want and that we often get what we do not want.

The fourth journey is personal, the inscape in which we do-or do not—look after ourselves, the weaving together of our four journeys *as* they go ahead through time and change. For some people this journey is spiritual, for others it may be re-creation through walking, playing sport, listening to music, gardening. At different stages of life this journey takes different forms. When there is a great deal of uncertainty to live with—especially when this has a heavy impact on the public journey—the personal journey can be neglected even though we know that giving time and attention to it would strengthen our grace in uncertainty.

In the rare blessed moments when these four journeys share the same path, we are whole: in one person's phrase "I can take myself everywhere I go". For most of us these are rare moments. The journey of the self has a life of its own: appearing to go ahead of its own accord, we all have an intuitive sense that our capacity to use our judgement to make decisions just grows and "nags" us when we do not or cannot find in work the challenges it needs. The other three journeys are kept on or blown off course by so many influences: in times of constant economic change the public journey at work can become all consuming; the private journey can make heavy demands when there are others to care for and/or their own journeys are especially difficult; the personal journey has its own inerrability in that it requires discipline to find time for it, it is all too easy to allow the demands of the public and private journeys to soak up the time and energy it needs.

The Journey of the Self

As I said, people's longing to use their judgement is a 'reservoir', a valuable source of latent energy for an organisation operating in uncertainty. Using judgement is about deciding what to do when you do not and cannot *know* what to do. So you have to discern the 'regular irregularities' that thread through even the most turbulent situations providing signals, indicators of the way things are going. 'Discerning' is being patient with uncertainty, using "that most valuable human skill the ability to see what might not be there... [it is] like moving softly through the forest tracking that beautiful beast, reality and discovering signs of its passage, the metaphorical broken twigs and bent flowers "[(Caron, 1996)"

"That most valuable human skill" is an essential capability for the viability of organisations in uncertainty. Releasing and harnessing it is one of the best starting points for building organisational capability. But it is a delicate process because each person discerns and uses his or her judgement most effectively when they are 'in flow'; as their capability grows, they seek new challenges and for each of us the pace of this growth is different, some peoples' capability continues to grow until they are in their seventies and beyond, leading them to seek wider and wider challenges. Other have the security of capability that matures earlier giving a clear sense of self and a contentment with familiar challenges. Evaluating individual capability to make decisions in uncertainty and pacing increase of responsibility in line with its growth is one of the most significant interventions that training and development can contribute to organisational capability.

Public Journey

Increasing uncertainty has numerous implications for this journey where peoples' capability is expressed, affirmed or constrained. An obvious impact is that fewer and fewer people will work for the same company for most of their working lives, they will have to become both multi-skilled and mobile, employable rather than employed by one organisation that can count on their loyalty and commitment and on which they can count for security.

This means that it is more difficult for managers to sustain coherence—the shared understanding of "vision" and priorities that gives meaning to work and is the touchstone for each decision. One of the effects of global investment can be heavy emphasis on short and medium profits as the primary purpose of an organisation. A study of companies that have consistently outperformed the US stock-market throws an interesting light on this. The authors (Collins and Porras, 1996) show that each these long-lived, successful companies has a "core ideology—core values and purpose beyond making money". What they call the "genius of the 'and'" lies in clear purpose and pragmatic pursuit of profit—"Profit is like oxygen, food, water and blood for the body; they are not the *point* of life, but without them, there is no life."

Managers can be helped to sustain coherence—purpose *and* profit—by teaching them about 'tasking', 'trusting' and 'tending'. 'Tasking' shares vision and intention, agrees resources and sets a completion time when a project can be reviewed. 'Trusting' entrusts people with the purpose and trusts them to use their own judgement in pursuit of it. 'Tending' is the continuous mindfulness that keeps purpose, people and processes aligned through time with all the uncertainties it brings.

Held in creative tension, tasking, trusting and tending build the judgement reservoir, coherence and a capacity to review what has been done, in particular how resources have been used, costs have been managed, how regulations have been complied with. This capacity to review makes for a 'learning organisation' which can make changes in its own time pre-empting the expense and pressure of review that comes from outside.

So, our public journey—and the public journeys of those who work to and with us—can be enriched and strengthened by learning about and practising 'the three t's'.

THE TRIPOD OF WORK

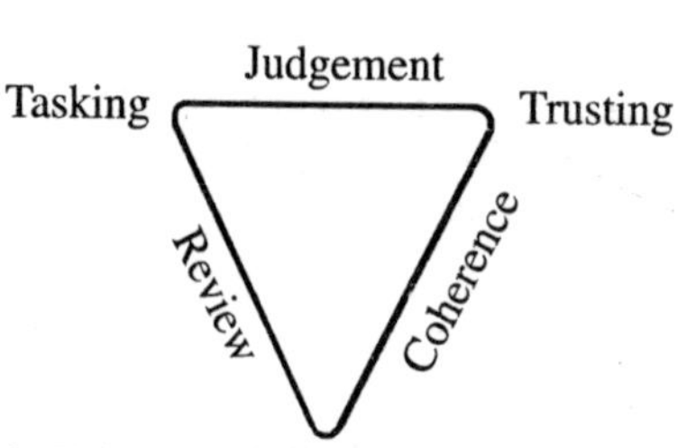

The Private Journey

The impact of uncertainty in our public journey on this journey that we share with close others can be very considerable. If change in our own working lives and the demands on time and energy become very great or if we are out of flow at work, then it can become very difficult to give time and attention to this journey. Different cultures have different traditions about the role of this journey in supporting one or the economically most significant of its members. Again, globalisation—especially through television and changes in the role of women—is having an impact in that many families now have more than one member working outside the home and living with the pressures of their own public journey.

One immediate implication of this is that the 'tending' of the habitat becomes a shared responsibility. There is no longer one person—usually a woman or a group of women—to ensure that the basic necessities are there when anyone needs them. Two tired adults at the end of a day realising there is no milk for anyone's breakfast cereal may need particular sensitivity to each other—and to the children—as they negotiate who is going to go out and buy it!

The pace of change and demands on our children—at different stages of their working lives—and the needs of elderly parents are all part of the joy and the expectations in our private journey.

Faced with continuous change and demand at work and the needs of others at home, we can lose sight of the delights of our private journey, coming to feel that there is no place where we are free of expectations. Guilty about neglecting and drawing on the support of our private journey and the people with whom we share it and sad that we are missing out on its joys, we may retreat form it rather than trying to refocus our time and energy.

In my work with people as they make significant changes in their working lives—particularly when they have been 'out placed' from an organisation where they may have worked for many years-1 find that they welcome the opportunity to reflect on the balance of their four journeys and whether there is anything they would like to do differently in the future.

Good training and development can offer people similar opportunities to pause and reflect about the balance between public and private journeys as it is and as they—and the people with whom they share both journeys—would like it to be.

The Personal Journey

This is the journey that weaves the others together and yet it is most likely to be neglected when continuous change draws time, energy and attention to the other three. Each of us will make our own choices about how we care for and develop ourselves and the emphasis will be different at different stages of our lives. This is the journey through which we 'tend' ourselves, not in the sense of being preoccupied with self but so that we can sustain the balance of the other journeys. However we choose to re-create ourselves (with others, alone, in sport, through music, craft) this is the source of our strength for living and working in life as it is—never quite what we anticipated or hoped for, sometimes more, sometimes less but always unexpected, always impossible to grasp, like a rosebush full of flowers but thorny if we grab it too tightly.

It is gradually becoming more common for people to think about developing themselves in some way. The many courses on stress management now on offer almost always introduce people to some way of questioning their thoughts, of "tethering the drunken monkey". All wisdom traditions have approaches to stilling the mind, a common thread seems to be the freedom that comes from learning to free ourselves *from* the idea that our conscious thoughts and endeavours are all there is, learning to be in touch with, to trust what one author (Milner, 1934), calls 'the answering activity', the inner resource that can deepen and widen our capacity to live with grace in uncertainty.

Giving time to our personal journey is especially important when we are not 'in flow'. Someone overwhelmed by the uncertainties of their role will often respond by trying to control every detail, every tiny incident, delaying decisions far too long or making them far too quickly in a desperate attempt to ward off anxiety. One of the ways we all try to cope with uncertainty is by attempting to control it, but someone overwhelmed by the challenges of their role can become totally preoccupied by the need to control—events, other people, what is said, what is not said—and this can do untold damage.

An important role for training and development here is, ideally, to support selection of people for roles in line with their capability so that the damage for the individual and the organisation is minimised. Or, when such a situation has arisen, an experienced human resource practitioner will know how to intervene in such a way as to restore the confidence of the individual and the capacity of the organisation.

Another way we all try to cope with uncertainty is to retreat from it into an 'empty self telling ourselves and anyone else who will listen that it is all beyond us, that we cannot cope. Again, gentle encouragement to give time and attention to the personal journey-perhaps simply to have time for oneself—can help the person to rediscover self-esteem and, with support, the best way forward for themselves and the organisation.

The part the personal journey can play in leadership is becoming more widely understood. For many years—perhaps especially in the US and the UK—leadership training has focused on 'skills', communication, behaviours. A recent study from the Army Research Institute in Washington DC (Me Intyre *et. al.,* 1994) indicates a very significant shift in this emphasis, suggesting that understanding the self is a primary 'tool' for leadership. The authors use somewhat heavy word "metacognition" to refer to the importance for a leader of knowing what he or she knows, how that knowledge has been formed and what can be done with it. To this I would add the importance—as Confucius pointed out—of knowing what you do not know, and of accepting with grace what is intrinsically unknowable.

A Quaker scholar (Palmer) puts the inner journey for leadership like this "A leader is a person who has an unusual degree of power to project on other people his or her shadow, his or her light. A leader is a person who has an unusual degree of power to create the conditions under which other people must live and move and have their being—conditions that can either be as illuminating as heaven or *v.* shadowy as hell. A leader is a person who must take special responsibility for what's going on inside him or herself, inside his or her consciousness, lest the act of leadership create more harm than good."

REFERENCES

Caron, P. (1996). Discernment Beyond the Church. *The Way Supplement,* 85.

Collins, J. and Porras, J. (1996). *Built To Last.* Century Business.

Csikszentmihalyi, M. (1998). *Optimal Experience.* Cambridge University Press.

McIntyre, R. *et al.*, (1994). *Toward a Theory Leadership: The Place of' Cognitive*

Stalls. TW 93262, Army Research Institute, Alexandria, Virginia, USA.

Milncr, M. (1934). *A Life of One's Own.* Chatto and Windus.

Palmer, Parker J. *Leading from Within.* Box 55063, Madison, Wisconsin, 53705 USA.

Vaill, P. (1998). The Unspeakable Texture of Process Wisdom. *In: S.* Srivasta and

D. Coopemder (eds.), *Organisational Wisdom and Executive Courage.* The *r* New Lexington *press,* pp. 37.

10

Building a Bridge between Academia, Industry and Graduates of the Future

Said Irandoust

INTRODUCTION

Of the many objectives for a university, the ultimate is to contribute actively to the sustainable development of society through knowledge generation and mediation. Education and research in a university give society the competencies needed to solve present and future global tasks and challenges.

The university plays a vital role in the development of its immediate region, and in promoting it internationally. Thus, co-operation with local and regional business and industry is essential in the very idea of the modern university. University staff are committed, together with students and with outside interested parties, to produce future employees, employment-opportunity creators, innovators and idea-generators.

A nation's economic survival and competitive power are now determined by its knowledge content, for which life-long learning is essential. Demands by society and industry on knowledge and competence change in pace with the transformations that occur outside our walls, and monitoring and analysis of the surroundings become ever more important.

In my opinion, the most promising orientation of a modern university should be based on education and research towards the sustainable development, strengthening the knowledge development and business capacity supporting the community economic development and its integration into the global economy.

Science used to speak to masses. Now it is different. Society talks back. This will transform the science and the research world. In a modern university there has to be an attitude of collaborative efforts where scientific research of high international quality can be combined with industrially relevant research programmes that form the basis of tomorrow's products, processes and national growth.

OVERVIEW ON HIGHER EDUCATION

Higher education both regionally and globally are undergoing fundamental changes. Universities are experimenting with new ways of funding through student fees, forging partnerships with private companies and engaging in mergers and acquisitions. Such changes can be attributed to four reasons, namely massification (democratisation) of higher education, rise of the knowledge economy, globalization, and lastly, competition.

The World Bank calculates that global spending on higher education amounts to $300 billion a year, or 1 per cent of global economic output. There are more than 80 million students worldwide, and 3.5 million people are employed to teach them or look after them. According to UNESCO statistics (UIS, 2004), the total student population in the world increased from 608 million in 1970 to 1.2 billion in 2000. Higher education accounted for 3.3 per cent of the total enrolment in 1970, while it accounted for 8.4 per cent in 2000. While in the 1960s and 1970s, both developed and developing countries made advances in expanding higher education; in the 1980s and 1990s, developing countries lagged behind the developed countries in terms of the expansion of the higher education system. The gross enrolment ratios in higher education doubled and trebled in the developed world between the 1980s and 1990s, the same in the developing world remained constant or marginally improved during the same period.

Asia is the top regional source for international students, constituting 43 per cent of post secondary international students studying in OECD (Organization for Economic Co-operation and Development) countries. It also provides four of the five top source countries. China, accounting with Hong Kong for 10 per cent (or 147,000) of all international students in the OECD area, has the most students abroad, followed by second-ranked Korea (5% or 70,500), third is India (4% or 61,000) and fifth-ranked Japan (3.8% or 55,000), eleventh-ranked Malaysia (2% or 33,000). The most popular OECD countries for Asian international students are the USA (receiving 44.3 % of the international students coming from Asia in the year 2001), Australia (12.5%) and the UK (11.3%). The most popular disciplines are business, IT, engineering, science and technology-related studies. Approximately two-thirds study at undergraduate level, the remainder at post graduate, although the proportions vary from country to country.

Countries in the Asian region are coming up with innovative forms of managing and regulating international education. Singapore is seeking to become a regional education hub, and is selectively encouraging foreign providers to attract international students and is also establishing operations in China. Malaysia is promoting itself as an education destination by establishing offices in China, Indonesia, Vietnam, the United Arab Emirates and South Africa. India is establishing transnational education operations in Sri Lanka and China. The growing number of middle class families willing to invest in higher education has further fuelled the market.

The total investment in higher education in the EU and Japan is about 1.1 per cent of GDP which is lower compared to those in Australia (1.5%), Canada (2.5%), US (2.7%) and Korea (2.7%). The differences in total investment are mainly explained by differences in the level of private investment. Private investment in higher education in the EU amounts to less that 0.2 per cent of GDP, compared to a weighted OECD average of 0.9 per cent. Private investment in higher education in the US is more than ten times higher (1.8% of GDP), and in Japan about four times higher (0.6%) than in the EU.

Universities play a critical role in catalyzing the technological innovations that fuels economic growth. Robert Solow, one of MIT's Nobel Prize winners in economics, estimated that more than 50 per cent of America's economic growth since World War II has derived directly from technological innovation. Knowledge is the core of today's social progress. Industry's survival and competitive power are now determined by its knowledge content, for which life-long learning is essential. Demands by society and industry upon knowledge and competence change in pace with the transformations that occur outside our walls, and monitoring and analysis of the surroundings become ever more important. In this context the universities play a major role in the development of its immediate region, and in promoting it internationally. Cooperation with local and regional business and industry is essential in the very idea of the modern university.

Universities lie at the heart of successful leading economies around the world. The OECD calculates that between 1985 and 1997 the contribution of knowledge-based industries to total value added increased from 51 per cent to 59 per cent in Germany and from 45 per cent to 51 per cent in Britain. The best companies are now devoting at least a third of their investment to knowledge-intensive intangibles such as R&D, licensing and marketing. Universities are among the most important engines of the knowledge economy. Not only do they produce the brain workers who man it, they also provide much of its backbone, from laboratories to libraries to computer networks. Harvard and seven other Greater Boston research universities infuse more than $7 billion into the regional economy. Tufts University President Laurence S. Bacow, who spoke on behalf of the universities at the launch of the economic study in 2003, remarked that "while the Midwest may produce cars and steel, and the South may produce textiles, paper, and citrus, we produce brains, new ideas, and new technologies".

PERSPECTIVES ON UNIVERSITIES AND SCIENCE

Today, questions are asked about the overall effect of universities on society. Although universities may be successful in their aims, they are viewed as failing in certain respects. Their efficiency is questioned, the academic disciplines remain isolated from one another and the connection to the real world is believed to be poor. Little evidence exists to support these views but, nevertheless, they are widespread.

Traditionally, science is viewed as the accumulation of new knowledge as a goal in itself. Research is planned and performed by independent and autonomous individuals; researchers have their own agenda, and outsiders see this agenda as a set of elitist, unpredictable and unmanageable activities. The alternative view, more and more common, is the societal perspective on science. Here, the ultimate goal is to produce knowledge for practical application with high relevance, utility and economic impacts. Research and education are managed to satisfy the needs of societal stakeholders; research is intentional, purposeful and manageable. Crucially, the agenda of the university and its staff is integrated with the agenda and desires of the stakeholders. In this model researchers are both individualists (free, critical and creative thinking) and team players.

I favour this societal perspective in which universities, as entrepreneurial institutions, are arenas in which knowledge is an intangible asset that increases when applied to different needs.

To create mutual trust in the relationships between the academy and its partners and in strategic alliances, it is equally important to communicate organisational goals to stakeholders, the community that supports the institution, and the individuals whose personal aspirations the university also seeks to support.

Successful research capacity building requires strong networking with other key actors, including private/public sector, other scientific communities, policy-makers, community and other stakeholders. Such networks also enable better use of research findings. Some important factors affecting the research capacity of the university include the following:

- *developing practice-focused research*—by developing the triple helix of university-private/public sector-government relations, developing university-private/public sector research consortia for work-integrated research and focusing on societal needs and economic development;
- *integrating scholarship with practice*—through increasing the number of adjunct professors and researchers from private/public sector; and by fostering the distinguished visiting scholar and fellowship schemes;
- *encouraging an entrepreneurial approach to research*—through the integration of knowledge-based innovation systems; by encouraging faculty entrepreneur-ship by designing appropriate recognition and reward systems; by favouring spin-out companies and business start-ups; by working for structures that accelerate the transfer and commercialisation of innovations; and by providing support for licensing, patenting, and the protection of intellectual property; and
- *practice orientation*—delivering demand and output-driven research for increased value and quality of work with the potential for better future implementation of the research outcomes; by supporting further incubation projects and the application of research, especially through consultancy activities.

Internationalisation of Innovation Processes: Internationalisation and Growth

Research and higher education policies are becoming more and more innovative and growth policies under pressure of globalisation and as a result of ongoing national restructuring. With continuing globalisation, the competitiveness of nations will increasingly depend on their abilities to innovate. Hence, it is necessary to reduce the gap between knowledge and innovations by better exploiting international excellence. Also, the future of our universities depends on creativity and innovation. The aim should be to better support ideas that bridge the gap between the theory and practice in knowledge creation and knowledge mediation through:

- supporting entrepreneurship through international co-operation
- bridging the gap between research and private/public sector to better foster innovation
- promoting consortia between firms, universities, and other research centres
- supporting efficient mechanisms for creating a critical mass of knowledge and competencies in research centres with an emphasis on heterogeneous capabilities. R&D intensive organisations require a wide range of skills and knowledge and diversity stimulates innovation
- financing projects and new ideas with high scientific quality, which face difficulties to attract financial support
- supporting projects stimulating demand for knowledge and innovation within SME
- investing in risk projects to support ideas with impact on regional/national innovation and competitiveness

These actions and approaches will:

- promote knowledge diversity and innovative performance in research and education
- improve the innovative capacity and performance of universities
- enhance the effectiveness of the innovation system

Internationalisation within higher education has many dimensions. It includes the type of courses offered, the teaching material, curriculum content, the students, the teaching staff in addition to the learning environment and context. But internationalisation is also a state of mind. We need to continue to invest in resources helping our staff to better cope with internationalisation activities if we want to take internationalisation beyond political rhetoric and better match policies with actions.

Internationalisation of Higher Education and Research

The aim of internationalization of higher education must be towards supporting various processes of integrating an international/ intercultural dimension into the teaching, research and service functions of the universities. This would result in the increase in the flow of ideas, attitudes, values, technology, economy and people across borders—all necessary responses to the impact of globalisation. In other words, internationalisation of higher education and research is considered as an agent of globalisation having impact on labour markets, knowledge-based economics, life-long learning, mobility of faculty and students, and the mobility of knowledge.

Developments in the "Knowledge Society" call for approaches that do not fit easily into traditional academic structures of scientific disciplines. It is in the border areas between various areas of knowledge that developments are most likely and most progressive. Knowledge is created not only in universities but also in the community by people working in professions.

This knowledge must be better integrated in the university context to enhance education and research. Integration of scientific knowledge and knowledge from professional practice, internationally, will require research questions generated from praxis fields. To provide opportunities for the development of advanced knowledge in fields which to date have had difficulties to make inroads in academia—artistic activities, innovations and entrepreneurship, to name a few—are among the most crucial challenges.

Internationalisation of industrial R&D must also be better studied since industrial R&D activities are increasingly carried out in other countries than the "home base" of the companies. International university-industry collaboration should be one of the areas of focus in order to gain access to other countries' industrial innovation systems and to facilitate the recruitment of scientists and engineers on an international labour market. Research activities are increasingly carried out at a few worldwide locations, close to "industry-friendly" universities, which imply a regionalisation of industrial research and development market.

Some major issues affecting the future development of the internationalisation of higher education and research are:

- impact of globalisation of the economy and society on the internationalisation of higher education and research.
- growing commercialisation leading to emphasis on the competitiveness.
- emergence of new, international and mostly private providers of higher education.
- emergence of new forms of delivery.
- emergence of international alliances and networks in higher education and research, between universities and between universities and private companies.
- less emphasis on physical mobility, more on curriculum and teaching and learning process.
- internationalisation of innovation.
- perspectives of different sectors in the society directly or indirectly related to higher education and research.

Some important activities to be discussed/considered are:

- Student mobility and student exchange programmes including work/internship abroad.
- Student-oriented training programmes.
- Student scholarship programmes.
- Recruitment of international students.
- Faculty/staff mobility programmes, both teaching and research.
- Joint and double degree programmes.
- International curriculum development programmes.
- Internationalisation of the curriculum.
- Language and culture training.
- Ph.D.-student-oriented programm-es including. Ph.D. student mobility.
- Joint and double appointments for research.
- International research agreements and projects.

- Joint research centres, universities and stakeholders.
- Staff training scholarship programmes/training programmes.
- Development of special programmes for stakeholders.
- Development of graduate and postgraduate training programmes for the international market.

Entrepreneurship, Leadership and Profession Orientation

Entrepreneurship, Leadership

Universities are key players in the generation of entrepreneurs who form start-ups and expanded businesses, thus creating new jobs and new income streams that catalyze further investment in the economy, which generates still more jobs, personal income and capital investment.

Successfully competing in the global economy requires the ability to innovate and to take calculated risks. To sustain economic development and provide sufficient quality jobs for the next generation, Asian economies must provide better conditions for new technology business creation. In this regard, universities must motivate and support new entrepreneurs and leaders who can capitalize on the opportunities of new technologies and who can reinvent the way Asian firms develop new products and services, go to market, connect with customers, and collaborate with their suppliers and share knowledge.

Moreover, bright young engineers and scientists from countries in the region that do not have the financial infrastructure to reward profitable business innovation have started up their companies abroad. There they find business incubators and venture capital firms that offer them a complete package of management skills and networking capabilities in addition to start-up capital.

Entrepreneurship—the ability to work effectively with high risk, high potential benefit projects and to rapidly take them from initial concept to realization—is not developed and supported through traditional educational programs.

Entrepreneurial and leadership education is the process of providing individuals with the ability to recognize commercial opportunities and the insight, self-esteem, knowledge and the skills to act on them. It includes instruction in opportunity recognition, commercializing a concept, marshalling resources in the face of risk and initiating a business venture. Although it also includes instruction in traditional business disciplines such as management, marketing, information systems and finance, entrepreneurship and leadership are sets of skills and attitudes that cut across disciplines and as such should be integrated into all programs to the extent possible.

Studies have shown that entrepreneurs and leaders prefer learning experiences that are short, to the point, content-oriented and taught by practicing professionals. While class-based knowledge input is a vital component of learning, the traditional lecture-based, didactic methods of teaching and learning alone are insufficient. Entrepreneurial and leadership education should provide opportunities for students to experience entrepreneurship and leadership first-hand by working alongside practicing entrepreneurs and leaders. This will require universities to be entrepreneurial university that fosters interaction and networking and embeds entrepreneurship and leadership in academic and management culture. It is important to integrate the concept of entrepreneurship and leadership across curricula and to tailor entrepreneurial and leadership education to local needs and marry the concepts of Asian entrepreneurship and leadership to those of the West.

Profession Orientation

With the shift from resource-based labour-intensive industries to more advanced, knowledge-based, technology-intensive sectors of production, there is a rise in the demand for more sophisticated education. This development will lead to greater affluence in some sectors, with a concomitant further increase in demand for higher education.

At the same time this situation will also create more and different challenges related to alleviating and abolishing poverty as well as massive urban and environmental problems. The quality of development in the region is hampered by the shortage of qualified human resources available at senior and middle management levels in both the public and private sectors. To address these circumstances close ties with industrial partners, providing a non-traditional approach to academics that emphasizes the eventual employability of its graduates must be encouraged.

Research programs must be developed by public and private sector and university researchers together. The programs must be pre-competitive, which means that although companies that take part in the programs may be competitors in the same market, the knowledge to be developed in the programs is the basis for a later generation of products, thus making it possible for the companies to work openly together.

The characteristics of a university of professions include among others the following: integration of scientific knowledge and knowledge from the professions; research questions generated from practical application; and encouragement to solve inter- and transdisciplinary problems. Some important considerations include: recognizing the validity of the vocational experience-based knowledge; engaging professions in partnership; emphasizing the criterion of relevance; forming strategic alliances; implementing new models of doctoral studies; and implementing an appropriate organizational structure.

University of Professions

Issues of relevance are often raised in academic discourse, such as the relevance of particular education or research, or the relevance of the university as a societal institution. The concept of a University of Professions rests on the conviction that partnership between the university on the one hand and the private sector and the public sector on the other hand, will improve the relevance of both research and education. Cooperation with different sectors of society and the new university could create a so-called win-win situation.

There is great potential to improve praxis in different ways through the strategy of cooperation. Partnership is, in a few words, about forming strategic alliances and sharing power and responsibilities.

Why a University of Professions?

Strong focus on the needs of stakeholders and the need to involve people from industry, public sector, researchers from national research institutes and from other academic institutions are important steps. Linking universities and other research institutes with industries and communities, with strong partnerships among them are crucial. I strongly believe in the need for research work having high relevance to the national and regional users. In my opinion, the focus should not only be on new knowledge and processes but also on their implementation. It is crucial to seriously deal with the barriers for the implementation of new knowledge, to enhance the quality of life and strengthen the economic development of the region. All these will require the university to develop into a strong, focused, collaborative and entrepreneurial institution.

- Developments in our "Knowledge Society" calls for approaches which do not fit easily into traditional academic structures of scientific disciplines.
- In the broader areas between various areas of knowledge, developments are most likely and most progressive.
- Knowledge is created not only in universities but also in the community by people working in professions.
- This knowledge must be integrated in the university context to enhance education and research.
- To provide opportunities for the development of advanced knowledge in fields which to date have had difficulties to make inroads in academia, e.g. artistic activities, innovations, entrepreneurship as well as providing new structures in teaching and nursing.
- To increase the number of people with doctorate degrees.
- To attract students from professions who are interested in developing their professional practice.

What are the characteristics of a University of Professions?

- Integration of scientific knowledge and knowledge from professional practice.
- Research questions are generated from praxis fields.
- Inter- and transdisciplinary solutions to problems are encouraged.
- Collaboration with stakeholders in private as well as public sectors of society.
- Diversity of students, staff, choice of research problems and methods.
- University core values.

University of Professions: how will it work?

Close collaboration with the professions involves:

- Students alternate/combine studies and work
- Staff alternate work in academia and in the professions
- Supervisors, lecturers, examiners come from both academia and the professions
- Tailoring of educational programmes to work needs by a closer integration of theory and practice, and increasing the time spent in professional practice
- Professional doctorate programmes, whereby people can advance their professional careers through relevant doctoral studies while still working
- By recognising the validity of vocational experienced-based knowledge
- By emphasising the criterion of relevance
- By engaging the professions in partnership
- By forming strategic alliances
- By implementing new models of doctoral studies
- By implementing an appropriate organisational structure
- Education providing competence required for professional careers in a global economy
- Education leading to internationally transparent and recognised qualifications
- Continuing education to upgrade skills, know-how, and knowledge according to new needs
- A valuable partner on the international educational arena

CONCLUDING REMARKS

The knowledge society needs new approaches. It would be a huge mistake if universities acted as if the creation of knowledge was their own monopoly. New ideas are today often born outside the institutes of higher education. It is an important mission for universities into the future to bring externally generated knowledge and new kinds of questions into the university setting, in a systematic and critical way. The university will actively integrate knowledge from the academic community and from the working world. It could be viewed as a new arena for knowledge management.

Since the problems encountered in working life are seldom classified within a single discipline, it is important that the institutes of higher education have structures that facilitate cross-disciplinary and cross-professional focus on problems. The bridging of academic subjects and scientific disciplines encourages creativity. It seems that increasingly scientists need to assemble a group of people with different perspectives in order to solve particular research problems.

These days there is discussion and debate on the subject as to whether we are witnessing a brain war between Europe, the United States and Asia in terms of the growing competition in research given that countries like China and India are emerging as new industrialized powers with advanced engineering skills. There is concern among certain European countries that given the lack of interest among the young generation for research, when countries such as China and India are producing large quantities of very high quality, hard-working researchers, it could lead to a situation wherein the developed countries, including the United States, will experience crises in scientific professional fields. To counter this, the European Union has set objectives for 2010 (The Lisbon Objectives), which include increasing the number of scientists, researchers, and engineers to 750,000 across all member nations. Therefore, competitiveness in research both in the region and globally is going to intensify into the future.

International universities are taking new directions in order to achieve two main goals for the future. One is collaboration between universities to be able to build competence of critical mass with qualified staff in different disciplines and advanced laboratory facilities in order to achieve top performance in producing new knowledge, PhDs and students for the different market places. The other goal is to achieve a much closer collaboration between universities and public and private sector, i.e. industry and society in order to increase the universities' accountability in different societies and to assure that the research has relevance to the future scientifically based and knowledge intensive industry.

Collaboration between universities will into the future go across scientific boundaries and disciplines as well as borders between nations and regions. Such collaboration means that the universities can specialize on different faculties and disciplines and avoid unnecessary and costly duplication of professor's chairs and thus spreading the limited resources too thin over the universities. By collaboration it is possible to compete with the best universities internationally. The selection of topics and disciplines has to be carefully done.

The new era of collaboration between universities and the public and private sectors will also enhance the role of the universities in building the new society. In order to be transparent to the society the university has to be well organized and if it covers on a top level the major subjects and fields of interest for the society it will be approached by national and international industry in virtue of its own competence. This will create a better financing of the research and the teaching. But also the positions and the employment in industry will be open to the students and the researchers because they are no longer foreigners or odd creatures living in ivory towers instead of in the real world. At the same time the industrialists will have a better understanding of the academic world with technology transfer career planning, publications in scientific, refereed journals and scrutiny of performance. It becomes especially interesting when leaders from industry can find a forum where industries can collaborate on a neutral platform provided by the universities. Industry collaboration by other means is very difficult and very rarely becomes successful.

It is common to refer to the primary missions of the university in terms of teaching, research and service. But these roles can also be regarded as the manifestation of the more fundamental roles of creating, preserving, integrating transmitting, and applying knowledge or as in the language of the computers, the university can be regarded as a "knowledge server", providing knowledge services, that is, creating, preserving, transmitting, and applying knowledge, in whatever form is needed by the society.

Clearly, as knowledge and educated people become even more the key to prosperity, security, and social well-being, the university has become one of the most important social institutions of our times.

I am certain that there will be forms of the university in the future that we might not recognize from our perspective today. It is difficult to suggest a particular form for the university for the 21st century. There will be many forms and many types of institutions serving our society.

Wisdom is the ultimate goal of a university education for every student—and therefore for every one of us—no matter what our career or other professional goals.

A university is not only a knowledge institution. It is something more. It is also about education. Education is enriching, a deepening of the personality, a stimulated curiosity and a certain love for learning. Education is wisdom. Wisdom means understanding oneself and other people in our society. It is to have a deeper appreciation of emotions.

11

Applied Longitudinal Thinking

An Exploration

Meenakshi Khemka and *Vinayshil Gautam*

INTRODUCTION

An interesting fact is that inspite of the numerous studies, both old and recent, managers of an organization still find themselves at the crossroads when it comes to designing an organization for the desired performance. This is despite taking into account the identified factors affecting an organization structure, its processes and growth. Very often, even after taking all the necessary precautions, the structure and processes of an organization fail to serve its needs and leaves the top management wondering as to why the same structure and processes that were successful in one organization do not work even moderately in the next one. More often than not, the reason for this is the negligence of an important factor—the context in the legacy with which the organization operates. This context and legacy differs from organization to organization and this needs to be taken into account for designing an effective organization. When this contextual factor and legacy factor is accounted for in the thinking process, it is leads to 'Longitudinal Thinking'. The understanding of this concept becomes all the more essential when we see organizations as continuously evolving entities.

LONGITUDINAL THINKING

Further, evolution is a universal phenomenon. Anything and everything evolves and changes with time. Human beings pass through various phases (childhood, adolescence, adulthood, old age) during their journey of life. This is true for living beings and organizations alike. The important thing to understand is that the present state is a result of the past state and the future state would be a result of the present state and the choices made today. This is to say that everything starts from a set of givens and nothing begins *ab initio*. This phenomenon is known as 'Longitudinal Thinking' (Gautam, 1999, 2000, 2003, 2005). Fundamentally, it implies taking into account the continuity factor. While the understanding of this concept is important both for living beings and organizations, it assumes critical significance for the success of an organization.

Talking in terms of equations, it may be important to recognize that 'Y', that is the trajectory of organizational growth, is not equal to 'mx' but 'Y' is more likely to be equal to 'mx + c'. In any work organization, in addition to the easily identifiable inputs, there is the unique presence of the heritage variable, which may be taken as the constant 'c'. It represents the appropriate definition of the situation and has to be factorized/scientifically decomposed and selectively built upon. In case of organizations, it can be by way of moulding influences at the early stage of its growth, contextual factors, personality variables of the leaders or the processes, and more, which left an impact on the structure of the organization (Gautam, 1999, 2000).

Talking of contextual factors leads to the understanding that even though the problems may be universal, the solution to these problems is very organization specific. This is because every organization has its own unique tradition, which has to be accounted for while deciding its future course of action. There can be no universal solution.

The longitudinal thinking approach, if properly put in place, can provide far-reaching insights into several elements which influence organizational growth and are at present not fully mapped. It also helps in deciphering of the organizational identity. This requires a careful scientific analysis. Carefully identified elements of tradition have to be fused with forces released on account of changing environment. Pressures of learning to cope with the imperatives of the future and better reprogramming of the directions of management action are greatly facilitated by drawing upon the lessons of the past and the defining characteristics of the context. This will enable the organization and all its personnel to be more productive and handle the appropriate contradictory pulls that they undergo. Given this approach, the comprehension of the complexity of the organization processes is facilitated and the reality is thereby better understood. An integrated approach hence evolves, not only to handle issues of structure but also of the process. Insights into organizational growth follow. This requires resorting to 'longitudinal thinking'. Longitudinal thinking is a very powerful tool and the understanding of its concept becomes important if one seeks to gain useful insights into the possible reasons for the success or failure of organizations.

CASE STUDY

In order to study the impact of longitudinal thinking in practical terms, a detailed case study and analysis was done in a major pharmaceutical organization of India. Data was collected by conducting extensive interviews with the senior management of the organization. This was supported, validated and extended by an intensive study of the documents of the organization right from the year of its inception. The documents studied included the annual reports, internal and external newsletters, minutes of meetings and other documents which the organization deemed fit to share. The details and the analysis are presented in the following section. The name of the organization has been kept confidential for reasons of anonymity.

ORGANIZATION A

As mentioned earlier too, the longitudinal thinking approach takes into account the historicity of the processes. Using this approach to analyze the organization, Table 11.1 was generated for Organization A. The table not only helps us to understand organizational change better, but also helps in identifying the different stages in the evolution of organization structure. It also helps in identifying the elements of continuity and discontinuity for organization growth. A point to be noted, however, is that the table, presented on the next page, deals with only the major changes in Organization A. This is because the other routine changes do not offer a broad insight into the various facets responsible for the change and affected by it. The major changes provide a good forum for the same.

The case has been analyzed using the longitudinal thinking approach. It can be seen that over the years, the structure of the organization has been modified and adapted to be in tune with the

Table 11.1: Organizational Change in Organization

		Original	*1993*	*1999*	*2002*
I	**Causative Factors**	Small family owned company	❖ Rapid transformation in domestic and global business environment threw up new opportunities and challenges ❖ To support the internationalization efforts ❖ To accelerate growth ❖ To build on the infrastructural strengths ❖ To aid good decision-making ❖ To provide flexibility in operational logistics ❖ To do business from and where the market was. For this purpose, four regions were created ❖ Focus on business development in core pharmaceutical markets	❖ The organization was benchmarked against leading organizations of similar profile ❖ Barriers to global effectiveness were considered against the improvement parameters identified ❖ To shift the focus to 'Growth' with operational efficiency in the background	❖ To build organizational capabilities in the area of therapy management ❖ To complement the existing strengths in brand building ❖ To optimize current brand portfolio ❖ To provide synergies of scale across various SBUs ❖ To be focused in identified therapies ❖ To facilitate the achievement of market share objectives in the medium term ❖ To attain leadership status in India by 2005

		Original	*1993*	*1999*	*2002*
II	**Features**				
a)	Job Design	Great autonomy, low standardization, frequent feedback	High autonomy, more standardization, need based feedback	Reasonable autonomy, great standardization, need based feedback	Reasonable autonomy, great standardization, need based feedback
b)	Organization Process	Informal communication, high team spirit	Formal communication, less team spirit, strategy of internationalization	Formal communication, low team spirit, strategy of internationalization, focus on R&D	Low team spirit and less informal communica-tion; Communication to seniors through proper channel and hierarchy, strategy of internationalization, increased focus on R&D
c)	Organization Structure	Conventional with a number of hierarchical levels	Matrix structure with four operating regions; Support functions like HR, Finance, R&D, Legal Services centralized	Shift to a transnational organization; teams operating across geographies to gain efficiency	Strategic restructuring of India region; Formation of 8 SBUs in terms of marketing offices in India (based on therapy)
d)	Information Flow (*Note: Formal and related information passed on quickly but a serious lack in informal information flow or information outside the scope of work*)	Informal	Typed letters and information on specific formats	Through emails, intranet besides paper based	Through emails, intranet besides paper based

		Original	*1993*	*1999*	*2002*
e)	Extent of Delegation (Decision Centers)	Highly centralized	Delegation for decision making	Delegation for decision making	Delegation for decision making but tight control from top management
III	**Extent of Continuity and Change**				
a)	Job Design	Great autonomy, low standardization, frequent feedback	Decrease in autonomy, increase in standardization, decrease in feedback	Decrease in autonomy, increase in standardization, decrease in feedback	Decrease in autonomy, increase in standardization, decrease in feedback
b)	Organization Process	Informal communication, high team spirit	Increase in formal communication, decrease in team spirit, core strategy remains the same	Increase in formal communication, decrease in team spirit, core strategy remains the same	Reduced team orientation and informal communication, core strategy remains the same, focus on R&D increased over the years
c)	Organization Structure	Conventional with a number of hierarchical levels	Decrease in hierarchy, flattened structure at the top, International Division reorganized in the form of 4 regions	Basic structure same, relocation of certain teams across geographies for greater efficiency like that of IPR, International Marketing Division	Reorganization of India region market into 8 SBUs—4 in Delhi and 4 in Bombay besides one unit for generic marketing in Delhi; other structure same
d)	Information Flow	Quick as it was a small group	Comparatively slow due to increase in size of the organization	Improved due to use of sophisticated technology, decrease in paperwork	Formal flow improved, decrease in paperwork

		Original	*1993*	*1999*	*2002*
e)	Extent of Delegation (Decision Centers)	Highly centralized	Increase in delegation for decision making	Greater Delegation for decision making	Decentralized but comparatively reduction in decision making authority
IV	**Company's Performance**	**Beginning-1993**	**1993 - 1999**	**1999-2002**	**2002-After**
	Sales (Rs. Millions)	171.2-5934.3	5934.3-15598.3	15598.3-28894.3	28894.3-35334.9
	Profit (Rs. Millions)	18-796.5	796.5-2562.5	2562.5-7304.8	7304.8-10041.1
	Market Position	Leader	Leader	Leader	Leader

long-term strategy of the organization concerned. However, the point to be noted is that, even though modifications have been made, they are not drastically apart from what the organization had been doing before that and ***in one case where a significant departure was required, the change failed to yield the desired results.***

In this particular organization, the long-term strategy has always been that of Internationalization.

In 1993, an International Division already existed in the organization looking after the issues of internationalization in the organization. However, it was then felt by the top management that different markets would need different customized strategies and hence the decision was taken to do away with the International Division (located in India) and in its place form units in different markets at their own place. The decision was taken to enable the organization to address the unique requirements of each market as well as approach the different markets in a focused way. For this reason, four regions were created based on the different markets that the organization wanted to focus upon.

To fulfil the objectives of this restructuring, that is—to aid in good decision making and providing flexibility in operational logistics—there was a decrease in hierarchy in the structure, particularly at the top, as well as greater delegation of authority. Functionally, a matrix organization was created. The line functions were the pharmaceutical dosage forms and bulk drugs business, to be operated through the Regional Head Quarters. The staff support functions were defined clearly to enable the organization to carry on its business world over, effectively. A new department of Pharmaceutical Strategy, Product Planning and Market Research was incorporated in the corporate office.

Business Development and Performance Monitoring continued to be a corporate support function. Logistic Management and commercial function were to be part of marketing services. R&D was aimed at providing thrust to basic research and biological science research. In addition to providing Medical Services, R&D was made responsible for Regulatory Affairs. Technical function was to provide support in areas of Quality Assurance, SHE and Technical Audit. For a considerable period, manufacturing was to be a corporate function. Finance, Legal Services were to be strengthened to provide support to regional management. HR function was made to be highly decentralized except for policy matters. The new department of

Strategic Planning was formed with an objective of carrying on integrative planning process and helping to decide future business options. On the research and technology front, the organization did backward integration fully to manufacture most of the critical drugs from their intermediate stages.

In 1999, the different international units were already in place catering to the needs of the different markets. However, it was felt that operational efficiency needed to be improved for certain process groups like IPR because India did not have the knowledge base required for the efficient functioning of this group. So, for processes/groups like these, it was proposed that they be situated in a country where the relevant knowledge pool was available but it would still be a part of the corporate structure of the organization in India. In other words, the organization decided to shift to a transnational mode of functioning marked by an integrated network with mutual interdependence rather than dependence on the center. This change was supported by the technological advances in the organization.

In 2002, the India region was already there. It was, however, reorganized into eight SBUs under two different hubs (Delhi and Bombay) to generate synergy and greater efficiency. A Strategic Marketing hub was created at the Regional Office to provide therapy focus and give functional direction to the Operational marketing function. The product portfolio across SBU's was harmonized along therapy lines. This not only involved brand shifts but also lead to the birth of two new marketing arms. Sales responsibility was decentralized at the SBU head level, with operational marketing under the Director-India Operations, providing the requisite marketing support to the SBU. The other business support functions apart from Marketing, such as Medical Affairs and Marketing Services were also centralized at the level of Director-India Operations to provide greater focus and economies of scale.

The strategic changes in the organization included the creation of a strategic marketing cell to streamline marketing across India region, initiating therapy management approach vis-à-vis brand building, carving out new SBU/task forces to give added impetus to key areas, new product allocation by division to follow therapy class/mass approach, and acquiring complementing therapy brands for inorganic growth.

The tactical changes included rectifying imbalances in product portfolio by shifting brands between SBU's, rationalizing field force numbers across SBU's, and phasing out obsolete brands and streamlining co-promotion activity.

An important point to note, however, is that this restructuring of the India region ***has not been very successful*** in delivering the desired results. The reason, mentioned by one of the respondents, was that this system called for a lot of coordination and teamwork among the different groups but team spirit has been constantly on the decline in the organization over the past many years. **This points out very clearly how the givens of an organization critically affect the functioning and performance of the organization.**

This also goes to prove that longitudinal thinking is an important concept and that organizations would do well to take the contextual factor(s) into cognizance while steering the organization into the future.

CONCLUSION

The paper first introduces the concept of longitudinal thinking. Thereafter a case study has been presented which looks into the changes in an organization over a time period of four decades. The changes have been studied both at a macro as well as at a micro level. The analysis has been presented in the form of a table. The study conclusively illustrates how longitudinal thinking is a very important concept for the functioning of an organization.

REFERENCES

Gautam, Vinayshil (1999). "Towards Longitudinal Thinking", *Abhigyan*, Vol. XVII, No. 3, Editorial.

——— (1999). "Towards Longitudinal Thinking—II", *Abhigyan*, Vol. XVII, No. 4, Editorial.

——— (2000). "Longitudinal Thinking—III", *Abhigyan*, Vol. XVIII, No. 1, Editorial.

——— (2004). Report on National Initiative On Institutional Competitiveness 2004, AICTE, New Delhi, pp. 3-4.

Report on Technology for Small Scale Industries—Current Status and Emerging Needs, (2001). SIDBI, Tata McGraw Hill Publishing Company Ltd, New Delhi, pp. 5.

Tamotia, S. K. and Gautam, Vinayshil (ed), (2005). *Essays in Longitudinal Thinking—Managing Change with Continuity,* Concept Publishing Company, New Delhi.

12

Psychological Types and Trainer Styles

John Cullen

INTRODUCTION

It is obvious that human beings possess many similarities and also exhibit many individual differences. These similarities and differences are usually explained in terms of genetic or cultural factors.

One major approach has been describing individuals based upon Psychological Types. There are many classification systems but the one that I have found to be extremely practical is the system described by the Italian Psychiatrist Roberto Assagioli.

Assagioli describes seven major types.

- Will
- Love
- Active—Practical
- Creative—Artistic
- Scientific
- Devotional—Idealistic
- Organizational

Applications to Management

My Primary interest is to apply these major types to Manager Styles.

Primary Management Styles

Examples

Type	*Primary style*	*Topics*
Will	Directive	Leadership
Love	Participative	Team building
Practical	Entrepreneurship	Finance, peak performance
Harmony	Intuitive	Conflict resolution
Science	Analytical	Charts/Graphs
Devotion	Charisma	Values
Organizer	Structure	Organizational design

These are examples of the primary styles and the areas that each type would possess skills or interests. It should be pointed out that is not one type but usually a combination of two or three.

The Types Personality Profile (TPP) is an instrument designed to assess one's major types.

TRAITS TO TRANSFORM

A major psychosynthesis task for each trainer is to identify traits that need to be transformed. Each type can overemphasize certain characteristics which can be detrimental to the success of the organization. The following is a list of traits to be transformed for each type.

Will

- ❖ Willfulness
- ❖ Desire to dominate or control others
- ❖ Unrelenting ambition for power

Love

- ❖ Giving in toc easily
- ❖ Too much study without taking action
- ❖ Fear because of over-sensitivity

Practical

- Wasted energy through over-activity and restlessness
- Manipulation and deviousness
- Intellectual pride

Harmony

- Too many "highs" and "lows"
- Over-eagerness for compromise
- Tendency to fight or to be contrary

Scientist (Analytical)

- Too much skepticism
- Intolerance of ideas which do not fit in with established knowledge
- Too much intellectual analysis and dissection

Devotion

- Uncontrolled enthusiasm
- Over-eagerness to trust and believe
- Over-learning on others

Organizer

- Over-concern for rules and regulations
- Subservience to habit and routine
- Over-concern for orderliness and detail

Exercise

Select from the list given on the previous page, the trait that is your highest priority for transformation. Take some time to center and imagine yourself in a typical situation when you express this trait. Get a sense of what this trait is for you in a specific training situation.

Observe your inner experience and your actual behavior. What sentences do you say to yourself when are expressing this trait? How do you sound? Maybe you sit in a certain way or express your body posture in a certain way.

What are your feelings when are expressing this trait? How do you think when you are in this role? How does your mind function in this role? What do you want?

Is there a particular talent or skill that is associated with this trait, something that you do well?

What are its primary weaknesses? How does it limit you? In what way is the trait incomplete? What are its missing parts?

Stay with this particular trait and allow an image to emerge which represents this trait to you.

Make a brief sketch of this particular trait and make a few brief notes. You might have a name for it. Write down any insights or recognitions that you obtained.

THE GULF INSTITUTE OF MANAGEMENT

The 9th Gulf International HRD Conference

Quality to Develop

Center yourself and identify with your own source of wisdom. Imagine above your head a symbol representing wisdom.

Imagine your mind opening up like a tulip. You are receptive to the intuitive understanding of your own source of inner wisdom.

Now ask a question. "What quality do I need to develop to transform this trait?" Listen in silence and allow a symbol to emerge which represents this quality.

When you have this symbol, take some time to draw it. Spend some time reflecting on the symbol and allow it to evoke thoughts within you as to its nature and steps that you could take to actualize it. Write down any of your insights and particularly your own program for achieving self-mastery.

The Trait Transformed

Center yourself and now see yourself with this trait transformed. See yourself manifesting the quality that you have identified. Identify with this quality. Experience it in your body. Experience it in your feelings. Experience it in your mind. Experience your entire personality being pervaded by this quality which has the ability to transform this trait which has been blocking your growth.

HIGHEST ASPIRATIONS

Each trainer also aspires to reach the highest level possible. The following list of Highest Aspirations for each type are indicative of the transpersonal nature of each type.

Will

I aspire to become a dynamic, powerful and benevolent leader, serving the greatest good. I aspire to liberate people from all forms of bondage and oppression.

Love

I aspire to a deep intuitive, loving-understanding of people, so that I can nurture them, and help them to unfold their highest potential.

I aspire to a wise understanding of life so that I car teach and illuminate others.

Practical

I aspire to great mental agility and resourcefulness, so that I can apply them creatively to intellectualiy challenging enterprises.

I aspire to arrive at truth through the power of deep thinking and careful reasoning.

Harmony

I aspire to express great artistry in every aspect of my life, thereby inspiring others to increase their sensitivity to beauty.

I aspire to be a mediator- a reconciler of human conflict and an instrument of peace.

Scientist

I aspire to become vitally involved in discovering solutions to Nature's mysteries through scientific research and experimentation.

I aspire to invent or develop those mechanisms, instruments, or technological improvements which will transform and uplift the quality of human life.

Devotion

I aspire to live with complete faith and commitment: true to my highest Vision of Right. I aspire to serve the God or the "highest ideal" with complete faith and utter devotion.

Organizer

I aspire to bring rhythmic order out of the chaos of human living by "grounding" progressive ideas in practical activity and "seeing them through" to perfected expression.

I aspire to take a practical, administra-tive role in redesigning and transforming the patterns of human civilization, so that a "New World of Order" may merge.

Exercise

Select from the above the quality that you chose as your highest aspiration. Take some time to reflect on your highest aspiration and make a few notes on the meaning to you of this aspiration.

Close your eyes and see yourself expressing the qualities of your highest aspirations. Not only see yourself but be there. You are that highest aspiration. Identify with the statement. "I am my highest aspiration." Be there in situations in the future when you are expressing this higher aspiration. Choose several situations.

Now allow a symbol of this higher aspirations to emerge.

Once this symbol has emerged allow the quality of this symbol to flow down into your personality vehicles. Allow it to flow into your mind evoking thoughts of how to manifest this quality.

Allow it to flow into your feelings evoking a desire to express this quality in your emotional life.

Allow it to flow into your body and experience your body being energized by this quality.

Once more, identify with your highest aspiration. "I am my highest aspiration." "I can express this aspiration in my daily life through my thoughts, my feelings and my actions."

Take some time to write down any of your experiences with this exercise and draw a picture of the symbol of your highest aspiration.

Repeat this exercise with your second and third highest aspirations and ultimately with all of them.

SUMMARY

Psychosynthesis Typology theory promises to be an effective approach to assessing leadership style, determining areas of growth and providing a vision of our higher potentials. It has also be used effectively to assess group process and organizational values.

NORMS FOR MALE AND FEMALE BUSINESS MAJORS ON THE HOLT TYPES PERSONALITY TEST (TPP)

Norms for MBA Females TPPNorms for MBA Females TPP

	WILL	LOVE	ACT	HARM	SCI	DEV	ORG
MAX (100%)	77	75	73	79	77	73	70
90%	63	69	60	66	64	59	64
75%	53	62	56	57	55	53	57
MEDIAN (50%)	47	52	49	47	45	45	52
25%	40	34	44	38	35	37	39
10%	35	43	40	30	28	33	31
MIN (0%)	18	25	32	21	22	23	18

Norms for MBA Males TPPNorms for MBA Males TPP

	WILL	LOVE	ACT	HARM	SCI	DEV	ORG
MAX (100%)	76	73	76	76	79	66	75
90%	68	61	66	55	69	57	67
75%	63	54	60	45	62	48	63
MEDIAN (50%)	56	40	53	39	53	28	57
25%	48	32	49	34	43	32	44
10%	37	26	44	29	35	28	35
MIN (0%)	17	20	34	23	21	23	18

Norms for UG Females TPPNorms for UG Females TPP

	WILL	LOVE	ACT	HARM	SCI	DEV	ORG
MAX (100%)	68	75	71	71	70	73	69
90%	61	68	60	58	61	64	65
75%	55	61	55	52	52	56	58
MEDIAN (50%)	45	51	50	45	47	49	52
25%	36	44	45	38	38	42	40
10%	27	34	39	34	30	34	33
MIN (0%)	15	22	32	27	21	27	24

Norms For UG Males TPPNorms For UG Males TPP

	WILL	LOVE	ACT	HARM	SCI	DEV	ORG
MAX (100%)	76	72	73	66	76	69	70
90%	67	65	60	55	62	61	60
75%	61	58	55	47	57	55	56
MEDIAN (50%)	53	50	50	41	48	48	47
25%	44	40	45	35	42	41	39
10%	36	32	39	30	34	37	32
MIN (0%)	15	22	34	20	19	23	20

July 12, 1989

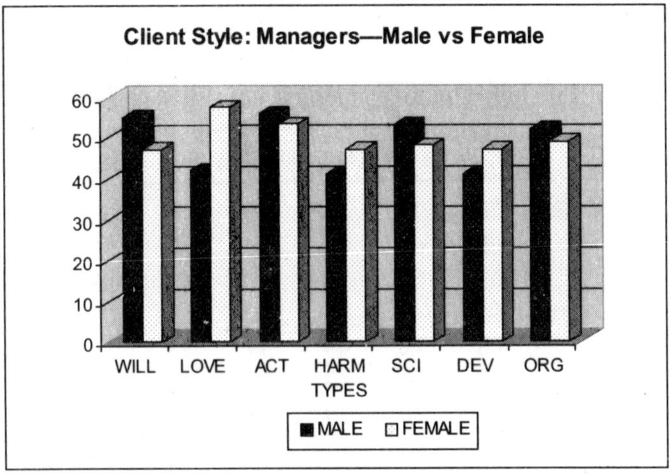

13

Leadership and Change Management

Annabel Beerel

INTRODUCTION

Organizations must remain **relevant** to their stakeholders if they wish to survive. To remain relevant requires the ability to read and respond to **new realities**. New realities are the forces that herald change. New realities are pervasive and are continuously arriving at our doorstep, whether we invite them or not. As we shall discuss, leadership and new realities go hand in hand.

To remain relevant and alive in today's world requires a shift in consciousness; new ways of perceiving the world, and new ways of wrestling with the challenges of change. We also need to understand that there are good and bad responses to change.

By and large we do not like change. Harder still, change usually tests our own self-esteem or sense of self. Adapting to change is hard work.

Since we live in a world of continuous change the only way to survive and even thrive under this perpetual challenge to who we are and how we see ourselves is to strengthen our **adaptive capacities**. This is not easy. It requires adaptive work which is different from technical work. The most important tasks of leadership are to identify the new realities facing the organization and to help build the organization's adaptive capacity.

GOALS OF AN ORGANISATION

All organizations, regardless of their purpose or mission, have one common, primary goal. That primary goal is to remain **relevant**. Organizations must remain relevant to their societies and relevant to the stakeholders interested in and affected by their actions. This key organizational purpose seems obvious and even trite, yet this essential requirement for continued organizational existence is often forgotten or overshadowed by fancy discussions about strategy, competitiveness and profits.

Relevance must be the major driving force behind all the actions of the organization. If relevance does not remain at the forefront of organizational thinking, the organization will soon lose its attraction to its markets and customers, slip into dysfunctional behaviors, decay, and ultimately disappear. Many, many organizations fade into the zone of non-relevance (for example well known Singer Sewing Machines or Digital Equipment Corporation) which despite all efforts, they cannot regain. The world has moved on!

Being relevant is about "engaged power." When something or someone is "relevant" this describes their relational significance. If someone is considered significant that means he or she has a "power" that has traction when engaging with others. With power one can do and achieve things. Powerless people or organizations are insignificant and readily become irrelevant. Power is a relational concept. Power as a force does not exist unless it can be exerted, expressed or used in relation to something else. Power and relevance go hand in hand. Being relevant generates power. Without power the individual or the organization "dies" (May, 1972).

The key challenge leaders of organizations facc is how to ensure their organizations remain relevant so that they have the power and the resources to do meaningful things. Leaders need to consider what "relevance" means from the perspective of the organization's mission or purpose, and to whom; which markets to target and where geographically they should position themselves. It is unlikely that any organization can be relevant in the eyes of everyone. Even the mighty Wal-Mart cannot make that claim. According to *Business Week*, July 2007, Wal-Mart retreated from the German market by selling 85 of its stores to the local competition. Wal-Mart could not adapt to German culture and was thus unable to become relevant to sufficient German consumers. The consequence: exit the market or die. It exited.

To remain relevant requires organizations to be adaptive, creative and innovative.

This means that the mission or underlying purpose of the organization must be made relevant through vision statements that lay out goals and strategies that cohere with the organization's competencies and above all address changing realities. Being in tune with new realities is what makes organizations adaptive and creative. This task is by no means easy. New realities are always arriving. Some realities are obvious and explicit, e.g. the looming retirement of baby boomers; some are not that readily obvious and more implicit, e.g. a change in the structure of households away from the traditional nuclear family model; and some changes slowly creep up on one and suddenly appear to be a big new reality although they have been arriving for some time, e.g. global warming and climate change. Often identifying the current reality is not easy. Identifying new realities when they are still new is even more difficult for the many reasons, some of which we discuss in this article. Easy or difficult, there is nothing more important for any system that wishes to remain alive and relevant than to orient its activities to responding to new realities.

THE FORCES OF CHANGE

Whether it is news on TV, the newspaper, discussion at the boardroom table or in the corridors of offices or manufacturing plants, everyone is talking about change. Change, they say, is the only constant. (Heraclitus, the Greek philosopher, told us this over 2000 years ago—no new reality!) Everyone claims to be in so called change mode. Products and processes are being revised, revamped, and re-engineered to respond to change. New industries are emerging, new types of companies being created; new partnerships forged; new territories "invaded"; new departments established, and newly skilled employees hired. Evidence of rapid and radical change is everywhere.

Change is pervasive. Many assert that never has there been so much change, such radical change, and such swift change as now. They insist we are facing change of new dimensions and proportions that exceed anything ever experienced. Is that true? Consider the time of the industrial revolution when seemingly overnight factories appeared; people left their traditional work at home to be employed by others; steam engines and automobiles replaced donkey carts and bicycles; and new types of medicines cured century old diseases. Songs and discussions on the local commons were supplanted by the gramophone and the wireless, and flying machines soon ushered in the jet age. People living in those times must have been overwhelmed by the impact of change and are likely to have said much of what we are saying today about the radicality and rapidity of change.

If we go further back in history we are likely to find many similar turning points where massive changes were the order of the day. If we look carefully we will note that not just every century, but every century heralded a series of spectacular changes.

The twentieth century brought with it a major change in our experience of space. One example is that thanks to advances in aerodynamic technology we can now travel faster than the speed of sound! This reality can hardly be grasped conceptually!

If we look back over the centuries we can mark our progress in the realm of travel. We evolved from walking, to riding the horse, to the donkey cart, to the bicycle, to the automobile, to the propeller plane, to the jet plane, and now to supersonic flight! Along with our new technical abilities, our consciousness has shifted in order to keep up with our changing understanding of distance. Distance, we know, relates to space.

Several hundred years ago, a once in a life time physical journey from say Casablanca to Mecca, would take months. Now this trip is possible within several hours. We can also repeat this journey weekly or even daily without undue hardship. Our twenty-first century understanding of journey is thus quite different to that of say four hundred years ago. There is no place on earth we cannot physically reach within twenty-four to forty-eight hours.

If for a moment we set aside the physical element of traversing distance and transport ourselves instead to the intellectual or mental plane, we recognize here too we have made dramatic strides. In earlier centuries we could only communicate face to face via passed on oral messages or handwritten briefs. Communication took time and space (distance had to be covered). Now, with the computer, the internet, and satellite communication, we can communicate almost instantaneously. There is no perceived space between us. Distance is collapsed into the immediate here and now. Space and time no longer exists. Everything is *virtually* here and now. The communication revolution has eradicated the "space between." Thus new happenings or new news is not new for long. We are relentlessly assailed with new realities. New realities are made known to us by seemingly instantaneous data feeds. No matter how much you and I might glue ourselves to the news or the internet, there is no way we can absorb, never mind grasp or embrace all the new realities being communicated.

The communication revolution is likely to continue. The speed of communication has stimulated the development in new technologies, which in turn has improved the technology of communication. The so called information revolution has resulted from these new technologies that have spawned and fed the ubiquitous world wide web. One important reminder is that the bombardment of information we experience does not guarantee its relevance or quality. Our new challenge is not paucity of information but how to sift out the grains of relevant truths from the mounds of data, facts and fanciful narratives. This too is one of the key challenges of organizational leadership. How does one lead in a virtual world? How does one identify the most salient information required for good decision making?

Judging by the enormous hype regarding the change we are experiencing one might be led to believe we are living in a new era. Well are we? What makes this time so spectacular, so different? Is "change" really a special phenomenon? Contemporary physics tells us that **everything, everywhere,** is **always** (and always has been) in perpetual motion and change. Nothing is static; everyone and everything consists of continuously vibrating molecules of energy. The cosmos comprises one pulsating mass of particles in continual movement toward new potentials, new possibilities and new outcomes (Capra, 1995 and Lazlo, 2007). Waves of change perpetually wash through the cosmos. If this is true, and the new science is the governing scientific paradigm at this time, then it is clear that change is inherent in all that we are and do. Change IS a constant; has always been with us, and will continue to dictate reality. In fact change IS the reality. Nothing can remain the same for any length of time. Change is as inevitable as night follows day.

So what is so different about our present time? Maynard and Mehrtens in their book, *The Fourth Wave* (1993), argue that we are moving from an era of interconnectedness (third wave) to an era of integration (fourth wave). (The first wave was the agricultural revolution and the second wave industrialization.) In the fourth wave, as we come to realize how integrated the world is, we experience a shift of consciousness. As we learn and experience that China, for example, is only a few jet hours away and that China's culture and industrial activity can be brought into our living rooms via TV, we apprehend China differently. The charming notion that the flap of a butterfly's wings in Brazil can impact wind currents over Asia is now understood as an existential reality. Our perception of what is and can be has altered. The combined forces of technology and communications have not only removed or destroyed old fences and archaic stereotypes but have ushered in a profusion of new possibilities and choices. Entrenched ideas have always been challenged, but never at the rate as now. Old technologies have always faded away, but never at the current pace. The more we realize how inter-related we are with one another and with the environment, the more inter-related we become. The collapse of space and time brings to our consciousness something the sages have always insisted on: the only thing we need to pay attention to is the present moment. As Peter Drucker claimed in one of the books he wrote at the turn of the twentieth century, the future is now!

Given this reality about change, the phenomenon of change is not what requires our attention as much as the impact and meaning of the change. Robert E. Quinn, author of *Deep Change, Discovering the Leader Within* (1996), writes "If we want to make the world a better place, we need to understand change." He claims that every person and every organization continually faces a core dilemma: deep change or slow death. Unless work is done to the contrary, all living systems move toward entropy or loss of productive energy. He claims if we do not make deep change we are doomed.

Many theories of organizational change exist. Christiane Demers provides a synthesis of some of the predominant change theories in her book, *Organizational Change Theories* (2007). In this book she illustrates how change theories have evolved over time and how our understanding of what initiates or motivates organizational change has changed from the 1970s to our present day understanding. I do not wish to provide a synthesis of her synthesis but simply to highlight some of the different approaches to organizational change that she mentions.

Change theories address the issue of change from a number of different perspectives. One perspective considers whether change is internally determined or environmentally determined. I argue that all change is and should be driven by environmental change. In other words, the stimulus for change always lies external to the system changing.

Another discussion about change rests on whether change is a radical or incremental phenomenon. Here the focus is on whether change is a transformational or evolutionary phenomenon. This theory looks into the implications of radical turnarounds as opposed to creeping strategic, structural and behavioral change. I argue that both types of change occur simultaneously in a far less definable and/or controlled fashion than we like to imagine.

Yet a further perspective of change focuses on the actions of management either selecting certain specific change strategies in a strategic and controlled manner or responding to crises and driving change through urgency and haste. In both cases change initiatives are considered highly rational and top down driven activities where leadership is exercised from the top. I resist this view of the management of change.

The late 1990s and the twenty-first century vision of change is different in that rather than it being deemed a one time event, it is seen as pervasive, continuous, and indeterminate. Here managers have less control as the organization grapples with change at all levels all the time. All members of the organization are caught up in change initiatives and everyone in the organization needs to see themselves as an agent of change. The life cycle approach to change is less relevant at this time as industries and organizations break-up or recreate new paradigms that do not follow the classic life cycle path. Change is less of a specific initiative in the strategic plan but a phenomenon of daily organizational life. Just like the atoms and molecules that are in continuous motion creating new possibilities, organizations are in perpetual change motion too. This latter approach is the most consonant with our discussions that follow.

CHANGE AND LOSS

If change is inherent in all things and is the order of each and every day, why are we so bad at it? Few would disagree that in general we dislike change and resist it if and when we can. We tend to favor the status quo. We provide all manner of reasons for justifying our preference for what currently exists, especially in the organizational context. At the personal level we may be somewhat open to trying out that new electric car and reluctantly acknowledging that our gas-guzzling SUV has to go. Times have changed. The cost of gas, not the cost of the automobile, is what now determines our buying decisions.

If we are part of the organization that is losing market share with its gas-guzzlers and is now retooling and recreating itself to become an electric car maker, we are likely to be even more resistant to the change from making SUVs to electric cars. Why are we so resistant to change? What ups the stakes? What makes organizational change so complex? To answer these questions let us begin by considering the nature of change.

As discussed earlier, change arrives by way of **new realities**. Realities by definition do not go away. They are **real** and must be heeded. We also know that new realities are **always** arriving. Some new realities have direct relevance and immediacy to us and our organization, and some less so. Because so many new realities are continuously arriving on so many fronts, we cannot apprehend or deal with them all. We have therefore developed coping strategies. Our coping strategies include screening out those realities we consider irrelevant or too insignificant to be concerned with. Often we identify new realities that will affect others, but thankfully not us! "Look what they have to deal with!" or "Thankfully that is not my problem!" are well known sighs of relief.

There are times when our coping strategies incorrectly screen out new realities that have direct relevance to us. This can occur due to inattention, negligence, overwhelm, distraction, denial or fear. Whatever the cause of the oversight, the ramifications of overlooking important new realities can range from inconvenient (I did not realize I had to fill out those new forms), to dire (I should have taken the opportunity to be retrained when it was offered to me).

Organizations screen new realities both formally and informally. They do this through formal processes, such as environmental scanning or strategic planning as well as informally via the collective consciousness of employees encouraged to be attentive to the changing environment. The result of these processes drive plans for change. Changes are usually initiated through the use of planning documents that layout goals, set benchmarks, calculate discounted cash flows and include other managerial techniques aimed at ensuring the change will generate a net positive contribution to the bottom line. The predicted addition to profits, however, does not guarantee success nor does it mean that the change initiative(s) will ensure enduring or even continued organizational relevance. Organizations too can omit responding to poignant new realities; respond to the wrong ones, or even to the right ones but in the wrong way. New realities are tricky business! As we discussed briefly, new realities can be obscure; can be deceptive; can arrive in a fragmented fashion; can readily mislead, and most importantly can be difficult or downright brutal to absorb. The bombardment of new realities contributes to making change so overwhelming. We have to continuously ask ourselves: Which new reality is the most critical one? How and why?

At the time of writing one existing reality is that North Korea, much to the alarm of many nations, is flexing its nuclear muscles. In response, the United Nations sponsored moves to tighten financial sanctions and to ban imports of luxury goods into North Korea. According to Economist World Report, the Kim regime has been the biggest customer for Hennessy's top cognac.[1] Cognac fell under the import ban. The brutal reality of losing this large market due to the embargoes must have been a challenging "new reality" for Hennessy to absorb and adapt to. Did Hennessy new realities' screening mechanism anticipate this challenge? How did Hennessy adapt one wonders.

New realities create **value tensions.**

All change, even good change signifies loss of some kind. And even "loss" as a consequence of a welcome new reality invariably has an impact on one's sense of self, or self-esteem. (Beerel, 1998; Heifetz, 1996).

Value tensions cut to the chase. They challenge who we are and the world of self-perceptions we have created around us. Often they pierce our most vulnerable spots and tear at the pillars on which we have built our world views, our sense of pride and our self-esteem. Identifying the value tensions that arise as a result of change is known as defining the adaptive challenge (Heifetz, 1996). Acknowledging the adaptive challenge is the beginning of the road of adaptive work.

New realities may require us to change our ideas; our belief systems; our loyalties; our concepts; our habits, and our skill sets. As one example we have only to look at the role of technology in our lives to grasp the value tensions that new realities can create. Many a specialized craft, managerial function, or professional skill has been replaced by technology of all sorts. For example, software tools of graphic and design have replaced the work of draughtsmen. Decision support systems can now perform certain planning functions that used

1. The Economist the World in 2007 report. "After the Bouffant of Pyongyang" London, England: *The Economist Newspaper*, 2006, p. 43.

to be the preserve of management. Medical systems can now diagnose diseases that used to be the responsibility of specialists in the medical profession. The most dramatic outsourcing we have and will continue to witness is not to India or China, but to the advance of wireless technology, advanced microchips and intelligent machines. How does it feel to know that a large portion of humankind's basic skill set can be replicated faster, more accurately, more reliably and more consistently by a machine? That truth is an old reality. The new tasks that machines will take over from us are destined to provide a stream of new realities in the foreseeable future.

ADAPTING CAPACITIES

In a world where change is constant and often radical we are constantly dealing with "loss" around our sense of self and who we are. This throws us into a continuous state of renegotiation with ourselves about ourselves. This is hard work – very hard work! It is not always pleasant work, as we are continuously asked to give up some things in favor of others. If we can develop our adaptive capacities by consciously engaging in adaptive work, new realities can bring us new freedoms and new opportunities for developing our infinite human potential. For example having to find a new job may mean we find new competencies and new strengths we never knew we had. In those cases where our sense of self or self-esteem is challenged we are provided with opportunities to consider whether they were grounded in healthy or sustaining values. If nothing else, having to respond to change in creative ways enhances our adaptive capacities, even when it hurts. Mature adaptive capacities provide us with resilience, and resilience is a capacity worth working for! Resilience improves the chances of healthy survival in a world of change.

Identifying and responding to change requires alertness, agility and energy. As we saw change is hard work. To be good at it, like all things, takes practice. We need to do it repeatedly. Jokingly we often say: "No rest for the wicked!" This well worn phrase refers to the need to continuously create, shift, change, rearrange, do whatever it takes, to keep up. The work of "keeping up" is never done. However, being adaptive is much more than keeping up.

To be good at responding to change refers to our capacity to adapt. As humans we are bestowed with innate adaptive capacities. These are part of our built in survival mechanisms as a species. As Darwin has explained to us, to ensure our legacy we need to adapt. To be sure some of the species (individuals or groups), will elect not to adapt or will not have the wherewithal to adapt, and will, therefore, die and disappear. Losing some is inevitable. The question for our consideration is: Do we want to be that individual who disappears? Does our organization want to be that group that falls behind and ends in the dustbin of history?

Adaptation is not the same as coping. Adaptive strategies are different from coping strategies. Adaptation refers to the ability to integrate new realities into one's worldview and to consciously work with the changes and value tensions these present. Adaptation means developing a new mindset and new skill sets that can integrate and competently handle new circumstances. Adaptation means being creative and active, not passive and submissive, in the face of change. Adaptation calls for working with the energy of change: guiding, shaping and harnessing that energy in innovative ways.

Coping strategies are less assertive, energetic and creative than adaptive strategies. Coping strategies imply a certain resignation to the inevitability of change whereas adaptive strategies are active, outgoing strategies that do the best they can to meet change on their own terms. Consciously developing our adaptive capacity is what makes us more competent at responding to change. It builds our resilience and our self-confidence. Developing our adaptive capacity also takes us out of the realm of simple survival to greater autonomy and personal moral agency.

Developing one's adaptive capacity is not something that is explicitly taught. Growing into adulthood is an adaptive process. Some do it well and some take a little longer. Even so, not all adults end up with the same adaptive capacities. In fact, our continued resistance to change, even though it is the essence of life, signals the need for us to become more adaptive.

From a leadership development perspective, MBA programs do not teach students how to read new realities and how to create adaptive responses. Regrettably, most MBA curricula place emphasis on technical and procedural, rather than adaptive work. Adaptive people and adaptive organizations can embrace the future with greater confidence and an enhanced sense of autonomy. If you think about it, there is no greater gift than to help enhance others' adaptive capacity. Isn't that one of the major responsibilities of good parenthood, good education, and good governance?

By now we understand well why people resist change. Within the organizational context peoples' resistance to change escalates. Let us look at some explanations for this phenomenon:

- ❖ People feel less in control when operating within the organization as they are part of a power hierarchy that has control over their future. The system is larger than they are.
- ❖ Usually there is someone else ultimately in charge of the change process, so there are usually power dynamics going on (*see* Chapter 5). Other peoples' issues have to be taken into consideration and these might take preference over one's own.
- ❖ The losses people experience as part of a change process may be more visible to others than if it is within the realm of their personal lives. Exposure makes them feel more vulnerable.
- ❖ There is fear that change may result in people losing their jobs and hence their source of livelihood.
- ❖ The group dynamic of the organization: Groups always fear for the survival of the group; employees are thus caught in the "groupthink" around resistance to change. (*see* Chapter 6 on the anxieties existent in organizational life.)
- ❖ Overall, change in the organization appears to higher the stakes.

At this point let us simply note that organizational change is more complex than personal change. Even where organizational leadership has clearly and accurately interpreted the new realities and devised appropriate strategies to move forward, organizational resistance to change can torpedo even the very best efforts. Identifying new realities is only the first part of the challenge of remaining relevant. These efforts must be followed by adaptive work or change initiatives will be sabotaged. Let us also for the moment note that "execution," A now popular concept, is not the same as adaptive work!

An important thing for organizational leaders and for executive management to grasp is that there is good change and there is bad change. Good change responds directly to new realities. Good change acknowledges the adaptive challenge and includes engaging in adaptive work along with the required technical work. Good change reinforces the organization's potency and relevance to its customers, markets, employees and shareholders. Good change sets the organization on a forward looking and healthy trajectory. Good change advances the adaptive capacity of the organization as a whole as well as that of its executives and employees. Good change is one recognized as an ongoing process.

Bad change detracts from the organization's potency and relevance. Bad change corrupts an organization's healthy trajectory and impairs its ădaptive capacity. Bad change affects morale and people's willingness to be adaptive in the future.

Bad change can be worse than no change, especially where it deludes the company into thinking it is a good change. Bad change is particularly "bad" if the organization has not truly dealt with the new realities that it needs to respond to in order to remain strategically relevant. Leaders that initiate badly aligned change initiatives do the organization serious damage. Alas, although examples of bad change efforts proliferate, many errant CEOs or executives are oblivious of the damage they have done and have moved on to their next big job, while the organization is stuck with reorienting and revitalizing itself.

It is possible that some change initiatives keep the organization on some course but not the most critical or salient one. That too is bad news. Not only has the organization used enormous energy and resources to achieve mediocre results, but the organization will remain convinced that it has changed and hence an important goal has been accomplished. Change is the means to an end and not the end in itself. Change is an ongoing process. The end of one change effort is the beginning of another. In the strenuous efforts around change initiatives, these truths are easily forgotten.

Here are several reasons for the low success rate of change projects in organizations:

- The change did not really respond to new realities, but rather was a response to the reality the CEO and strategic management wanted to perceive was occurring rather than that which was really occurring.
- The change required in order to truly respond to the new realities was not fully understood, as the new realities were not adequately "reality tested".
- The change engaged in was a technical fix to an adaptive problem (refer Chapter 4).
- People involved in implementing changes did not truly believe

that the change project was responding to new realities, so they were coerced into action rather than feeling self-mobilized.

- The anxieties inherent in the organization impeded its ability to adapt and learn.
- People's resistance to change was not properly dealt with.
- People affected by the change were not included in the decision making processes.
- Leadership did not or could not convey the urgency of the requirement to change resulting in poor timing around change.
- The extent of the change initiative was not fully thought through, hence shortly after launch trouble spots creating further stress occurred.
- The full impact on stakeholders to the change initiative had been only superficially explored.
- The focus on the change was strategic, tactical and technical but not ethical.

Identifying new realities and managing the change process is the critical task of leadership. When leadership is exercised effectively the organization's change initiatives will be effective and there will be "good change". When leadership is exercised ineffectively, change initiatives will be mediocre, ineffective or fail miserably.

Organizations need to be adaptive, creative and innovative to survive and prosper. Being adaptive, creative and innovative requires enormous attention and energy. To sustain these efforts demands a culture of openness to change. The adaptive and creative work cannot be the sole responsibility of the CEO and strategic management or that of a single division or department. The adaptive and creative mindset must pervade every corner of the organization to make it effective and sustainable.

A change mindset must permeate the entire organization:

- Due to the amount of energy and focus needed to be adaptive and creative, organizations need to optimize group synergy around creative efforts.
- Departmentalizing creativity creates artificial barriers that foster a "them versus us" attitude.
- Organizations are only as progressive as their weakest link; therefore, their weakest link had better be adaptive and creative.

- Organizations need to encourage the creative potential of all their employees, not just those in special functions or departments.
- A culture of openness to change heightens the organization's awareness of new realities and reduces resistance to change.
- In order to foster a learning organization—see below—all the individuals in the organization need to bring their adaptive capacities to bear.

Many organizations claim they have the characteristics of a learning organization.

They insist they are creative and innovative and engage in healthy risk taking. Creating a learning organization takes more than this! True learning is to "know differently". It is the process of exploring, enquiring, searching, reflecting and in the end "knowing the place for the first time."[1] The learning process alters the way a person constructs meaning and re-charts her mental maps. True learning results in transformation, not the addition of more information. True learning does not concern acquiring new skills or new technical solutions. True learning creates new understandings, new paradigms and new adaptive strategies and new behaviors.

Let us take a simple example; learning to drive a motor vehicle. Think back on the adaptive work and learning that took. There was certainly all the technical work; learning how to use the pedals, what the information on the instrument panel meant; using the rear view and side mirrors; what lay under the hood; how to change a tire and so on. Well and good. Prior to learning to drive you had no doubt been driven around by your parents, teachers and friends. Now you are to take over and drive for yourself. This is big! There is a lot of adaptive work here too. You are going to be responsible for your actions behind the wheel. You have new autonomy and thus a new sense of self. You are a real grown up now as you can take yourself places on your own terms. On the other hand, now you will be asked to fetch and take other people. You may even lose some of your freedom. Driving has opened up a whole new world of opportunities and responsibilities.

Recall the first days of driving. You get in behind the wheel and now you are driving. Yes, you know all the technical stuff, but putting it all together is another matter. You run out of hands to activate the

---

1. T.S. Eliot. *Little Gidding*, 1942.

turn signals, you brake too late and nearly miss the stop sign, you forget to look in the rear view mirror when you make a turn and nearly hit an overtaking car… and so it continues for quite some time. You also learn about your understanding of speed. What it means to push the pedal to 80 mph; you feel exhilarated and scared. What it means to stop and how long that can take if you are driving too fast. You learn that reading the map while you are driving is not a good idea as you will most likely miss the turn off. Driving in a thunder or snow storm presents a whole other number of challenges.

Learning to drive changes your world. It changes the way you feel about yourself and it changes your relationship with others. You have a new understanding of go, speed and stop. You have a new awareness of yourself and your ability to multi-task in this environment. You know why you cannot drink and drive or should not drive when you are drowsy. You know this through the deep personal understanding of being in control, or not, of this metallic capsule that hurtles you and others through space. No-one can really grasp the mindset of driving unless one drives. Driving requires an "altered state of consciousness."

IDENTIFYING NEW REALITIES

When thinking about **new realities** it is easy to fall into the trap of trying to predict the future as if it is a one time event. The future is not a one time event. It is **always arriving!** It is as ceaseless as the waves that wash up on the sea shore. And the future is the past before we know it. No sooner has it arrived, it is past. There is no way and no point in trying to stargaze and anticipate future out of the blue events. Everything we wish to know about the future is being revealed to us in the present. Remember, every minute now, was in the future a minute ago!

The future lies in the present; the future is now. Our understanding of the future and new realities depends upon our ability to pay attention and understand what is going on now. If we read today's tea leaves correctly we will see the new realities unfolding.

Organizations that excel, work intensively with current realities. Their mindfulness and attention to developments both in their markets and in others provides them with insights into new solutions and new creative opportunities. These organizations are observant and curious. They tend to investigate corners where others are not paying attention.

They are essentially idea driven, rather than market share or profit driven. They continuously change the rules on themselves to avoid complacency and arrogance. They see change as an opportunity. The entire enterprise is committed to change and action. Above all they employ adaptive, creative, self-motivated people.

Gary Hamel in his article "Be Your Own Seer" provides some profound advice on how to be alert to new realities and how to respond effectively. He advocates the importance of freeing oneself from the stranglehold of the familiar by leaping over our mental constraints. We are prisoners to tradition and our eyes are dimmed by precedent, he claims. Familiarity is the enemy. He stresses the importance of imagination, curiosity and creativity that comes with learning to see and be different. He suggests that we become novelty addicts and heretics, willing to challenge the status quo and to proactively shape the environment.

Hamel insists it is essential to become "addicted to change" and to perpetually seek new possibilities. Predicting the future is for fools; what is important is to develop strategies to deal with unpredictability. He argues that the future is different rather than unknowable. Opportunities lie by looking where others are not looking and that requires really paying attention. He advocates we should challenge our mental models and deconstruct existing beliefs.

John Kotter of the Harvard Business School insists that the central issue is never strategy, structure, culture or systems. The core of change lies in changing the behavior of people. And behavior change happens mostly by speaking to people's feelings. The task of leadership is primarily about dealing with people's adaptive capacity to new realities, i.e. their ability to transform and change.

Leadership is about facilitating, guiding, and managing change. Where there is no change, we do not need leaders. Exercising leadership concerns mobilizing oneself and others (the group or the organization) to adapt to the new realities of change (Beerel, 1998).

The first responsibility of the leader is to define reality in collaboration with others in the organization. This requires sizing up the current situation as it really is; not as it used to be, or as people would like it to be. It is essential that the current realities are viewed from every angle; that bad news is confronted, and that creative attention is given to new realities that are continuously arriving.

Max De Pree, ex-Chairman of Herman Miller, describes in his two well-known books, *Leadership is an Art* (1989), and *Leadership*

Jazz (1992), an approach to leadership that resonates with this attention to new realities. In his book, *Leadership is an Art*, his advice for leadership is deeply consonant with the systemic and inter-relatedness concepts of the new science discussed earlier. He claims that the first step of the leader is to define reality (De Pree, 1989, p.11). According to him leaders should also liberate people to do what is required of them: to change, grow and strive for their potential. They can only do this if they are aligned to the changing realities of the world and are in touch with the consequences.

Defining reality is difficult as we tend to mute or downplay those parts of reality we do not want to deal with. Entire organizations and even entire societies (see below) collude in this fashion. In order to define reality effectively, therefore, leaders need to reality test their perception of what is changing. Reality testing means involving others in dialogue and investigation so as to arrive at a co-created understanding of the current new reality. Leaders must include views and opinions of people across all sectors of the organization; across all disciplines, and preferably across all points of view. Frequently the organization's outliers have insights into "reality" that others may not see or grasp. Leaders must also persist in exploring current new realities that are being ignored, no matter how trivial they may initially seem.

Jared Diamond gives us some interesting insights into the devastating results of ignoring new realities and how and why this occurs. His recent book, *Collapse: How Societies Choose to Fail or Succeed* (2005), chronicles the collapse of past civilizations. He reveals how humankind's use and abuse of the environment throughout the centuries reveal the truth behind the world's greatest collapses. History, he claims is filled with patterns of environmental catastrophes. The processes by which past societies have undermined themselves include deforestation and habitat destruction, soil problems, water management problems, overhunting, overfishing, the effects of introduced species on native species, uncontained human population growth, and increased percapita impact of people on the local environment.[1] And we are calling these phenomena new realities!

His examples include the history of Easter Island, Norse Greenland, and the Native American Mayan society. In recounting the events that led to their demise he highlights the warning signals that were present

1. Jared Diamond Collapse page 6.

and visible but ignored by the population and its leaders. In fact some of the leaders' strategies exacerbated the situation rather than raising it to public attention or confronting the signal of impending doom.

Diamond asks the question: Why do some societies make disastrous decisions? He refers to the collapse of the Easter Island society who cut down all the trees on which they radically depended. Easter Island was discovered by Jacob Roggeveen on Easter day, April 5, 1722. It is famous for its gigantic stone statues of human faces. Over several centuries the islanders systematically destroyed their forests. Without constraint they used wood for building houses and canoes, wood for platforms to haul the enormous statues across the island and bark for ropes. Clans competed to build bigger and bigger statues destroying forests as they sought to outdo one another. The result of the native tribes' overexploitation of resources and destruction of a fragile echo system led to the society's eventual demise.

SYSTEMIC LEADERSHIP

In this text we focus on the Systemic Leadership approach. Systemic leaders focus on keeping the organization fine tuned to new realities. They understand the impact of new realities and change, and help (members of) the organization to work with the value tensions presented, adapt, learn and develop their adaptive capacities.

Systemic leaders are transformational leaders, concerned with strengthening the organization's capacity for learning. They understand that the organization's capacity for learning will determine its resilience and continued competitive strength. They recognize the consequences of Easter Island myopia.

Understanding the philosophy of Systemic Leadership and the tasks of effective systemic leaders will preoccupy us in the next chapters. In essence Systemic Leaders understand the critical necessity of holding the organization's focus on new realities that keep arriving and dealing with value tensions before technical and procedural work is embarked upon.

Based on this text, here are some of the essential aspects of the Systemic Leadership approach:

- Organizations are human systems formed to achieve a predetermined purpose or goal. In order to survive in the longer term, organizations must remain relevant.

- Change arrives by way of new realities. New realities are always arriving and will not disappear.
- The only constant in the world is change. Change challenges existing structures, forms and paradigms. In order for people and organizations to survive meaningfully they need to respond to new realities and adapt.
- New realities are driven by forces in the external environment. Failure to identify the source of new realities can result in the organization responding to the wrong ones.
- Change always creates value tensions. These value tensions represent both gains and losses. Change will always represent loss in some form or another. Identifying value tensions is known as defining the adaptive challenge.
- In order to enhance their adaptive capacity people and organizations need to define the adaptive challenge and then do their adaptive work. These activities enhance their adaptive capacities.
- Adaptive capacity is a function of the organization's ability to deal with the value tensions that change always implies.
- The prime task of leadership is to identify the new realities and to consider the value tensions they imply for various stakeholders.

FURTHER READING

Ackoff, Russell L. (1999). *Recreating the Corporation: A Design of Organizations for the 21st Century*. New York: Oxford University Press.

Beerel, Annabel (1998). *Leadership Through Strategic Planning*. London, United Kingdom: International Thompson.

Charan, Ram (2007). *Know-How*. New York: Crown Business.

Conner, Daryl R. (1998). *Leading At The Edge of Chaos: How to Create the Nimble Organization*. New York: John Wiley & Sons, Inc.

Diamond, Jared (2005). *Collapse*. New York: Penguin Books.

Drucker, Peter F. (1999). *Management Challenges for the 21st Century*. New York: Harper Business.

Kotter, John P. (1996). *Leading Change*. Boston: Harvard Business School Press.

Senge, Peter *et al*. (2008). *The Necessary Revolution*. New York: Doubleday.

14

Adopting Competition Policy in Appointments for Top Management Positions in Government Bodies in the Republic of Yemen Pilot Experiment at the Ministry of Civil Service

Nabil Shamsan

FIRST
PREFACE - JUSTIFICATIONS FOR THE PILOT

The Republic of Yemen is witnessing a multi-direction dynamism aiming at achieving overall development, reform and modernization in all political, economic, administrative, social and legislative aspects along with branching procedures and institutional building.

Within the framework of this paper, we shall very briefly address two milestones of these developments in two directions; the first: is related to political directions and transitions seen by Yemen recently, and the second: regarding organizational and administrative reforms of the basic government structure.

First Direction: Political

The Republic of Yemen adopted the democratic choice in the ruling regime of the country. This choice resulted in the provision of political and social environment for political pluralism, basic pillars for electoral process and related establishment of constitutional and legal organizations to supervise and administer the elections process. The ultimate outcome of elections is the peaceful exchange of power.

Reaching this conviction and social era means that governance of the country will transfer from a party to another in a certain time period as determined by the constitution. Therefore, necessary measures and steps should be taken especially in the field of developing administ-rative and organizational systems to cope with these political trends and to ensure maintaining strength and integrity of the administrative body of the government and its accumulative experience as well as continuation of its tasks effectively and efficiently. Appropriate level of service should be maintained in terms of quality, efficiency and simplicity regardless of the ruling regime of the country.

Despite the fact that there are still some principles, policies and systems to be developed and materialized, but the following principles are of crucial importance:

- Apply the principle of neutrality in public job from highest levels down to technical and vocational jobs and to lowest job level.
- Apply the principle of merit, efficiency and competition for public positions, the key of which are top management posts.
- Establish foundations of scienti-fic and objective legislations of clear and transparent procedures for public jobs regardless of those occupying these jobs.

Consequently, creating these princi-ples and foundations represent, transitionally, the minimum limit of required organizational environ-ment to cope with peaceful exchange of power.

Otherwise, the door will be open for all parties alternating in power through ballot boxes to give preponderance to political loyalty in public jobs on the account of absolute standards of professional and occupational capacities and skills for occupation of public jobs. This will result in complete removal of existing staff and replacement by others. Such practices will result in damages to the society not the least of which is the destruction of accumulated experience of the government body in addition to adverse effects on human and social aspects.

For all above, establishing scientific and objective system for selection and appointment of human resources in state agencies in different levels based on competition rules achieving merit, neutrality and equal opportunities principles is an essential demand that complements and copes with democratic system leading to peaceful exchange of power.

SECOND DIRECTION
ORGANIZATIONAL AND ADMINISTRATIVE REFORMS OF GOVERNMENT BODY

The Republic of Yemen is going through an overall reform and modernization process using various tools and methodologies and piloting model experiments in different modernization and improvement areas. Adopting restructuring and re-engineering methodologies represented the backbone of this experiment.

During the last period of the Civil Service Modernization Project, various activities were undertaken to achieve its objectives including restructuring and re-engineering process for seven government agencies (ministries, authorities and boards) including the Ministry of Civil Service.

The Ministry of Civil Service restructuring study came out with results that represent a root change in its functional and structural position. These results were reflected in a new organizational regulation for the ministry identifying three main sectors with various technical and specialized departments under each sector.

For the purpose of filling in these leadership posts with efficient and qualified staff able to achieve objectives envisaged of the reform process, a decision was taken to make appointment in these positions subject to competition system among the maximum possible number of applicants from Yemeni citizens meeting required conditions either from the staff of the ministry, other government agencies or the private sector and then select the best candidates.

We conclude from above preface that political choices and approaches witnessed by Yemen in its current phase imposed on those responsible for the overall reform process to adopt coping and consistent policies and methodolo-gies for the administration of government agencies, building institutional and human capacities in different organizational levels.

Under this broad and integrated vision, the idea of our experiment emerged. The principle of this idea is to adopt competition basis for appointment in leadership positions at the Ministry of Civil Service and Insurance as a transitional pilot case to be rolled out to other government agencies in later times. This is based on the conviction that such experiment will cope with overarching political and reform trends followed by the government of Yemen especially if we refer to the principles of:

- Neutrality in public jobs.
- Merit and fair competition in filling in public jobs as key conditions to boost democratic practices and peaceful exchange of power in the country. On the other hand, it aims at creating reform-friendly environment to make successful all administrative and organiza-tional reform initiatives.

Since the early stages of thinking in this option, a material and essential issue was to be decided before initiating practical steps for the experiment. This issue was to ensure the alignment of the experiment and its procedures with the constitution and applicable laws. The process of searching and enquiry resulted in identifying various constitutional, legal and organizational provisions that represent constitutional and legal basis. These may be summarized as follows:

Constitutional basis:

Articles 24, 25, 28, 41 and 42 of the Constitution of the Republic of Yemen included social and cultural foundations of the state and its philosophy, principles and values as follows:

- Article 24: the state guarantees equal opportunities for all citizens politically, economically, socially and culturally and issues laws to ensure that.
- Article 25: the Yemeni society is built on social solidarity based on justice, freedom and equality.
- Article 28: public service is an assignment and honour for its occupants. While performing their tasks, employees shall target public interest and service of the people. The law determines conditions for public service, rights and duties of its occupants.
- Article 41: all citizens are equal in public rights and duties.
- Article 42: each citizen has the right to participate in political, economic, social and cultural life. The state guarantees

freedom of thought, expression of opinion by voice, writing, and picturing under the limits of law.

Legal basis:

Provisions and conditions of Law No. 19 of 1991 and its executive Regulation No. 122 of 1992 regarding civil service included the following:

- Public jobs are assignments for their occupants. Sincerity and dedication in public jobs is a national duty imposed by public interest. The aim is to serve people honestly and diligently and preponderance of public interest over private interests. Public jobs should be practiced according to the law and applicable regulations. All employees are citizens entrusted by the state to achieve this objective and implement its policies in all political, economic and social areas each in its relevant position.
- Occupancy of public job and management of personnel affairs is based on equal opportunities and rights for all citizens without any discrimination. The state shall adopt control means to ensure application of this principle. Conditions and specifications required by job nature are not considered as discrimination.

Political and reform basis:

Coping with policies and approaches included in the electoral programme of H. E. Ali Abdullah Saleh, President of the Republic, the general programme of the government and principles and objectives contained in the Civil Service Modernization Strategy, National Wages and Salaries Strategy, Civil Service Law No. 19/1991 and Wages and Positions Law No. 34/2005, the key of which are:

- Review mandate and functions of the state to make it more focused on main activities and tasks. Provide receptive environment to attract investments, give opportunity to the private sector and civil society organizations to contribute in development as to strengthen capacities of national economy and support sustainable growth opportunities.

- Eliminate structural oversize of government body towards reducing expenditures, minimizing waste of resources and energies by removing duplication and overlapping in competencies and tasks between government agencies and adopt rationalized, effective and consistent administrative structures simplifying governmental service provision.
- Build government body having ability to develop strategies, draw policies and plans, and implement the same with high degree of efficiency and responsiveness to expectations of people and beneficiaries of these services of high quality and efficiency meeting their satisfaction.
- Apply the national wages and salaries strategy, evaluate phased implementation and utilize outcomes to achieve objectives of administrative, financial and institutional reforms.
- Build main and sub-databases, network connection and design information systems using modern means and technologies for human resources management. Improve efficiency of public expenditures, performance, its economic returns and eliminate all persistent imbalances and shortfalls in public jobs.

Organization and modernization basis:

In implementation of the compre-hensive study for restructuring of the Ministry of Civil Service and the articulated executive regulation of the Ministry No. 235/2007, mission, vision, objectives and values of the Ministry are determined as follows:

- *Mission*: Prepare, develop and activate an efficient and effective system for civil service based on principles of transparency, decentralization, merit and accountability and able to serve the objectives of socio-economic development, support public units in its implementation, adhere to its values and principles. Work to follow up sound implementation and propose continuous modernization to ensure provision of high quality service.
- *Vision*: The Ministry of Civil Service and Insurance shall become the most professional agency among all counterpart civil service bodies in Arabian Peninsula and Gulf Region by the year 2025.

- *Strategic objectives of the Ministry*: The Ministry shall work to upgrade performance in public service units and improve management level in government agencies in general based on its mission and vision by assuming the following strategic tasks:
  - Manage civil service system, develop and modernize its legislations, systems, regulations and procedures based on scientific develop-ments in management concepts, mechanisms and approaches in government organizations worldwide.
  - Manage human resources system, develop and modernize its legislations, systems, regulations and procedures based on renewing scientific developments in concepts, mechanisms and approaches of human capital and investing human resources in public service units.
  - Manage the system of social insurance, develop and modernize the system to ensure optimum investments of its funds.
  - Manage civil service system to train and develop human resource, prepare and develop administrative leaders in government sector.
  - Build and operate databases, manage scientific research systems in civil service, HRD areas. Manage insurance and pension systems to create sound platform for developing these systems and support decision making at national level.
  - Provide support and assistance to public service units in applying new legislations, systems, policies and procedures and address any performance obstacles. Provide advice and technical expertise to these units in their efforts to improve and develop performance.
  - Monitor and evaluate performance of public service units to ensure they provide services efficiency and effectively and comply with approved regulations and procedures to achieve their objectives.
  - Develop an effective system for insurance and pensions meeting requirements of sustainability and ability to ensure stable life for public service employees after referral to retirement.

- *Strategic approaches of the Ministry to modernize the concept of civil service*: The Ministry works seriously to affirm and activate the following strategic approaches and follow up compliance at all public service units:
  - Transformation from "authority" concept to "service" concept in all functions and tasks of civil service.
  - Affirmation of citizens' rights to obtain public services easily and effectively and involve them in the management of public service units, assign appropriate functions to private and community sectors according to applicable legislations.
  - Change from stagnant ideology to positive diversity allowing every main public service unit of forming its performance styles and achieving their objectives in a manner consistent with the nature of their activities, their work environment and targeted clients.
  - Abandon the logic of viewing public service units as organizations spending their budget allocations and adopt the logic of conside-ring them as units aiming at achieving economic management of their available resources and reach economic-efficiency in their activities and services.

Values

The Ministry believes and adheres to the following values and works to spread and affirm these values in all public service units and all administrative units covered by the civil service law:

- *Transparency*: by making available all information on systems, regulations and decisions and make clear justifications and motives behind government actions in civil service Issues.
- *Responsibility and accountability*: all civil servants at all levels should be responsible for their acts and subject to accountabi-lity on their results.
- *Equality*: affirm that all citizens are equal and have right to have job opportunities in public service units or dealing with these units to obtain their services with equality and non-discrimination for whatever reason.

- *Social responsibility*: affirm that all public service units are participating in national development and are continuously responsible for providing better levels of social welfare.
- *Scientific methodology*: adopting scientific research as basis for study and objectiveness as basis for preparation of plans, programmes and decision making.
- *Objectiveness*: all decisions and actions shall be based on objective analysis of data, technical studies and documents.

THIRD
VALUES AND PRINCIPLES ADOPTED FOR IMPLEMENTING THE PILOT EXPERIMENT

***Transparency and publicity principle*:** represented in preparation and publication of the following information:

- *Ministry related information*: name of ministry, its organizational regulation and address with all contact numbers to the Ministry.
- General conditions for the competition and specific conditions for each post.
- Job description card for each advertised post.
- *Competition-related information*: including date and time for receiving applications and closing date. Place for submitting applications and name of responsible employee for receiving applications. Rules and forms for competition, means for sending applications, stages and standards for each stage.

Equality, scientific methodology and maximize women participation: through the following:

- Preparation of general and special conditions for the competition by international consultancy company.
- Discussion and approval of conditions through meetings, workshops and approval from the Council of Ministers.
- Competition did not include any political, social or geographic conditions or criteria for selection.
- Support women participation by giving them preference in case of equal scoring with men.

Neutrality: Management of the competition was not assigned to one party but to various parties in different stages:

- *Conditions preparation*: done through international firm assisted by specialized technical team.
- *Conditions approval*: done through meetings, workshops and approval of the Council of Ministers.
- *Announcement, receipt and review of applications*: done through a multilateral committee formed of Ministry of Civil Service, Premiership, Presidency of the Republic and Ministry of Legal Affairs.
- *Scoring of participants*: Arab Administrative Development Organization - Arab League.

Simple rules for entry: Adopting simplified procedures such as:

- Right to compete for two jobs
- Simple participation: applications may not necessarily be delivered personally but could be delivered by:
    - Post
    - Email
    - Fax
    - Personal delivery

FOURTH
RULES AND PROCEDURES OF COMPETITION

Advertisement

For the sake of accurately and fully clarify to potential applications the method of application and preparation of complete files, the advertisement was prepared to include an accurate and comprehensive explanation for all employment grounds to be contained in the file as well as some standard forms such as the C.V., position to apply to, application form and form of covering letter to be submitted by applicant.

More details on the announcement could be reached by viewing the advertisement published in newspapers and the Ministry website. Briefly, contents of the advertisement were as follows:

- *Title*: Competition for selecting candidates for Top Management Posts at the Headquarters of the Ministry of Civil Service and Insurance.
- *Introduction*: stating that the competition is announced as a result of the instructions from H.E. Ali Abdullah Saleh, President of the Republic, and H.E. Dr. Ali Mohammed Mujawar, Prime Minister.
- *Number and titles of posts*: 19 posts were advertised as follows:
- *Heads of sectors*: 3 positions:
  - Head of Technical Advisory Services
  - Head of Policies Research and Development
  - Head of Monitoring and Performance Appraisal
- *General Managers*: 16 positions:
  - General Manager of Technical Advisory Services - Central Authority
  - General Manager of Technical Advisory Services - Local Authority
  - General Manager of Communications and Coordination
  - General Manager of HR Training and Development
  - General Manager of Organizational Development Research
  - General Manager of HR Management Research
  - General Manager of Service Development
  - General Manager of Monitoring and Evaluation of Central Authority Units
  - General Manager of Monitoring and Evaluation of Local Authority Units
  - General Manager of Service Quality
  - General Manager of Grievance and Dispute Settlement
  - General Manager of IT Center
  - General Manager of HR Units Development
  - General Manager of Internal Audit
  - General Manager of Secretary & Documentation
  - General Manager of Relations and Regional and International Organizations

Invitation to submit applications

The Ministry of Civil Service and Insurance invites employees of the

Ministry and those who meet above conditions and willing to fill in any of the advertised posts to visit the website of the Ministry www.mocsai.org to review the organizational regulation of the Ministry and to know more details about set conditions for each advertised post as indicated in the job description cards. This is in addition to obtaining samples of required CVs and to fill in the application form. The following should be followed:

- Identify the job applying to fill (each applicant may compete for two jobs).
- Prepare the CV as per provided sample published on the website of the Ministry.
- Prepare copy of supporting documents for data included in the CV.
- Fill in the application form published on the website of the Ministry.
- Prepare a complete file containing all required documents and arrange these documents in a file as follows:
    - List of documents contained in the file of applicant
    - 2 new coloured photographs 4×6
    - Original application form
    - Original CV in hard and softcopy
    - Copy of the Personal ID card
    - Copy of scientific qualifica-tions (equalizations and translations)
    - Copy of experience certificates and appointment decisions
    - Copy of participation certificates in sessions, conferences and workshops
    - Other documents
- Put the application form in a sealed envelope containing required documents and send it by post to the address of the Ministry as shown in this advertisement or personal delivery to Mr. Mohammed Ablan, Committee Reporter, who shall be present in the Ministry Headquarters during official working hours starting from 08:00AM Wednesday 2 July 2008 until 12:00PM Saturday 12 July 2008.

Latest Application Deadline

The Ministry confirmed to all potential applicants that applications received after 12:00PM Saturday 12.07.2008.

Competition Stages

Selection process will be undertaken as follows:

- Preparation of minutes by the end of the last reception day in light of provisions of Civil Service Law, its executive regulation and the decision of the Cabinet regarding appointment in public jobs at 03:00PM Saturday 12.07.2008 indicating all received applications by post (and all applications sent by post but not yet delivered to the Ministry provided that the Ministry should have received by fax the application letter, CV and the postage receipt).
- Review of submitted applications to determine:
    - ◆ Names of applicants meeting conditions of filling in these jobs to move to second phase of competition
    - ◆ Names of applicants not meeting conditions and eliminated from competition
- Evaluate qualifications and experiences of applicants meeting required conditions against job description cards.
- Announce names of candidates for interview and define time and place of interview.
- Conduct the interview.
- Announce results and names of winning candidates to fill in these positions.
- Confirmation that those selected will have motivating benefits and privileges during their employment.

Receiving applications

The task was assigned to a special team to receive applications. Received applications were 304. Applications review against conditions of job. The review was conducted as follows:

- Formation of a main committee by a ministerial resolution as follows:

  - Vice-Minister of Civil Service - Chairman
  - Representative of Presidency Office - Member
  - Representative of Premiership - Member
  - Representative of Minister of Legal Affairs - Member
  - General Manager of Human Resource Reporter
- Formation of assistant technical team headed by reporter of the main committee, general manager of human resources at the Ministry.
- Review process was conducted and concluded the following:
  - Applicants for head of section post are 89; of which 43 are meeting conditions (48.3%) and 46 are not (51.7%)
  - Total applicants for general manager post are 215; of which 114 are meeting conditions (53%) and 101 are not (47%)
- Applicants were notified by the result of review against general conditions.

Evaluation of qualifications, experience and skills of applicants meeting conditions: to ensure neutrality, this task was assigned to the Arab Administrative Development Organization, Arab League.

Conducting interviews: This task is assigned to the Arab Administrative Development Organization, Arab League.

Announcement of successful candidates.

Issue appointment decisions.

FIFTH
ACHIEVED AND EXPECTED BENEFITS

Medium and long term benefits of the competition may be summarized as follows:

- Materialize principles of equality, efficiency, merit and equal opportunities among citizens as contained in the constitution and laws.
- Being more specific in job conditions.
- Link appointment to existence of approved jobs in organizational structure.

- Raise capacity of top management employees.
- Boost loyalty of employees to their organization.
- Enhance hope with employees that appointment in top management posts is competitive.
- Acceptance of government to review appointment system in public jobs.
- Encourage use of ITC in government organizations by providing ITC literacy conditions for top management posts.

JOB DESCRIPTION CARDS FOR POSTS TO BE FILLED

During preparations for the pilot experiment, job description cards were developed for all advertised positions, namely:

- 3 jobs for heads of sectors
- 16 jobs for General Managers in the three sectors as indicated in the advertisement

Due to space constrains, only two sample job description cards will be quoted in following pages:

- Job description card for head of sector position
- Job description card for general manager in one sector

The aim of developing these job description cards was to complete an important element of advertisement components and to serve as a guide for applicants.

Therefore, job description cards were integral parts of the advertisement. Potential applicants were requested to review and read all contents of job description card for the applied job and make sure they have required capacities and skills for related positions.

SAMPLE JOB DESCRIPTION CARD FOR HEAD OF SECTOR POSITION

The following are sample job description cards:

Position:	Head of Policies Research Development
Group:	Top Management
Level:	Level One/Grade One
Location:	Headquarters of the Ministry of Civil Service and Insurance - Capital Sana'a

Role

Prepare and establish civil service policies and procedures to ensure meeting vision and objectives of the Ministry of Civil Service.

Assigned Strategic Objectives

Ensure achieving level of efficiency and performance in public service units as to achieve national objectives.

Minimum qualifications, experiences and skills required:

Education: University degree in business administration, economy or any related field. It is preferred to have higher degree or researches in administrative reforms and development.

Experience: Should have experience post university degree as follows:

- 19 years post first university degree out of which 11 years at least in public administration field
- 15 years post Master degree out of which 9 years at least in public administration
- 11 years post Ph.D. degree out of which 7 years at least in public administration.

Skills:

Management skills:

- Strategic planning (e.g., five-year plans)
- Operational planning (annual department work plans)

IT skills:

- Word processor (MS Office)
- MS Excel
- Email and internet

Communication and HR skills:

- Dispute resolution/negotiation/ communication

- Team building
- Staff appraisal (job performance)

Legislations and Administration:

Familiar with legislations regulating public jobs and related legislations.

Knowledge and technical skills:

- Wide knowledge of international developments
- Understanding of international or regional experiences in public administration reform

Acceptance criteria

- No criminal precedents
- No negative inspection reports
- No less than "good" score in annual appraisal for two last years
- Record of achievements
- Demonstrate ability to learn
- Understand public administra-tion ethics and principles
- Respected by peers and colleagues

Role:

Manage and provide technical advisory services to ensure successful implementation of new policies and procedures in all central authority units.

Objectives:

- Establish structure and mechanism for management of relations with all public service units.
- Facilitate the process of expanding authorities transferred from the Ministry to public service units.
- Provide advisory services to facilitate applying rules and procedures of civil service, HR system and social insurance in all public service units in central authority.

Minimum qualifications, experiences and skills required:

Education: University degree in public administration or any related field. Should have successfully completed a four-week basic course in civil service.

Skills:

Management skills

- Strategic planning (e.g., five-year plans)
- Operational planning (annual department work plans)

IT skills

- Word processor (MS Office)
- MS Excel
- Email and internet

Legislations and administration

Familiar with legislations regulating public jobs and related legislations.

Communication and HR skills

- Dispute resolution/negotiation/ communication
- Team building
- Staff appraisal (job performance)

Experience

Should have experience post university degree as follows:

- 13 years post first university degree out of which 8 years at least in public administration field
- 9 years post Master degree out of which 5 years at least in public administration
- 5 years post Ph.D. degree out of which 3 years at least in public administration.

Acceptance criteria

- No criminal precedents
- No negative inspection reports
- No less than "good" score in annual appraisal for two last years
- Record of achievements
- Demonstrate ability to learn
- Understand public administration ethics and principles
- Respected by peers and colleagues

15

Addressing Tomorrow's Need of Human Capital Competency Based Continuing Education for the Knowledge Society

Bambang Supriyanto and *Anton S. Wahjosoedibjo*

INTRODUCTION

One hour of yesterday is not slower than one hour of today and tomorrow; it's exactly the same sixty minutes. But the values, products, and services that we could create or destroy or things that could happen and change in one hour today, let alone tomorrow, by far excel what we could expect to happen in one hour of yesterday. This is just to illustrate that things are rapidly moving and changing in today's world, even more and more in tomorrow's world. Thanks to the advancement of man-made technology, information has been spreading much faster and the world loses its boundary. As a consequence, people are becoming more interdependent, cross-cultural matters are turning into way of live, information can be instantly made available, and the role of people to lead and manage changes to serve their needs has been increasingly challenged. In other words, the need of quality human capital grows into the utmost importance.

Accordingly, one of the key success factors of tomorrow's organization to excel and achieve its vision and accomplish its mission is to have competent, knowledge based human resource (HR) professionals with solid and high performing team spirit that involved throughout the planning and deployment processes of organization policies and strategies. Future organizations need leaders and managers at any level to deal with the human resources aspect or the human capital as an integrated part of their duty and responsibility.

The role of the HR organization has rapidly evolved from merely doing administrative and technical jobs to providing professional supports and services throughout the organiz-ation lines to enable the organization to employ, develop and maintain competent, high quality people to carry out their assigned roles; maintain conducive working environment; and create harmon-ious industrial relations. These impose challenges but at the same time offer opportunities to HR professionals in the organization to enhance their professionalism and competency level, and to be recognized at equal stand as their professional counterparts in legal, finance and accounting, engineering, and others.

Driven by above conceptual perspectives, a group of HR practitioners and professionals in Indonesia with full support from University of Atmajaya Continuing Education in Jakarta have developed competency based Certified Human Resources Professional (CHRP) programme. The objective of CHRP programme is to equip HR professionals with knowledge, skill and attitude and enhance their professionalism and confidence in meeting future challenges and creating growth opportunities. The CHRP programme is an integrated competency and knowledge based training and development initiative in which programme facilitators, instead of instructors, facilitate and mentor participants in the process of education (knowledge enhancement) and development of skills and attitude through a combination of applied theory and practical study cases in various HR functions.

This paper outlines detailed background of the Atmajaya University CHRP Programme and presents the programme syllabus, how it has been developed, deployed, and reviewed for continuous improvement. It also provides results of assessment and measurement of previous programme performances.

THE CHRP PROGRAMME

As part of the Continuing Education Programme and in its efforts to take a proactive role in enhancing the quality of human resources management in Indonesia, the Catholic University of Atmajaya in Jakarta, Indonesia, had organized a group of academic and practicing HR professionals and company executives to develop a competency based certified human resources professional programme.

The scope of human resources activities is very broad. In order to be able to carry out the entire spectrum of human resources activities well and professionally, it is necessary that human resources practitioners learn the entire human resources functions the right way and in accordance with best practices in industries. With average economic growth rate of six to seven per cent per annum since 2000, Indonesia's need of human resources professionals is eminent. Therefore, an intensive human resources development programme is required, either to equip fresh graduates with practical knowledge and behavioural attitude required to carry out the job or to provide HR practitioners with academic and applied theories to broaden their knowledge base and enhance their performance.

The Certified Human Resources Professional (CHRP) programme is a comprehensive, intensive, and competency based programme which covers three basic functions in the spectrum of human resources management that are delivered as an integrated programme. The three basic HR functions are: Human Resources Development, Human Resources Management (Compens-ation and Benefits, Industrial Relations), and Human Resources Supplements.

The programme has been designed to provide basic and broad based knowledge, practical skills, and attitude necessary to effectively manage human resources and human capital in an organization or company, covering aforementioned HR functions in an integrated manner. By having competent HR professionals, with integrated and broad-based knowledge, skill and attitude in HR functions, the organization or company will benefit with improved quality of performance, easier job rotation in human resources functions, and better, well-planned and targeted human resources development.

Participants of the CHRP progra-mme are required to have at least a bachelor degree (4-year college education) in any discipline, preferably with at least one year working experience. They can also be HR practitioners or those projected to occupy position in human resources function in the organization.

The CHRP programme facilitators are structured as a team consisting of experienced - active or retired - practitioners, senior consultants, and executive in human resources with at least 15 years of experience in large or multinational companies; former senior government officials of the Ministry of Manpower; and senior lecturers of the University of Atmajaya in relevant field of HR discipline. To reflect the competency base of the programme the composition of the facilitators are maintained at a ratio of approximately 70 per cent well seasoned HR practitioners and 30 per cent university lecturers.

The Atmajaya University CHRP programme has been developed with the following unique characteristics:

- The CHRP programme is an integrated, competency based human resources training and development programme which provides effective lesson to learn through combined instruction, facilitation and monitoring in applied and practical key functions in managing company human resources.
- The key functions in human resources management are categorized in three groups: Human Resources Develop-ment, Human Resources Management (Compensation and Benefit, Industrial Relati-ons), and Human Resources Supplement. Each group or subgroup consists of several modules of specific topics. There are 31 modules - Human Resources Development: 14 modules, Compensation & Benefit: 7 modules, Industrial Relations: 7 modules, and HR Supplements: 3 modules. Each module is given in one session of two effective hours.
- To obtain the certificate, participants should pass competency assessment, conducted through written examination and presenting thesis paper under the guidance of programme facilitator commensurate with their specific expertise.

The CHRP Programme consists of 31 topical modules which are grouped in four categories. The modules reflect the syllabus of the entire CHRP programme as shown below:

Module	*Topic*	*Session*
Human Resources Development		
1	Strategic Human Resources Planning	1
2	Managing Organization Development	5
3	Effective Recruitment and Interview Technique	2
4	Case Study: Organization Development	13
5	Managing Career Development	11
6	Managing Training and Effective Learning	8
7	Organization	7
8	Competency Based Human Resources	17
9	Case Study: People Development	16
10	Leadership Development Programme	3
11	Strategic Performance Management	12
12	Talent Management	15
13	Knowledge Management	14
14	Human Resource Audit	19
	Case Study: Succession Planning	

Compensation and Benefits		
1	Total Compensation Concept	20
2	Job Evaluation	21
3	Salary Structure Design	27
4	Salary Survey	26
5	Rewarding Employee Performance	29
6	Case Study: Job Evaluation	23
7	Case Study: Compensation. Wrap-up	30

Industrial Relations		
1	Legal Aspect in Industrial Relations, Employment Agreement, Techniques for Preparing Employment	6
2	Agreement	9
3	Collective Labour Agreement and Company Policies	10
4	Industrial Relations and the Synergy between the Union and the Employer	18
5	Industrial Relations - Dispute Resolution	22
6	Employment Termination and Suspension	28
7	Industrial Relations Court	25
	Case Study: Industrial Relations	

Supplementary HR Knowledge and Skills		
1	Employee Pension Plan	24
2	Company Merger and Acquisition	4
3	Corporate Culture	31

Each module takes one session of facilitated interactive discussion or problem solving of a case study, preceded by a brief classroom instruction. Each session lasts for 2 (two) hours. The CHRP programme applies global concept with due consideration to local culture and values. Therefore, most discussion and classroom materials are written in English but conducted in Indonesian. This way the programme attracts participation from national as well as multi-national companies.

To ensure that participants attain the maximum benefit of the learning process during each session, both facilitators and participants should observe certain ground rules for the session.

Facilitators', not teachers', primary role is to help participants, not students, learn and to assist participants through coaching and educating on specific topic towards productive sessions. Facilitators' responsibility include, among others: (a) Keep discussion focus on the topic of the session; (b) Help guide and encourage participants to take active part in interactive discussion and problem solving process; (c) Observes participants' learning behaviours and progress and realign the learning process as deemed necessary.

Participants are expected to be proactive and actively participate in the discussion to get the maximum benefit of this programme and to tap the knowledge, experience and wisdom of facilitators who are experts in their respective field. Participants are primarily responsible for learning, be prepared for the upcoming session and take active participation in every session. Of course, participants have to comply with administrative terms and conditions.

To pass the CHRP programme and obtain certificate of achievement, participants should meet the following academic requirements:

- Eighty per cent (80%) attendance of all 31 sessions.
- Obtain a minimum score of 60 (out of 100 maximum score) for each examined module.
- Acceptance of thesis paper by the faculty on Human Resources Development, Compensation, Industrial Relations or other supplementary modules given in the programme. The paper can be written in English or Indonesian language.

Participants who do not score passing grade for certain module may retake the examination one time or participate in the final examination of the next batch.

Exhibit-2 shows examples of selected topics of papers prepared by participants.

As an example, topics of examination for CHRP Programme Batch #4 are as follows:

- Organization Development (Strategic Human Resources Planning, Managing Organizational Development, Recruitment)
- People Development (Competency Based HR, Career Development, Managing Training, Knowledge Management)
- Leadership (Leadership Development, Performance Management, Talent Management)
- Total Compensation Concept
- Salary Structure Design and Rewarding Employee Performance

- Job Evaluation and Salary Survey
- Employment and Collective Labour Agreement
- Labour Management Cooperation and Industrial Relation Dispute
- Termination and Industrial Relation Court

The entire one batch of the CHRP programme takes six effective weeks for 31 sessions, including examinations. Typical schedule of CHRP Programme is as follows:

Exhibit-1 shows detailed schedule of CHRP Programme, Batch #7 which will commence on 15 October 2008. Sixty participants have registered; there will be 2 parallel sessions to limit participants below 30 per class to ensure that effectiveness of each session.

Date	*Activities*
5 July 7 July - 30 August: Every Monday Thursday from 18:30 to 20:30; Saturday from 08:30 to 15:45	Programme Opening Classroom Instruction (31 sessions), including examination
4 August	Deadline for submitting topic of the term - paper and name of tutor
25 August	Finalization/submission of paper
12 September	Programme Closing/
	Graduation

In summary, the University of Atmajaya Certified Human Resources Professional programme is a "learning while doing" process. Because of the time constraint, the learning process for each topic of CHRP programme is lacking in-depth, but the CHRP programme gives a strong basic concept and philosophy of each HR function so that participants can readily apply what they have learned and experienced from the CHRP programme in their respective job and career. Since various basic concepts of HR functions are addressed in a well coordinated and integrated manner, in one package, participants can be expected to comprehend the whole picture of HR functions in an organization much easier and more long-lasting.

To get more in-depth knowledge of specific topics given in the CHRP programme, participants are encouraged to attend workshops or seminars on specific areas of interest, which are offered by many professional associations or commercial training organizers.

CHRP PROGRAMME EVALUATION

To-date, there have been 6 (six) batches of the Atmajaya University Continuing Education (AUCE) CHRP Programmes delivered with more than 250 participants from various industries such as banking, manufacturing, oil and gas and other energy industries, insurance, airlines, government institution, leasing, hotel, retail, hospital, and management consultants. The seventh batch of AUCE CHRP will commence on 15 October 2008 and there have been 60 participants registered and enrolled. The committee plan to conduct two parallel sessions, each session will be limited to not more than 30 participants to ensure effectiveness of each session.

The AUCE CHRP Programme committee has committed to make the programme excel in quality and in delivering value to participants and the industry that supports them. This commitment has been taken seriously by employing continuous quality improvement practice. Upon completion of each batch of the CHRP Programme, the programme committee conducts opinion survey from participants, facilitators, as well as programme stakeholders or industries that support CHRP participants. Results of the survey are evaluated, appropriate plans of improvement actions to the programme formulated, and feedback given to the programme stakeholders.

Questionnaires to participants on the overall CHRP Programme include 10 questions which could be summarized into the following key programme evaluation criteria:

(a) Materials of the Programme Module; (b) Qualification of Facilitators; (c) Benefits of the Programme; and (d) Achievement of the Programme Objective. More than 90 per cent of responders (average of survey after 6 batches of CHRP Programme) state that the CHRP Programme is very good to excellent in term of the benefit of the programme, quality of facilitators, relevancies of the programme to their job and profession, and meeting the programme objective. Regarding the Programme Module, 75 per cent of responders show the module is very good to excellent. The only drawback is lack of depth due to time constraint and insufficient time to cover one module in 2-hour session.

Questionnaires to evaluate each facilitator of the CHRP Programme by participants include the following opinions: (a) Mastery of the materials; (b) Systematic of materials presented; (c) Ability to deliver the materials with clarity; (d) Time management; (e) Ability to respond to questions; (f) Ability to use learning media; and (g) Overall assessment rating. Also, more than 90 per cent responders state that almost all facilitators are very good to excellent, particularly those practitioners and lecturers who have had practical exposures in HR functions in the industry or government.

Some encouraging comments from the survey and events are:

- Hope there will be advance level of the AUCE CHRP Programme in the future
- The company of one of the participants stated that they planned to set a requisite for their HR staffs to participate in the CHRP programme
- The 1st batch of AUCE CHRP programme was attended by 26 participants and participants of the 6th batch had been doubled. This shows increasing interest in the CHRP Programme
- CHRP alumni are enthusiastic to attend thesis presentations at the following CHRP closing session to learn to new ideas that have been generated in the CHRP programme

CONCLUSION

The CHRP Programme of Atmajaya University Continuing Education is a unique "learning by doing process" or competency based human capital enhancement programme, specifically tailored for development of HR professionals.

The CHRP programme is a comprehensive, intensive, and competency based programme which covers three basic functions in the spectrum of human resources management that are delivered as an integrated programme. The three basic HR functions are:

- The certification is granted based on competency assessment that include attendance record in classroom instruction, interactive discussion and case study sessions upon which their behavioural attitude can be evaluated;
- Successfully passing written examinations; and

- Thesis presentation on HR functions modules.

The Atmajaya University CHRP Programme has been a success story, proven by industry acceptance and growing participation. It is a dynamic "learning by doing process" that combined academic excellence and practitioners' competence and wisdom. The programme quality and stakeholders satisfaction are kept up through opinion survey which results are used to develop better future programmes through continuous quality improvement process.

The Atmajaya University CHRP Programme can be further developed into a regional or international joint cooperation CHRP programmes among universities, private institutions and public sector, within the context of continuing education. It is believed that through this CHRP Programme and other similar and better CHRP programmes, the professionalism and competency of HR practitioners in the organization can be enhanced to the level that they will be recognized at equal stand as their professional counterparts in legal, finance and accounting, engineering, and other professionals.

At this opportunity, the authors wish to thank Atmajaya University Continuing Education for the unrelenting supports to the CHRP Programme and for permitting the authors to share the information of this unique programme to the honorable participants of the 35th International ARTDO Conference 2008 in Cairo, Egypt.

REFERENCES

Programme Director, Atmajaya University CHRP Continuing Education Programme, Lecturer at AU Faculty of Law.

Programme Advisor AU-CHRP, President Director - PEN Consulting, Chairman - PEN Alliance, Energy Group of Companies.

Human Resources Development, Human Resources Management (Compensation and Benefits, Industrial Relations), and Human Resources Supplements.

16

Upgrading Small and Medium-Sized Enterprises (SMEs) in the GCC Region

Rudy Yaksick

INTRODUCTION

The Arabian Gulf (Gulf Cooperation Council–GCC countries) region inherited the world's largest known reserves of petroleum and natural gas. Over the past 50 years, the efficient management of these reserves has brought a dramatic increase in the standard of living to the citizens of this region. However, the fact that petroleum and natural gas are finite resources, coupled with the constant development of competing energy technologies, presents the region with a challenging problem: how should the GCC region diversify their economies in an intelligent, strategic manner in order to become and remain globally competitive?

What do we mean by the term globally competitive? Over the past two or three decades a new interpretation of competitiveness has emerged in response to the globalization of production. Now, most firms tend to break the production process into stages, locating each stage in its most profitable location. The resulting ensemble of stages is called a value chain, with logistics and internet-based communication linking the stages–some of which are co-located in industrial clusters; others are spatially dispersed throughout the globe. Within the value chain, structured exchange relationships– rather than the arms-length transactions consummated via markets–tend to dominate buyer-supplier relationships at both the level of international trade and domestic economies. This new interpretation highlights the role of a dominant lead firm that coordinates and determines the global production and trade patterns by setting and enforcing the rules of the game: product and process standards, delivery terms, determination of inclusion/ exclusion of subordinate trading partners in the supply chain, etc.

Yet, paradoxically, each stage derives its profitability by exploiting positive economic "spillovers" (cost reductions and knowledge diffusion leading to more rapid innovation) generated by the specific spatial proximity/agglomeration with other firms, even those from other industries. For example, innovation tends to be geographically concentrated in industrial clusters since tacit knowledge ("know how" that is learned via close personal contact and trust, as opposed to written instruction) is more effectively exchanged through local social/ professional networks and trade associations. The examples

that immediately leap to mind are computer industry clusters in Silicon Valley and Bangalore as well as the oil and gas cluster in Houston, Texas. Historically, the pattern and benefits of Small and Medium-sized Enterprises (SME) spatial clustering were first observed in the 1980s in the Emilia-Romagna district in northeastern Italy.

From this modern perspective, Harvard Business School Professor Michael Porter (1998) argues that national competitiveness is created by increasing the productivity of the national (regional) economy via innovation and learning in **industrial clusters** that possess external linkages to the world economy via global **value chains**. In contrast, the classical view of international trade and competition (initially formulated by David Ricardo in 1817 with a competing theory developed by Bertil Ohlin (1933) and Eli Heckscher) argued that global competiveness and trade patterns were generated solely by a nation's **comparative advantage** stemming from labour productivity (Ricardo) and endowments of natural resources (Heckscher-Olin). In short, a nation's comparative advantage stems from its labour productivity and inherited supply of natural resources, e.g., oil and natural gas in the case of GCC countries. Recent trade flow data refute this classical theory; it has been replaced by the "New Economic Geography," based on Paul Krugman's (1991) seminal analysis of the interaction between trade and geography. Based on his path-breaking synthesis, Prof. Krugman was awarded the Nobel Prize in Economics in 2008.[1]

The purpose of this article is to present an alternative, empirically-based regional development strategy, drawing on the insights of Professor Krugman and Professor Porter. This new strategy stresses the interaction of the organizational structure of production (clusters and global value chains) and their respective governance structures (control and coordination mechanisms) in determining the ability of SMEs to upgrade and, thereby, obtain a **competitive advantage.**

Why the focus on Small and Medium-sized Enterprises (SMEs)? SMEs play a critical role in the development of a national economy. That is, SMEs tend to be responsible for most job creation as well as make significant contributions to innovation and productivity. Can SMEs continue to play this critical role in the context of the new global competitiveness framework? Motivated by this question, this article addresses the broad issue: how can industrial clusters and global value chains be used to upgrade GCC SMEs? That is, to increase the productive efficiency and value adding activities of GCC SMEs in order to gain a sustainable competitive advantage in a global economy. The remainder of this article is organized as follows. In Section I we discuss the basic concept of competitive advantage and formulate the SME manager's competitive advantage strategy problem. Section II describes the menu of upgrading activities available to SMEs. Section III analyzes the opportunities and constraints imposed on upgrading activities by clusters and their interaction with global value chains. This section addresses the question: does the insertion of a local industrial cluster into a global value chain enhance or impede local SME upgrading strategies? We pay particular attention to the interaction between these two modes of coordination and control of SME production and the interaction's impact on SME competitiveness potential. Section IV summarizes various obstacles to upgrading–Financing, Legal and Business Practices–that appear in both GCC and Asian countries. After developing an understanding of these obstacles, we conclude (Section V) by recommending several policy interventions to facilitate the upgrading of SMEs located in the GCC region.

SME MANAGER'S COMPETITIVE ADVANTAGE STRATEGY PROBLEM

According to Michael Porter (1998), continued growth in productivity is the fundamental source of national and regional competitiveness in a globalized economy; not cheap labour or access to natural resources.

By specializing in exporting primary goods and raw materials as suggested by the classic comparative advantage theory–countries can become trapped in low-wage industries. Instead, Porter's theory stresses that sustainable and superior economic performance is determined by a country/region/ firm's competitive advantages.

What is a Competitive Advantage?

What is a competitive advantage for an SME? The term competitive advantage describes the SME's ability to outperform its competitors in the same industry or market. Simply put, competitive advantage is the ability to stay ahead of current or future potential competitors. How does a SME obtain a competitive advantage? Broadly speaking, the SME must formulate and implement a corporate strategy/business plan that upgrades its production resources and exploits opportunities (such as use of robotics and/or membership in industrial clusters and global value chains) in order to create competitive advantages, e.g. production costs lower than the industry/market average. And, rivals must not be able to match these advantages.

In Porter's theory a very important source of competitive advantages is membership in industrial clusters. Specifically, Porter argues that cluster membership for existing SMEs provides two competitive advantages: (1) increased productivity arising from both the internal and external economies of scale that accrue to SMEs located inthe cluster and (2) future growth in productivity that is induced by the cluster's ability to promote and accelerate the pace of innovation.

Clusters also provide several competitive advantages for entrepreneurs considering the launch of a start-up SME venture. For example, barriers to entry tend to be relatively lower, given the supportive business environment and large, talented labour pools attached to clusters. Similarly, financial capital may be easily accessible on cheaper terms since local "angel" investors and financial institutions are familiar with the competitive advantages offered by the cluster. In short, the perceived risk of entry and exit for SME start-ups tends to be lower. Finally, there is a positive feedback loop at work as well. The entry of innovative, new firms strengthens the cluster's collective pool of resources relative to those possessed by rivals at other locations.

The SME Manager's Competitive Advantage Strategy Problem

SME corporate strategy is the decision-making tool that SME

managers use to manipulate their unique resources and opportunities, such as industrial cluster membership, in order to create competitive advantages. Formulating such a strategy in a globalized economy is a non-trivial problem: the manager of a SME has to take into account both international trade flows and geographical (firm location) considerations. The interaction between these considerations is important for two reasons. First, the interaction determines the structure, composition, and location of clustered economic activities within a country or region. Secondly, the location of the clusters (within a country or region) determines those possible clusters in which the SME can seek membership, given the SME's location relative to the location of the cluster.

It is within this context, that we present a very simplified version of the SME manager's competitive advantage strategy problem. In particular, the manager's problem is:

> Maximize profits by choosing feasible upgrading activities that produce competitive advantages in the manager's target market (domestic or international)

By feasible upgrading activities, we mean those upgrading activities (such as upgrading the production process) that are compatible with the upgrading opportunities that are provided by various clusters and value chains which offer potential membership to the SME Manager. For example, captive value chains hinder functional upgrading. Later, in Section III we address the issue: Do cluster and chain governance ("rules of the game") reinforce or block each other's upgrading opportunities?

The key elements of the problem and solution process (recipe) are illustrated in Fig. 1. The manager's first choice is to decide the target market for the SME–either domestic or international. Secondly, the manager then chooses which cluster and/or value chain to enter. The candidate clusters and value chains are taken as "givens" (i.e. "parameters" in mathematical modelling jargon) by the manager. In other words, our formulation of the problem assumes that clusters and value chains already exist at a particular geographical location in the manager's target market. The SME manager is not being asked to form either clusters and/or value chains from "scratch".

Having selected a cluster and/or value chain, the manager is then left with a list of feasible upgrading activities. That is, the governance structure of the cluster/value chain eliminates various upgrading activities that are incompatible with the cluster/value chain "rules of the game". After this winnowing out process, the manager is left with a set of feasible upgrading activities to pursue in order to maximize profits.

The solution to the manager's problem is a set of profit-maximizing upgrading activities. These activities yield sustainable competitive advantages arising from both internal and external economies of scale that accrue to SMEs embedded in clusters and/or global value chains. The source of these scale economies is discussed in Section III. Finally, we call this set of profit-maximizing upgrading activities an optimal upgrading strategy.

MANAGER'S MENU OF UPGRADING ACTIVITIES

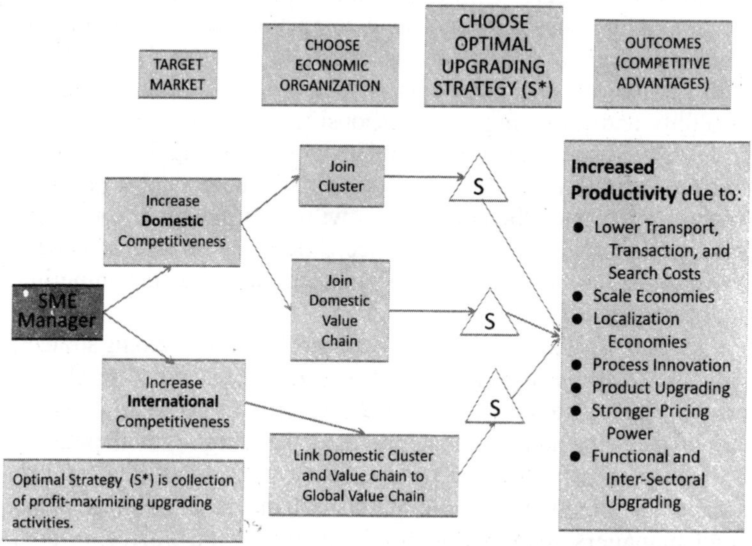

Fig. 1: SME Manager's Competitive Advantage Strategy Problem

Following the structure of the manager's competitive advantage problem, we begin by reviewing the different types of upgrading activities that can be undertaken by SMEs. By upgrading, we mean facilitating process and product innovation as well as a shift towards higher-value activities/functions and consumer markets in order to increase productivity and value-added in SMEs. There are four types of upgrading activities:

Production Process Upgrading: Reorganize production systems or adopt superior production technology in order to more efficiently transform production inputs into products.

Product Upgrading: Produce more sophisticated, valuable products. For example, upgrading from selling apparel to discount chains to supplying high-end department stores.

Functional (Vertical) Upgrading: Acquire new, more complex functions (such as design or marketing) in the cluster or value chain and/or jettison existing lower value-added functions. Upgrading from producing shoes to designing shoes to marketing your own brand.

Inter-sectoral (Horizontal) Upgrading: Transfer competencies acquired in a particular segment of a cluster or value chain to a new, more valuable segment. For example, applying the skills used to make TVs to make computer monitors and then laptops, as Taiwan has done.

Upgrading, thus, gives SMEs a competitive advantage either in terms of lower total costs or the ability to produce differentiated products/services, e.g. higher performing products, having increased reliability and providing more responsive after-sale service. Lower costs translate into higher profits relative to competing firms. Product and service differentiation enables SMEs to command a premium (higher) price since the consumer is willing to pay more for unique and superior products/ services. Hence, differentiation results in higher profitability, as long as costs remain comparable to competing, undifferentiated firms.

In short, SMEs embedded in industrial clusters containing strategic industries–linked to regional and global value chains-will have a higher probability of survival and sustained growth, with increase in employment and household income. And, these high-growth potential SMEs are exactly the type of investment opportunity that quickly attracts the attention of astute merchant bankers and private equity fund managers responsible for identifying and nurturing such opportunities.

UPGRADING OPPORTUNITIES AND CONSTRAINTS: CLUSTERSAND VALUE CHAINS

The purpose of this section is to identify feasible upgrading activities for the SME manager. We begin by first explaining how clusters and value chains provide competitive advantages for SMEs. Then, we address the question: does the insertion of a local industrial cluster into a global value chain enhance or impede local SME upgrading activities?

On the one hand, a fertile environment for SME upgrading can be created by the interaction of local industrial clusters and global value chains. Local clusters generate efficiencies that are internal to the cluster. Global value chains (VCs) can also provide opportunities for upgrading as local SMEs are exposed to the higher production and quality standards required by international buyers (chain lead firms) and their end-use customers. On the other hand, these external determinants of competitive advantages are not always available to local SMEs, as we shall discuss below. Hence, the interaction of these two modes of coordination and control of SME production are a key determinant of the opportunities and constraints imposed on SME upgrading activities and resultant competitiveness.

Armed with this information (a menu of feasible upgrading activities), the manager can then decide: what feasible upgrading activities should I undertake in order to generate one or more competitive advantages, thereby maximizing current and future profits? This set of feasible, profit-maximizing upgrading activities constitutes the manager's optimal upgrading strategy.

Industrial Clusters: SME Competitive Advantage via Agglomeration Economies

Intuitively, an industrial cluster is a set of linked economic relationships among one or more large industrial companies (key firms) and several nimble SMEs, along with associated supportive business services (e.g. legal/consulting), within one geographic area. Specifically, the SMEs provide intermediate production inputs/services and components to be used by the core of the cluster: the industrial company(ies) exporting from the cluster. In addition, the small scale of the SMEs enables them to anticipate and quickly respond to–even anticipate-the changing requirements of the core industry.[2]

Cluster Competitive Advantages

Firms that are co-located in a cluster enjoy a competitive advantage since their production processes become more efficient, exhibiting increasing returns to scale (i.e. IRS is present when the average production costs decrease as the scale of production increases). Some of these economies of scale are internal to each firm, e.g. larger plant size enables a steel mill owner to negotiate volume discounts from its suppliers.

Other scale economies are external to each firm but internal to the industry/cluster. The geographic concentration of firms (clusters) creates IRS via three forces collectively called localization economies:

Sharing of Inputs: The sharing of a larger, more dependable pool of specialized labour permits firms to provide specialized intermediate goods and services tailored to the needs of their buyers.[3]

Matching: Expansion of the range of industry-specific skills enables a closer match between the distinctive needs of cluster producers and pool of workers. In turn, workers are attracted to the cluster by increased real wages and a reduced probability of unemployment, given the presence of many potential employers. Likewise, expansion of the variety of intermediate inputs enables a closer match between the needs of final-goods producers and intermediate producers.

Learning: Spatial proximity amongst firms provides immediate access to competitors in the same industry. This access, in turn, accelerates the spillover of knowledge about current market conditions regarding customers and suppliers. Also, the spatial proximity permits the transfer of tacit (face-to-face) knowledge.

These scale benefits (equivalently competitive advantages) arise since the cluster's economic interdependence generates lower production costs (broadly defined to include transaction and information search costs). Also, increased SME efficiency (increasing returns to scale) is created by the combination of SME joint action (i.e. horizontal and vertical linkages amongst suppliers, subcontractors, traders and buyers within the cluster) and the SMEs ability to exploit external economies (cost reductions) generated within the cluster (e.g. easy access to specialized, skilled labour and specialized knowledge about technologies and markets). In short, an industrial cluster creates a virtuous circle for its members, with increased interdependence and interaction leading to lower (not higher) costs as each member firm increases its output.

Paradoxically, local circumstances become even more important determinants of a nation's economic prosperity in this era of increased global competition. In sum, the cluster generates a competitive advantage for its members via a variety of agglomeration economies, e.g. more rapid information flows and networking which lower transaction costs, spawned by an efficient spatial and industrial organization of the cluster. Note, however, that the SME's local "business environment" (e.g. legal and regulatory framework) must provide a supportive platform for cluster formation and growth in order for the SMEs to be able to reap the benefits of cluster membership.[4]

Empirical Studies of Scale Economies

Do all industries exhibit the agglomeration economies described above? In other words, if you were a cluster designer, which industries would be your target candidates for membership in your cluster? Several empirical studies documenting the presence (or absence) of scale economies in various countries have bearing on this question, as summarized in the recent World Bank publication: *World Development Report - 2009.* These studies support the following general conclusions. Internal increasing returns to scale are found in manufacturing and services. The internal scale economies range from negligible or low among light industries (e.g. footwear, apparel, leather products, textiles) to high among heavy (petroleum, transport equipment, cement products, electric power generation) and high-technology (pharmaceuticals, engineering, instruments, commercial banking) industries.

Global Value Chains: Constraints on Upgrading Choices

Complementing the local (internal) sources of competitive advantages present within industrial clusters, are the global (external) sources of competitive advantages stemming from SMEs (and related cluster) participation in global value chains. What is a Value Chain (VC)?A value chain (sometimes called a supply or commodity chain) is a series of coordinated economic activities (product design–production marketing–distribution–quality standards–consumer support) needed to: turn raw materials into finished products/services, sell the products/ services, and recycle them. Value chains can be contained within a single geographical location (i.e. embedded within a cluster) or spread over wider areas. When SMEs from several countries participate in a value chain, the chain is called a Global Value Chain (GVC).[5]

Membership in a value chain can foster (or inhibit) a SME's ability to learn from global leaders (either buyers or producers) of the chain.

The potential for SME learning is determined by the coordination and distribution of economic power (i.e. governance) within the chain. Intuitively, governance refers to the setting and enforcing of the rules of the game: who produces what, how, where, when, and according to what quality specifications?[6] Other potential sources of upgrading via value chains include: (i) Final product (downstream) buyers promotion of the capabilities of developing country (upstream) producers, and (ii) Entrance into value chains with more demanding customers forces the SME to improve quality and service standards and, more generally, to "raise the level of its game". In general, the sources of competitive advantage stem from inter-firm cooperation within the value chain, instead of advantages stemming from spatial proximity (as is stressed in the cluster literature).[7]

The important point is that the upgrading opportunities and constraints faced by SME managers vary across the types of value chains.[8]

Captive (Quasi-Hierarchy) Value Chains

For example, captive (quasi-hierarchy) value chains, such as the export crafts chain, provide SMEs with the greatest opportunity to experience process and product upgrading. However, captive value chains tend to hinder functional upgrading. The reason is that the dominant buyer exerts a high degree of monitoring and control over product specification, trading rules and innovation by the SME suppliers.[9]

Market-based Chains

This type of value chain appears to offer the most possibilities for upgrading, particularly functional upgrading. However, for the upgrading to occur, case studies of horticultural clusters in

Northeastern Brazil have demonstrated that local action–in the form of business support services provided by public agencies–may be required (Humphrey and Schmitz, 2000). These services are needed to provide information about international market requirements, since wholesale markets and international commodity auctions (e.g. flower auction market in Aalsmeer, Holland) do not consciously disburse information about quality standards.

Relational (Balanced) Chains

Relational chains are characterized by fairly equal decision making among many buyers and suppliers as well as balanced cooperation. Relational chains are, thus, said to have a balanced network governance structure. Thus, balanced chains (such as the global organic coffee chain) tend to provide ideal conditions for all forms of upgrading.

In sum, we can make two general statements linking the two classification schemes. Buyer-driven chains tend to be coordinated via market or network (modular or relational) governance structures. In contrast, producer-driven chains tend to be coordinated via vertically integrated hierarchical and captive governance structures. Hence, the upgrading possibilities available to SMEs are determined by the form of governance used to control the value chain.[10]

GCC OBSTACLES TO UPGRADING: FINANCING, LEGAL AND BUSINESS PRACTICES

In this section we identify several obstacles hindering the upgrading efforts of SME managers in the GCC countries. These obstacles–which are also present in Asian countries impede the efficient working of the capital markets. Hence, these obstacles limit the effectiveness of SME financing and investment activity by commercial banks and private equity firms, respectively.

Obstacles to SME Financing

Perhaps, the most common obstacle to upgrading in the GCC and Asian countries is the failure of banking and capital markets to provide sufficient funding to SMEs. This obstacle is referred to as a SME Financing Gap. Intuitively, a Financing Gap is present when, "there are significant numbers of SMEs that could use funds productively if they were available but cannot obtain finance from the formal financial system." (OECD, 2006, p. 9). However, much debate in the development finance literature surrounds a precise definition of this concept. In this section we briefly summarize these demand and supply side obstacles to the efficient allocation of equity (risk) and debt capital by competitive capital markets and commercial banks.

Supply-side Obstacles

- Credit Rationing due to Informational Asymmetries: HiddenKnowledgeandEffort.[11]
- Potential Borrowers Inability to Provide Acceptable Collateral.
- High Transaction Costs to Execute Financing.
- Financiers' Aversion to High Risk of SME Investing.
- Limited (though rapidly expanding) Credit Information on SMEs.

Demand-side Obstacles

- Entrepreneur's Control Aversion: refusal to cede control of his/her business to outside investors.
- Few "bankable" projects: Business plans lack accurate, verifiable data and convincing strategy.

Legal Obstacles

- Limited legal rights of creditors.
- Resolution of conflicts surrounding debt and bankruptcy tends to be slow, cumbersome, and unreliable with weak enforcement by the courts of collateral and debt agreements.

Business Practices

- Owner's Reluctance to Cede Ownership/Control to non-Family Investors.
- Unrealistic Expectations Regarding Venture Valuation.
- Relational and Reputation-Based Business Cultural Practices.
- Scarcity of Managerial Talent to Execute Business Upgrading Strategies.

IMPROVING SME COMPETITIVENESS: UPGRADING POLICIES

In this section we briefly catalogue three sets of policies that aim to facilitate the upgrading of SMEs. The first set of policies aims to support industrial cluster formation. The second set is more specific, customized to fit different types of industrial clusters. Finally, the third set of policies focus on strengthening SMEs' competitiveness within value chains.

Forming Clusters

Several policy interventions can be used to promote cluster formation amongst SME firms, including:

- Create and enhance trust among firms.
- Promote the establishment of collective projects.
- Create and strengthen business associations.
- Strengthen the local supply of financial and non-financial services.
- Facilitate the external connections of the cluster.
- Promote innovation.

Strengthening Clusters: Policies by Cluster Type

Policies can also be formulated that are targeted to different types of clusters.

- Manufacturing Clusters
  - — Ensure consistency between SME upgrading policies and programmes and the national macroeconomic policy.
  - — Promote linkages among firms.
  - — Promote access to new, competitive value chains.
- Natural Resources Clusters
  - — Promote public-private collaboration in the execution of Research and Development projects as well as dissemination of results to SMEs.
  - — Improve skills and abilities of producers in the backward stages of the value chain, e.g. agriculture and breeding.
  - — Facilitate the entry of SMEs into markets and value chains.
  - — Promote the adoption of quality and sanitary standards and environmental regulations.
  - — Enforce quality inspections and adherence to regulations
  - — Promote access to foreign markets and overcome non-tariff barriers.

  - Improve the supply of and SME access to physical and social infrastructure.
- Complex Products Clusters
  - Promote the active role of network brokers within the cluster, especially with regard to facilitating the relationship between the large anchor firms and the local SME suppliers.
  - Design incentives that reward large firms which source their intermediate inputs and services from local SMEs as well as support their suppliers' upgrading strategies.
- Specialized Suppliers Clusters (e.g. Software clusters)
  - invest in highly skilled professionals.
  - intensify industry-academic research collaboration.

Value Chains

To increase the competition of SMEs within VCs, the following policies should be pursued:

- Induce the dominant firm of the chain to become a member of the industrial cluster, using financial incentives/subsidies such as the public-private cost sharing of SME product and process upgrading.
- Strengthen the skills and abilities of the suppliers occupying the backward production stages in the chain.
- Facilitate interaction within the Value Chain by the use of business associations and consultants as intermediaries between suppliers and the dominant firm.
- Assist SMEs in meeting international standards.
- Promote SME access to competitive value chains and new markets via, e.g., facilitate participation in international trade fairs.

CONCLUSION

This paper addresses the following issue: How should the inherited energy wealth of GCC countries be managed in order to create sustainable prosperity for the GCC countries? Motivated by this issue, we propose a new approach to managing inherited energy wealth.

That is, GCC economies should be diversified based on the idea of competitive (as opposed to comparative) advantage of SMEs. This new approach calls for a reorientation away from a trust fund mentality approach (i.e., risk-averse investing in order to protect inherited wealth) for managing inherited energy wealth towards a more entrepreneurial, private equity approach. In this new approach, industrial policy makers must adopt the perspective of private equity Fund Managers, designing and implementing policies that create and exploit growth opportunities for SMEs in order to create diversified, sustainable sources of wealth.

The aim of this private equity approach is to upgrade SMEs by facilitating their entry into and competitiveness within local industrial clusters and global value chains. This new approach is, thus, in synch with current patterns of global trade and production location that have emerged over the last few decades. Hence, the new approach promises to deliver sustainable prosperity to current and future generations of GCC citizens. However, a word of caution is necessary: clusters of SMEs will not always benefit from entry into global value chains (GVC). As we have argued above, the governance (control and coordination of production) of value chains is a key external determinant of SME cluster competitiveness. For example, a quasi-hierarchical governance structure tends to facilitate process and product upgrading but hinders functional upgrading. In short, the GVC governance structure can either hinder or encourage the local (cluster-based) upgrading of SMEs.

Moreover, the competitiveness of the lead firm in the cluster or the global value chain is a critical determinant in achieving the national development objectives of increased incomes, employment and sustainable economic growth. Competitive SMEs linked to an uncompetitive, declining global value chain or lead cluster firm should switch to a GVC or a cluster possessing (or able to build) a global competitive advantage.

The fundamental role of government in this new approach is to aid SMEs in making good upgrading choices when striving to attain a competitive advantage. That is, governments should provide incentives and a business environment that remove obstacles hindering the upgrading in clusters and global value chains as well as promote healthy competition-cooperation amongst SMEs. The conventional industrial development policy tools of locational subsidies and "strategic" industry protectionism (e.g. the recent protection of the yoghurt industry in France) are misguided. These out-dated policies enable SMEs to avoid the necessary investment in innovation, organizational learning, and prudent risk-management behaviour required to develop a sustainable competitive advantage.

Finally, our formulation of the SME manager's competitive advantage strategy problem is very generic. That is, the upgrading constraints can be easily be reformulated to capture the cluster and value chain industrial structure of Asian countries. Likewise, the financial, legal and business practices in Asian countries can also be reviewed to identify obstacles to SME upgrading.

FOOTNOTES

1. Brakman and Garretsen (2009) provide a concise summary of Prof. Krugman's three seminal papers on trade and geography that garnered him the 2008 Nobel Prize in Economics. Note that Krugman's 1991 paper, which is the intellectual foundation of the "new economic geography," was motivated by Prof. Michael Porter's path-breaking work on clusters.
   As Krugman explained, "Michael Porter had given me a manuscript copy of his book on Competitive Advantage of Nations, probably late 1989. I was much taken by the stuff of clusters, and I started trying to make a model...I got stumped for a while by the analytics, and tried numerical examples on a spreadsheet to figure them out. It all came together in a hotel in Honolulu."
2. Clusters can take several forms, as categorized by Markusen (1996): Marshallian (Italian industrial districts, Banglore), Hub-and-Spoke (Toyota-Aichi Prefecture), Satellite Platform (IT cluster in Kyushu Region), and State Anchored (biotech cluster in San Diego, California). Of course, these are ideal types. The reality is that clusters tend to have characteristics from more than one category.
3. The formation of a specialized work force is called "Marshallian labour pooling" in honour of the great 20th century British economist Alfred Marshall. He first observed this pooling phenomenon and related positive, external benefits in England's industrial districts.
4. At this point, the careful reader may be asking three related, fundamental questions regarding cluster formation and stability:
   - ? In the presence of increasing returns to scale that are INTERNAL to firms, why aren't all goods in each industry produced by a single, very large firm? In other works, why don't we see industries composed of one large firm per industry? ANSWER: Transportation Costs.
   - ? Why do industrial clusters form? ANSWER: Localization Economies.
   - ? What is the economic "glue" (centripetal forces) that binds together the cluster over time?

   More specifically, what keeps a cluster together (centripetal forces) in the presence of transport costs, scale economies internal to the firm, and localization economies? As clearly discussed by Fujita (2008), when economies of scale are large and unexhausted (i.e., cluster firms are not producing at the minimum efficient scale level of output) and firms compete on both price (although price competition is muted even though the firms are co-located) and product differentiation dimensions (i.e., monopolistic competition), then virtuous circles of causation arise of their own accord within the dynamics of the cluster. In sum, when the two opposing forces of clustering (centripetal) and dispersion (centrifugal forces such as transport costs and congestion) are in balance, we observe a spatial equilibrium in which industrial clusters are optimally located throughout the nation.

5. Bair (2009) contains an excellent survey of the global commodity and value chain literature. The classic reference is Gereffi and Korzeniewicz (1994). Pietrobelli and Rabellotti (2006) contains several case studies summarizing the Latin American experience in upgrading via clusters and value chains.
6. Gereffi (1999) defines governance as, "the functional integration and coordination of internationally dispersed activities." The term captures the basic idea that some kind of steering of economic activities is undertaken by a firm, either with regard to its internal activities and/or the activities of other firms with whom the original firm has an economic relationship.
7. A cluster can be thought of as a "local" value chain that does not impose the inflexibilities of vertical integration or the
5. management challenges of creating and maintaining formal linkages such as networks, alliances, or partnerships. (Porter, 1998b,p.80)
8. Researchers initially classified value chains as either buyer-driven or producer-driven. In buyer-driven chains (e.g. garments, shoes, toys), the dominant firm (such as NIKE) owns the strategic asset such as an international/regional brand reputation or privileged access to consumer markets via a large retail distribution system (Wal-Mart). Producer-driven chains are characterized by high-technology and capital-intensive production facilities that tend to produce components, e.g. the automotive and aircraft industries. For these chains the dominant firm is the producer/manufacturer (multinational firms such as General Motorsor IBM).

   This dichotomous classification has two limitations. First, the classification is unable to capture the diversity of organizational relations, e.g., networks as opposed to vertical linkages, connecting firms in the chain. Secondly, the classification scheme has less descriptive accuracy regarding the current trend of global production relationships. Producer chains have begun to behave more like buyer chains and *vice versa.*

   To overcome these weaknesses, we group Value Chains (VCs) into the following five-categories:

   Market-based VC : The simplest form of VC governance, characterized by uncomplicated arms-length transactions: goods exchanged for money at a market determined price. Since the ability to codify transactions is quite high, there is a very low level of explicit coordination. Hence, the cost of switching to new trading partners is quite low for buyers and sellers.

Modular-based VC : This is the first of three network-based VCs. The VC contains transactions that are more complicated than the market-based VC. One of the key distinguishing features of a modular VC is that it is very easy to codify (or "template") information required to execute the transaction. Hence, only a modest amount of cooperation and coordination are required in order to execute complex transactions.

Relational VC : In this network VC, complex transactions between buyers and sellers are also consummated. However, this complexity requires a high degree of mutual dependence and high levels of asset specificity. The mutual dependence is regulated through reputation or family and ethnic ties. Often the participants are co-located since the spatial proximity supports the trust and reputation needed to sustain the mutual dependence. One well-known example is the industrial district in northeastern Italy.

Captive (Quasi-Hierarchy) VC: In this network VC, small suppliers are dependent on much larger, dominant buyers. The terms of the relationship, which tend to be unique to each buyer, are dictated by the buyer. Consequently, the buyer (lead firm) coordinates the chain by engaging in a high degree of monitoring and control.

Hierarchical VC : The polar opposite of Market-based VCs. The VC form is vertical integration; all transactions occur inside the single dominant firm. Finally, note that even though non-market based coordination is costly, buyers prefer to organize network-based chains when they perceive a high risk of supplier failure. And, risks are high when competence differentials are high amongst chain members.

9. Humphrey and Schmitz (2000) summarize the experience of a captive value chain-the Sinos Valley shoe cluster located in the southern region of Brazil. By the late 1980sasignificant number of Sinos Valley firms were large by international shoe industry standards, employing more than 500 people. However, in the early 1990s Chinese producers undercut Brazilian products in the US market. Unfortunately, Brazilian producers did not retaliate by implementing their competitive advantages. Neither the Brazilian producers nor the dominant US buyers (who purchased over 89% of the cluster's output) had an incentive to encourage functional upgrading of marketing because that was the core competence of the US buyers.
10. This relationship begs the question: what determines the form of governance within a value chain? Humphrey and Schmitz (2000, p. 17) convincingly argue that, "the key determinant of the governance form (of the value chain) is not the intrinsic characteristics of the product, such as its complexity or its closeness to the technology frontier but rather the risks faced by the final product buyer. These (risks) arise from the level of probability of poor performance and the consequences of that poor performance. Where the (expected) loss (the probability and level of loss) is greater than the cost of tight governance, quasi-hierarchy is adopted." Of course, this proposition has to be empirically validated.

11. Entrepreneurs typically possess superior private information that can easily be hidden from bankers and investors. Consequently, bankers/investors have great difficulty distinguishing–prior to providing financing–between high quality/growth potential "winners" and low quality/failure prone "losers" enterprises. Economists call this the adverse selection problem.
    In addition, after the financing is provided, entrepreneurs can reallocate the financing away from the business to finance a life style of the "rich and famous" and/or shirk on effort. Economists call this the moral hazard problem. Potential lenders (bankers) and investors rationally respond to these adverse selection and moral hazard problems by rationing credit.

REFERENCES

Bair, J. (ed., 2009). *Frontiers of Commodity Chain Research*. Stanford University Press.

Brakman, S. and H. Garretsen (2009). Trade and Geography: Paul Krugman and the 2008 Nobel Prize in Economics. CESifoWorking Paper No. 2528. Munich, Germany.

Fujita, M. (2008). Formation and Growth of Economic Agglomerations and Industrial Clusters: A Theoretical Framework from the Viewpoint of Spatial Economics. Appears as Ch. 2 in *The Flowchart Approach to Industrial Cluster Policy* by A. Kuchiki and M. Tsuji (eds.). Palgrave MacMillan.

Gereffi, G. and M . Korzeniewicz, eds. (1994). *Commodity Chains and Global Capitalism*. Praeger Publishers.

Gereffi, G. (1999). International Trade and Industrial Upgrading in the Apparel Commodity Chain. *J. of International Economics*. 48:37-70.

Humphrey. J. and H. Schmitz (2000). *Governance and Upgrading: Linking Industrial Cluster and Global Value Chain Research*. University of Sussex Institute for Development Studies. W.P. 120.

Krugman, P. (1991). Increasing Returns and Economic Geography. *J. of Political Economy*, 99:483-499.

Markusen, A. (1996). Sticky Places in Slippery Space: A Typology of Industrial Districts. *Economic Geography*, 72:293-313.

OECD (2006).*The SME Financing Gap*, Volume One: *Theory and Evidence*. Paris.

Pietrobelli, C. and R. Rabellotti eds., (2006). *Upgrading to Compete: Global Value Chains, Clusters, and SMEs in Latin America*. Harvard University Press. Cambridge, Mass.

Porter, M.E. (1998a). *The Competitive Advantage of Nations* (2nd ed.).The Free Press.

Ibid (Nov/Dec1998b). Clusters and the New Economics of Competition. Harvard Business Review, pp. 77-90.

World Bank (2009). *World Development Report 2009: Reshaping Economic Geography*. The World Bank.

17

Strategies of Establishing E-learning System for Public Sector

A Case of Regional Civil Service Development Institute, Central Personnel Administration, Executive Yuan, Taiwan

Chen Chung-Chih

INTRODUCTION

Regional Civil Service Development Institute, C. P. A. in Taiwan is founded to provide training to more than 100 thousand local civil servants in Taiwan, and the annual training capacity has reached 35,000. For the purpose of breaking the constraints of time and space and bringing new learning opportunities to local civil servants, the Institute has designed an e-learning system to its training programmes.

By adopting "shared learning platform" strategy, the Institute began to produce a number of e-learning courses in other public agencies' learning platform in 2003. The professional courses are mainly for personnel, household registration, land administration and health management. Thirty-seven e-learning courses, total 82 e-learning hours have been introduced in two years. The accumulated experience lays down a solid foundation for e-learning system.

The Construction of e-learning System

In order to construct an integral e-learning system, the Institute employed four strategies in2006:

"Top-down first, then bottom-up" Model

In order to put sufficient pressure to subordinates, organizational leaders have to demonstrate the determination to support e-learning programme, therefore, a top-down first strategy is necessary. On the other hand, e-learning activity is closely related to the staffs' information technology literacy and organizational culture, and organizational members will have the feedback loop to organization. No matter it is positive or negative feedback, organizational leaders must seriously take it into consideration, then provide resources in time and declare the determination again.

The Institute adopted such a strategy to assist local governments setting an annual e-learning plan, and according to their business activity specialization, civil servants were required to take a number of professional courses. At the beginning, a reward incentive mechanism was initiated to let civil servants have a pleasant learning experience. Trying to create a positive correlation between training and performance and establishing the legitimacy of e-learning, it also encouraged organization members to improve their performance with e-learning.

Reducing thee-learning Gap

Based on 'The Readiness Rankings' yearly report of 2006 and 2007 by the Economist and IBM, the ranking of Taiwan was 23 and 17 respectively, and it indicates that the condition of promoting e-learning is mature. However, in order to speed up local civil servants' participation in e-learning and to reduce digital gap, it is necessary to set exclusive e-learning system and to broaden bandwidth to allow sufficient on-line learning at the same time. To reduce e-learning gap successfully, it also needs to balance distribution of learning resources and train seed teachers.

Knowledge Management Practice

The e-learning experience will enhance the personal working effectiveness; therefore, it should be systematically accumulated and organized as organizational common knowledge. Knowledge management practice has already been introduced to Taiwan's public sectors for many years. If e-learning can integrate with knowledge management, there is no doubt that it will add knowledge sources to organizations, speed up the creation of learning organization, and increase organizational competitiveness.

Integration of External Resources

There are 52 public sector e-learning websites which have been constructed in Taiwan webs by February 2007. The contents of e-learning programme include not only officially required knowledge and skills but also other courses such as language, computer, health, tourism and culture. If these agencies could integrate and exchange their resources, and form strategic alliances, it could save a lot of money and the learning effects could bealso multiplied. After adopted these four strategies, seven action programmes have been presented accordingly.

An Exclusive Institute-owned E-learning website

The institute has provided core professional training courses to local civil servants for a long time. Due to the increasing demands of e-learning and problems of shared learning platform, the Institute decided to create the "E-Learning Centre" which is an exclusive platform for local civil servants to learn online in November 2006. Its advantage is to have more than 45 Mbps bandwidth which can afford 2,000 people to learn on line simultaneously. On February 10, 2009, the platform has been updated from 'ORACLE E-learning' to 'Moodle 1.93.' The bandwidth has also been broadened to 1,000 Mbps, and the number of online learning can reach to 4,000 people which can meet the needs of e-learning from local civil servants. Meanwhile, "E-Learning Centre" is in line with the public sectors e-learning single sign on (SSO) mechanism which allows members to use the same log in account and password to access all e-learning website resources in order to integrate digital resources effectively.

Facilitating Local Government to Implement E-learning

"Programme of promoting local governments to implement e-learning" was designed by the Institute in 2008. This programme includes the following activities, such as "assisting local government implementing e-learning", "cultivating talented digital people", "benchmarking", etc.

Furthermore, the main purposes of this programme are to help local governments to promote e-learning, to provide high-quality learning environment for civil servants, to offer core knowledge and skills for learners' professional development, to save training costs and to create knowledge economy. To fulfil these purposes, professional consulting team was organized to give advice to local governments.

E-learning CompetitionActivity

The Institute connects e-learning with performance appraisal system of Central PersonnelAdministration, Executive Yuan. In 2006, the Institute used "E-Learning Centre" website to hold the "E-Learning Competition of Local governments" and set rewards for

"The Most Participating Group", "The Most Effective Group" and "Contribution of Best-led person". From 2007 to 2009, it also rolled out "Award for the most effective person", "The best-led group in public forum", "E-Learning Material DIY competition", etc. and all 23 local governments in Taiwan were actively involved.

Cultivating E-learning Talents

Since 2007, the Institute held education training programme for local government e-learning prospect lecturers. The list of qualified lecturers was delivered to local governments to solve the lecturer shortage problem. In 2008, the Institute held basic and advanced courses for how to make e-learning teaching materials yourself, and 1,290 civil servants were trained and e-learning materials were also produced for training purpose. The Institute also prepared necessary materials such as manual of website operation, teaching materials and promotion films for teaching and promoting purposes.

Expanding Blended Learning

In 2007, the Institute developed an annual blended learning plan to integrate "e-learning centre" with actual classroom courses.According to the plan, blended learning modes of "E+C" and "E+C+E" were proposed. It is a learner-oriented strategy and will have a synergy coming out from the learning platform. During this period of time, accompanied with incentive mechanism, civil servants were encouraged to study designated e-learning courses before they went to the classroom, to help them to study online, to discuss with other participants through "public forum", and to establish a communication channel among teachers and learners. Hopefully, it could stimulate learning atmosphere, and enhance the learning effect.

Establishing"PublicForums"

The Institute added "public forum" function to "E-Learning Centre" in 2008 in which an exclusively individual forum for each local government was designed, and each local government may at lcast select four discussion subjects and assign six moderators to manage the forum. Based upon the number of articles published, 9 grades were created to keep the game competitive. At the end of the year, the Institute will reward those members who belong to the highest degree. In 2008, the total articles published in the forum were 186,559, and 22 administrative cases were produced from them.The Institute launched "Elite Internet Forum" hosted by professors from different colleges in March 2009, and 3 subjects were scheduled to be examined in every quarter. For the purpose of rewarding, according to the content of article, 3 categories of above average, good and excellent were employed, and gave "knowledge token" of 5, 10 and 15 accordingly. The "knowledge token" mechanism not only helps to improve the discussion, but also is expected to produce more valuable administrative cases from the forum.

Enriching E-learning Courses by Multiple Methods

Based on training needs oflocal civil servants, the Institute cooperated with professors from various universities and experts in public sectors to develop e-learning courses systematically, and transformed core professional knowledge into e-learning courses beforehand in order to enhance the effectiveness of classroom training. In addition, it is also important for the Institute to regularly purchase high-quality e-learning courses to provide learners studying online promptly. Furthermore, owing to the fruity of e-learning resources in public sectors, the Institute established a reciprocal exchange mechanism among agencies such as: Directorate-General of Budget, Accounting and Statistics, Executive Yuan, National Palace Museum etc. and it did help to transform information instantly. Now-a-days, "E-Learning Centre" has 150 regular courses and they are kept updated continuously.

Cost-Benefits Analysis of "E-Learning Centre"

"E-Learning Center" website was created on November 9, 2006. Combining with action programmes, the e-learning system of local civil servants was completed gradually. The cost-benefits are presented as follows:

Tangible Benefits

From the day of opening "E-Learning Centre" website on May 31, 2009, the number of member log in reached to 146,174, and the total certificated hours amountedto4,356,871.Among them, 112,490 members which are 76.95 per cent are local civil servants. This data indicates that the goal of establishing "E-Learning Centre" is fulfilled.

Participation Rate

According to the statistics, in February 2007, the ratiooflocal civil servants who participated in e-learning was under 3 per cent. After the e-learning competition practice was initiated in March 2007 and the number of civil servants participated in e-learning activities increased to 32,437 which constituted about 30 per cent in total in July 2007. At the end of the same year, the number of civil servants participatingin e-learning boosted to 83,978 and the ratiois77.08 per cent. In fact, the "E-Learning Centre" website becomes the best website compared with other public agency website.

Average Certificated Hours

In 2007, there were 108,945 local civil servants who totally received 856,308 certificated hours and the average of certificated hours per person is 7.86 hours which is far beyond the officially required 5 hours. In 2008, the total number of civil servants participating e-learning was 110,470 and the total certificated hours amounted to 1,626,182. In average, local civil servants received 14.72 hours certificated per person. The changeis substantial.

Cost-effectiveness Evaluation

The annual cost invested by the Institute is about NT$ 18,421,465 (equal to US$ 562,316) (including personnel cost (per staff cost annually NT$ 774,495 * 7 persons = NT$ 5,421,465), and the cost of building and maintaining platform (NT$ 6,000,000 per year),and the cost of creating e-learning courses (NT$ 7,000,000 per year).

The benefits are as follows:

Make up the shortage of training needs, and reduce training costs

The training cost of the Institute is NT$700 per day. If NT$700 is used as the calculation baseline, then converted the certificated e-learning hours to days in classroom (6 hours = a day) and it appeared that NT$114,611,000 (US$ 3,498,504) of training cost in 2007 and NT$ 238,163,800 (US$ 7,269,957) in 2008 weresaved.

The reduction of personnel cost

The saved personnel cost was NT$ 26,418,347 (US$ 806,421) which was equal to 34.11 manpower in 2007. In 2008, the savings were double and amount reached to NT$ 54,897,819 (US$ 1,675,758) which wasequalto70.88 manpower.

The reduction of the costs of teaching materials, papers and printing

In this category, the amount of NT$ 1,109,885 (US$ 33,879) was saved in 2007 and the amount of NT$ 2,508,366 (US$ 6,568) was saved in 2008.

The reduction of travel expenses

Based on the single travel expense of NT$ 1,000 per person, the total amount of NT$ 54,576,666 (US$ 1,665,954) was saved in 2007 and the amount of NT$ 113,411,333was savedin 2008.

The reduction of the cost of contracting out

The Institute has exchanged 97 courses (total 216 learning hours) with other public sectors, and saved NT$18,514,286 (US$565,149) in production cost.

If the investment costs (NT$ 18,421,465) are deducted from the above savings, the result is NT$ 196,808,719 saving in 2007 and NT$ 409,074,139 (US$ 12,487,000) saving in 2008. [The exchange rate: US$: NT$ = 1:32.76 (June 10, 2009)].

The cost of certification per person per hour in "E-Learning Centre" is decreasing yearly. Based on the annual investing cost of NT$ 18,421,465, the total certificated hours were 982,380 in 2007 and the average cost was NT$ 18.75 (US$ 0.57). The total certificated hours amounted to 2,041,980 in 2008 and the average cost decreased to NT$ 9.02 (US$ 0.28) which is less than half of 2007 cost. JI HUI QING (2007) reported that GoLearn of the US (the US federal government's Public Service-Learning Website) spent 3 years to decrease the cost of per person per e-learning course from US$ 150 to US$ 0.7 and it only took two years for the Institute to break this record.

IntangibleBenefits

- To construct a fair learning environment among local public servants and shorten the gap between urban and rural areas.
- To strengthen local civil servants ' knowledge management and work improvement ability.
- To develop an active learning attitude in civil servants, and update their working knowledge timely.
- To integrate public sectors e-learning resources.
- To provide a lifelong learning channel and let the public understand public policies and Institute business.

Future Prospects

E-learning will continue to develop and become the new mainstream of public sector learning system. To build a time and space barrier-free e-learning system is one of the missions for the Institute. To increase lifelong learning resources continually for civil servants, to offer high quality digital learning resources and to assist public servants to improve their service quality and efficiency through e-learning are the Institute's goals in the future.

The Institute will take the following efforts on e-learning in the near future.

Producing Shareable Courses

In the recent years, Taiwan government and the academic organizations have taken their efforts to implement SCORM standard. The first step for "E-Learning Centre" to programme their future courses is to make sure that the necessary knowledge of local civil servants is identified, then, scholars are invited to design courses with these components and finally, private manufacturers are responsible for the development of multimedia courseware. In this case, Shareable Content Object (SCO) rather than multiple sets of customized courses that cannot be divided is produced. Owing to the unified style of these courses and SCORM standard, it can be re-composed with any teaching needs. If the courses have to be updated in the future, the only thing the Institute has to do is to renew the necessary parts. It is not only cost saving but also fasten the speed of courses update.

Introducing the Non-linear Learning Model, and Establishing Knowledge Management and Searching Mechanisms

Problem Based Learning Mechanism (PBLM) is a mechanism which allows learners no longer to rely on professional experts but rather is a mechanism for civil servants to construct an ability to solve problem, to make appropriate judgments and decisions by their own active exploration, and to learn how to feed-back. This is a model that put LMS in the central part of management and takes controlofthe linear digital-based curriculum database and problem-oriented knowledge base, then adds outside experts into the system accompanying with incentives to constitute a virtual and physical, as well as linear and non-linear co-existence learning model.

E-Learning Centre will introduce Business Intelligence (BI) in 2010 to facilitate the convenience, speed and accuracy of knowledge searching and final goal is to make knowledge searching and quotation barrier free.

Providing a Mechanism for Wireless Learning

The usage of 3G (UMTS, CDMA2000) mobiles has become more popular and the environment settled for faster transmission of 3.5G (HSDPA) and 3.75G (HSUPA) is rapidly mature. These devices are easy-carrying and internet installed and will become the universal digital information receiver and transmitter in the future. Therefore, e-learning will be extended to the action (Mobile) e-learning, even streaming audio and video-based e-learning courses will not be a problem. This allows local civil servants to become "mobile" workers and learners.

CONCLUSION

To acquire global competitive advantages, one of the most important steps adopted by countries in the world is 'to speed up digital economy or knowledge (or intelligence) economy.' According to the "e-learning promoting programme of the Executive Yuan", the e-learning programme is divided into "introduction, development and promotion" stages. Due to central and local governments' efforts to promote e-learning activity during these two years, this programme has been stepped up into development and promotion stages, and it demonstrates that Taiwan's public servants are gradually adapt to e-learning and also can gain knowledge from it.

As a result, our government will continue to include e-learning promotion into national policy and our civil servants must continue to study to enhance performance effectiveness and to create more public value.

18

Managing Talent in a Borderless World: Challenges and Opportunities

Tanvi Gautam

> "The traditional organizational map describes a world that no longer exists". *(Hirschhorn & Gilmore, 1992)*

50 years ago, the US economy accounted for 53 per cent of the global GDP, however today it accounts for less than 28 per cent of the same. The world economy is coming to be dominated more and more by players who were not a part of the traditional in-group of nations or large companies that cornered the world market. The rise of BRIC (Brazil, Russia, India and China) and other emerging economies is being felt strongly across the board. 30 of the *GECD* member countries made an investment in cross border mergers and acquisitions in excess of $1.8 trillion in the year 2007 alone. This coupled with the fact that some of the larger well known firms, such as IBM, Fuji film, Nestle, Unilever, Intel, Xerox, among others derive more than 50 per cent of their revenue from outside their home country (Briscoe *et al.,* 2009) is a strong indicator that talent management in today's world cannot be understood without the reference to the issue of globalization and the role played by the emerging economies in it.

While on the one hand, the world trade map has become more diversified, the nature of employment contract and the employee profile itself has undergone a tremendous change. The age and gender profile of the workers is also shifting dramatically. In mature economies like US, Europe, and Japan the baby boomers generation (age today between 45-63) is beginning to retire (Aguiree *et al.,* 2009). It is predicted that by the year 2025 generation Y (born between 1979 and 1994, now between 15-30 years of age) will form between 60-75 per cent of the workforce. This generation is also more gender balanced with more women entering the workforce and the issues of work life balance start to assume centre stage (Aguirre *et al.*, 2009).

HR professionals can no longer rely on the traditional one-firm-long-term employment contract with employees. Knowledge and skills of employees along with their loyalties have started to belong more to the profession than to 'a' firm. Companies too have started relying on a large contractual workforce and off shoring or outsourcing arrangement to meet the skill and talent gaps that emerge due to the changing priorities of firms and the exodus of talent to other places. This in turn has created issues relating to the management of relationship and knowledge of the contingent workforce. The rise in temporary work structures, such as the project form of organizing work require that talent identification and deployment happen at a much faster rate than we have been traditionally used to.

Under the circumstances discussed, the traditional models of managing talent and human capital which focused on forecasting supply/ demand of talent through extensive data analysis and predictions are being challenged. This is because the traditional models assumed a certain stability and predictability of the work environment and employees, which is a luxury that is simply unavailable in today's environment. Moreover, any model of managing talent today needs to account for the large global component that has come to characterize the field of human capital management. What is needed then is set of strategies that help us in correcting our course as we traverse the choppy waters of managing talent in a borderless world. The ability to acquire talent and utilize it may seem like a shifting target but by acknowledging the management of talent as a process rather than a static model to be analyzed, we can hope to improve our chances of getting what we want.

Before we address the challenges presented by the new work order and the trends that have emerged to manage them, it would be useful to dwell upon the concept of boundaries. This is because in some ways the challenges encountered with the new work structures and globalization are symptoms of the issue of managing boundaries.

The Concept of Boundaries

A boundary is any distinction, however big or small that distinguishes and separates one unit from the other. The boundary could be of *language,* for instance a Japanese employee trying to communicate with an Indian manager. It could be of *culture,* for instance a French firm trying to acquire a Latin American company. It could be *functional background,* for instance a marketing person trying to talk to an engineer. It could be *hierarchical,* for instance a senior HR manager trying to bring a new employee onboard. Boundaries could even emerge from a seemingly sterile object such as technology.

The boundaries serve a specific purpose. They unite those who are within the boundary, such that communication and interaction become easier for those within the boundary. For instance, the HR managers all are united by their professional boundary and find it easy to communicate with their acronyms and trade jargon with each other. At the same time, however, boundaries divide the group 'within' from the group 'outside' the boundary. This idea has been prevalent in the management literature for quite some time (Lawrence & Lorsch, 1967; March&Simon,1958).

What research has shown us is that people on either side of the boundary not only know different things but they also know things differently (Tiwana *et al.,* 2003). This has major implications for managing a global workforce and work alliances. It requires that each time we encounter a

boundary, no matter of what type, we need to work towards the creation of a common ground before any meaningful exchange can take place. For instance, when it comes to attracting talent from emerging economies, the strategies that work in the developed world may not work for the values and priorities of the former. The creation of the common ground then can be a key factor in our ability to communicate with, reach, manage and retain the talent in the new world and work order.

Challenges and Opportunities of the New Work Order

While there are several challenges and opportunities in managing talent and human capital under the new work order, I shall focus on two important trends that are quite pervasive and need attention when we think about effective management of human capital. The first is high availability of the international/multi-cultural and younger talent base and the other is the rise in the temporary workforce and work structures.

The International Talent Pool: Crossing the Cultural Boundary

It is exciting to imagine that today one is able to source the best code writers from Germany and the best analysts from Japan to solve your talent management problems. Countries like China are making up for strategic competency gaps by acquiring companies in the US and other parts of the world. They have chosen the 'buy' approach when they can't 'make' the talent themselves. Indeed this may be a useful strategy to get over the important gaps in the competency portfolio of a firm or a country. The differentiation in the new workforce is not just cultural it is also a more younger age group that is going to dominate in the years to come. A firm's ability to recruit and more importantly 'engage' the younger and more multicultural workforce can depend on your capability to deal with questions about:

(a) *The Winning Value Proposition:* What is the value proposition that you can offer the diversified workforce that they should join your firm and not another? While this is the challenge you will face even with domestic workers, it only gets compounded with multi-cultural workers because they will in the process of their work cross more boundaries than they would in a domestic setting. Additionally, is the value proposition something that the prospective employee cares about? For instance, in France where the managers prefer to have office space right in the middle of their workers in order to facilitate supervision and coordination, there is no value for the corner office.

(b) *Integration and Engagement Concerns:* How do you ease the transition of the younger and more diversified workforce over to your side of the boundary? In other words, how do you create the common ground that will ensure that you are able to help the employee contribute their best performance? Again, while expatriate management has examined these issues in detail, a long term process view has to go beyond the operational and tactical discussion of relocation packages, language lessons and cross-cultural training. We are now walking into the realm of 'integrating' the multi-cultural workers into your firm. If the employee does not engage with your side of the boundary and experience the same passion and zeal that you do for your mission, they will be much quicker in jumping ship to a place that will provide them the right environment. Engagement concerns also arise when dealing with a differentiated younger workforce which does not believe that 9-5 is the best model for their career aspirations and is as comfortable working and learning online as it is offline.

The Transitory Work Structures and Workforce: Crossing Affiliation and Continuity Boundaries

Increasingly there is a heightened recognition that the organizations whether they be manufacturing or consulting need to be recognized as a web of inter-relationships and interconnected knowledge bases. This is more true of the knowledge economy today where every business can be conceptualized as a knowledge business. Consequently, we are seeing a sharp increase in the organization of work around transitory structures, such as projects, which allow a firm to draw on knowledge and skills from where they are abundant to where they are needed most. project is defined as a time limited, goal directed, major undertaking requiring the commitment of varied skills and resources (Meredith and Mantel, 2000). The project is a structural form that pervades across industries (Construction, IT, R&D labs, health care). This trend in working towards the project form of organizing work will be on a rise due to the talent utilization advantages that it provides to corporations.

Accompanying the rise of the project form of work is the rise of the transitory workers. A transitory worker is any worker who is available to the firm on a fixed contract term basis and often does not enjoy the benefits of employment security that traditional workers do. The range of skills brought into the firm by the transitory worker can range from the low paying janitorial workers to the high end consultant brought in for specialized skills. The contingent workers provide flexibility with the option of just in time skills at often a lower cost. Reliance on the external workforce is most visible in the stellar growth of the outsourcing industry. For instance, the knowledge intensive business processes outsourcing market is expected to grow from $1.2 billion (2003) to $12-$14 billion by 2010 (Datamonitor, 2008). The growth of this sector can be attributed to the cost advantages available from outsourcing, as well as its ability to fill gaps in skills, knowledge and resources of a firm. Increasing pressure of global competition has ensured that outsourcing will not be seeing a slow down any time soon. Firms may outsource work to other companies whose employees may or may not be physically part of the everyday functioning of the company.

While the lure of getting the right skills, at the right time, at a lower cost is very attractive, the firms often fail to realize the complete benefits that are available from transient workers and projects due to the role played by affiliation of employees (permanent *vs.* transitory) and the drawback created by traditional models of talent recognition and staffing. Identification and utilization of talent for projects is as critical as it is difficult. This is because project work often require crossing of multiple and coinciding boundaries (organizational, geographical, cultural, technological, temporal). Expertise and knowledge recognition, access and utilization is as difficult due to lack of common ground between people on different sides of the boundary (Vlaar *et al.,* 2008; Carlile, 2002). Some of the challenges of managing project and transient workforce lie around:

(a) Project Structures and Deployment of 'within firm' Talent: How can one ensure that projects are staffed with the best available talent within the organization? Putting together a team of experts for different project requires that an organization be current not only on the skills and knowledge of its employees but have a reasonable idea of who would benefit most by being staffed on a particular project. Another important question that arises is whether repeat staffing of people in their areas of core competency is the best way to manage the performance of the project. Additionally how does one ensure that the organization has the ability to meet project needs in an environment where skill requirement forecasting is becoming increasingly tougher?

(b) Project Structures and the Management of the 'between firm'/ Transitory Talent: How can one ensure that the transient workers who enter my firm collaborate effectively with my permanent workforce? In order to preserve the transient worker's external affiliation boundary, they are often not given sufficient training or adequately on-boarded to be able to contribute to the extent they can. By denying the transient workers the ability to grasp the process and contextual knowledge associated with the firm, the hiring organization is unable to reap the benefits of this external talent. The permanent employees also may not be willing to share knowledge with the hired hands as they see the transient employee as a threat to their job and possibly the recipient of more exciting opportunities in high end work. Here again when the preservation of the affiliation boundary coincide with the preservation

of the cross-cultural boundary, the gap created is even larger, and this becomes a big stumbling block towards the utilization of talent.

Navigating the New Work Order

In this section we shall discuss some key trends utilized by companies to address the issues noted above, as well as propose some concrete actions that you can undertake today to prepare yourself to be a more proactive player in the talent game. I would like to propose that the new strategies of talent management be formulated around the three levers of people, process and technology (*see* Table 18.1).

Table 18.1: Challenges and interventions for managing talent: some suggested strategies

	People based interventions	*Process based interventions*	*Technology based interventions*
Global workforce	Cultural shift in thinking	- Cross-cultural on-boarding - Creating global rituals	- Flexibility and connectedness.
Project talent deployment	- Tunnel and helicopter Vision	- Talent portfolio approach - Rotation and mentoring	- Web 2.0 - Talent repositories
Transient workers	Reducing fault-lines	Dual socialization	- Portals - Document repositories

(a) *Attracting and Engaging the Global Workforce:* As corporations become more global and look beyond their shores to get the best talent, it is very important that the people in the organization undergo a *cultural shift in their thinking.* Often organizations use cultural filters to identify and promote talent. The white middle aged male at the top of a hierarchy is a common filter that is used when deciding top spots in several western firms. These filters may be subconscious and may arise from a preference for *the familiar.* However, to attract top talent from a diversified workforce the organization must send a clear signal that it views the world through the filter of talent recognition, and not that of race, colour, creed or gender. Seimens, for instance launched the global leadership organization of women (GLOW) in March 2009 to expand global visibility of women employees from across their international location and initiate change practiced aimed at recruiting and retaining top talent. The company plans to identify 100 'diversity' ambassadors to act as role models. The other important idea to remember is that the shift in thinking has to be signalled at all levels and not just at the top. The fresh entry level recruit from China should feel valued and welcome just as much as the mid-level manager recruited from France. Practices such as skip level lunches with senior employees and the international workforce is another way of sending the signal that all members of the organization have access to top management rather than a select few.

The process of cross-cultural empathy and sensitivity training has started to catch on. However, rather than just sending employees on a three-day training programme organizations should consider more immersion based activities as well. In Tata Consultancy Services (a large Indian multinational) often send employees from acquired firms overseas to its headquarters in India to become familiar with cross-cultural nuances of a global headquarters. Creating rituals such as announcing promotions on the same day across the globe, or launching international products simultaneously are other ways of creating a one firm feeling. Also for operations in other countries the signal that the firm is genuinely interested in *investing in and not just harvesting local talent* is extremely important for attracting talent from emerging economies (Ready *et al.*, 2008). It is equally important for HR managers be training in cross-cultural values, and practices to develop recruitment strategies that appeal to the citizens of other countries.

Finally, technology can be leveraged to create and enhance opportunities available to the global workforce. International consulting firms such as Mckinsey and Booz Allen Hamilton create internal job postings on their HR intranets as means of encouraging employees to apply for roles and positions across the globe. The ability to offer challenging and global careers to the young diverse talent can make all the difference between winning or

losing the talent war. Technology can also be leveraged in global mentoring and training programmes which enable people from different global locations to interact and interconnect enabling the smooth transition between cultural boundaries.

(b) *Managing Talent in Project Forms of Organizing Work:* The crux of project organization is to be able to utilize the best available talent within the firm. For this it is critical that employees at all level practice both the ability to see the end result of 'a' particular project (tunnel vision) but more importantly are able to locate the relevance and criticality off the project in the overall strategy of the firm (Helicopter vision). This skill is particularly critical for HR which as a unit should keep tab on the skill mix available within the firm, new skills being added as well as identify projects as opportunities for development of internal skills. A project presents within itself a manifold learning opportunity of not only gaining new skills from the existing project but transferring relevant skills to newcomers. If needed, companies should not hesitate in investing in projects that may have low return in the short term but a high learning potential for the long term.

In his famous book, 'The talent management problem' Peter Capelli proposed a portfolio based approach to talent management. Just as a stock market portfolio is balanced with different capabilities so should a firm's talent management strategy. Given that the demand for all positions cannot always be accurately predicted, he suggests that it is better to invest in multiple stocks of talent in the same portfolio rather than focus all energies on one stock. In other

words, it may be very useful to create a talent management strategy where employees have broad generic capabilities and a strong learning mindset which can then be effectively tapped into when opportunity presents itself. Related to this issue of investing in multiple stocks is the idea of repeat staffing on projects. Companies often prefer to staff projects with individuals who have had prior experience in an industry and or client. However, not only can this technique lead to loss of motivation and lower learning for the employees, it also has been shown to adversely impact the ability of the team to utilize external knowledge. Research shows that while it staffing projects with people who have extensive prior experience in a field helps in acquiring new knowledge, it is the same prior experience that can interfere with the utilization of that knowledge for effective execution (Gautam, 2009). This may be due to pre-conceived notions or mindset that might persist from prior projects. Consequently, rotation of staff through projects and transfer of knowledge through mentoring initiatives is an important means of managing not just motivation but also performance on projects.

By creating talent inventories online that are updated by employees

HR can shift to the self service mode of technology utilization and updates. In an era where employees are starting to take greater responsibility for their careers this should be fairly simple step to execute. More and more organizations are starting to rely on talent management systems. For instance, Novartis the healthcare company tracks 14,000 high potential employer through a system called organization and talent review which rates not only the skills and abilities but also the employees' learning agility, people skills and ability to obtain results. HR should be quick to jump on the potential of web 2.0 where user generated content as well as the networking potential created by social technologies allows employees to be more aware of talent and opportunity availability within the firm.

(c) *Management of Transient Talent:* While it is true that transient employees will eventually return home to their home organizations, it is important to reduce the *psychological distance* that exist between them and the permanent employees. There are several important reasons for the same. Firstly, while the two sets of employees belong to either side of the boundary the goal that they are trying to achieve is the one and the same which is the achievement of firm goals. Secondly, often times the outcome of the hiring of transient employees depends on the collaboration that takes place between them and the permanent employees. Finally, the ability to integrate the high end transient employee, able it to a limited extent, may impact their ability to craft solutions that are relevant for the existing context of the firm.

One important means by which the distance can be reduced is through the process of *dual socialization* of leaders of such teams. Socialization provides project leaders with familiarity regarding the 'frames-of-reference' used by the hiring firm, and s/he in turn can use this frame of reference to bring the rest of the transient team on board. Variations in the level of dual socialization can be practiced depending on the level at which the transient worker skills are classified. For instance, this strategy is most effective with high value adding transient workers such as consultants. Additionally, by using this strategy with the key members of the home team one can enhance their ability to gain maximum value from the skills of the transient workers. Dual socialization, therefore, is a learning mechanism which bequeaths on the project leader an advantage that is not available through training, documentation or other codified mechanisms. Socialization to both sides enables the creation of mutual knowledge and appreciation of the other party's perspective (Carlile, 2002; Nelson & Cooprider,

1998). Deeper appreciation of the expectations and limitations of the other party should enhance collaboration and performance. Dual socialization also helps direct the attention of the leader to those aspects of the firm environment that are most significant for the task at hand.

Technology based solutions such as creating an integrated portal pertaining to the task and/or project at hand that is utilized by both permanent and temporary employees can be utilized. Such portals remove the common irritant of 'restricted' access that constantly reminds the transient employees of their outsider status. It would also be highly useful to create document repositories that reduce the dependence on transitory workers. Ultimately, the knowledge created on projects through these employees can add value to the firm on future projects as well. Instituting robust handing-and-taking over processes will also ensure that the knowledge generated on the project is available to the firm in the future.

CONCLUSION

We are entering a new era of talent management. Not only are boundaries and flow of trade and commerce shifting but so are the characteristics and availability of talent. It is up to the HR managers of today to wake up to these new realities and adjust their compass accordingly. The firms that will win the war on talent are the ones who recognize that the old maps can't help you in new territory. By utilizing and building on strategies presented above, the managers can start the change that is so critical the way talent and human capital is managed in firms today.

REFERENCES

Aguirre Deanne; Laird Post; Sylvia Ann Hewltt (2009) The talent innovation imperative, *Strategy and Business,* Issue 56.

Carlile, P. (2002). A Pragmatic View of Knowledge and Boundaries: Boundary Objects in New Product Development, *Organization Science,* Vol. 13: 442-455.

Datamonitor (2008); India's march towards knowledge process outsourcing; http://search.ebscohost.com/login.aspx?direct=true&db=buh&AN=33776781&site=ehost-live;Accessedon October, 2008.

Gautam, Tanvi (2009), *Project leader's dual socialization and its impact on team learning and performance: A diagnostic study.*

Hirschhorn, Larry and Tom Gilmore (1992) The new boundaries of the boundaryless corporation, *Harvard Business Review,*May-June1992.

Lawrence, P. & Lorsch, J. (1967). Differentiation and Integration in Complex Organizations, *Administrative Science Quarterly,* Vol. 12: 1-30.

March, J.G.& Simon, H. (1958). *Organizations.* New York: Wiley.

Meredith, R. J. & Mantel, S. J. J. (2000). *Project Management: A Managerial Approach* (Fourth ed.). New York: John Wiley & Son.

Nelson, K. M. & Coopriider, J. G. (1996). The contribution of shared knowledge to IS group performance. *MIS Quarterly,* 20(4): 409-432.

Schuler, Randall, Briscoe, D. and Claus Lisbeth (2008) *International human resource management,* Routlege, Third edition.

Tiwana, A., Bharadwaj, A., & Sambamurthy, V. (2003). "The antecedents of IS development capability: A knowledge integration perspective," Proceedings of the 24th International Conference on Information Systems B2 - Proceedings of the 24th International Conference on Information Systems): 246-258. Seattle.

Vlaar, P. W. L., van Fenema, P. C., & Tiwari, V. (2008). Co-creating understanding and value in distributed work: How members of onsite and offshore vendor teams give, make, demand and break sense. *MIS Quarterly,* 32(2): 227-255.

19

Strategic Human Resource Development: An Empirical Study in Taiwan

Irving Yi-Feng Huang

INTRODUCTION

It's a prevailing thought that training and development can help organizations to retain and cultivate talents to enhance organizational competitiveness. But, many analysts of training and development programmes contend that much of the money being spent for training and development is not being well spent. Most organizations neither assess their training and development needs adequately nor evaluate the benefit of training to the organization (Kunder, 1998; Brinkerhoff and Gill, 1994; Rothwell, 1994). According to Brinkerhoff and Gill (1994), most organizations never assess whether the money spent on employees' training and development has actually advanced the organization's overall productivity or improved individual performance. It is a critical issue to know the linkage between T & D activities and the achievement of organizational goals. Employees can be beneficial from the T & D activities which organizations provided. But, it's also necessary to know their perception towards those resources and activities worthy to spend.

LITERATURE REVIEW

The competitive environment within which firms operate is to prompt senior management to take a greater interest in the development of the organization's human resources. The value of employees to the organizations is related to the uniqueness, capabilities and skills. Competitive advantage is secured when organizations possess skills and competencies that are unique and difficult to implicate or imitate by other competitors (Rainbird, 1995). HRD is best seen as the strategic management of training, development and of management/professional education interventions, and to achieve the organizational objectives, and also to ensure the full utilization of the knowledge and skills of individual employees.

The concept of Strategic Human Resource Development is relatively new to the training and development literature. Firstly, SHRD facilitates the development of core competence which is paramount and critical in developing and also maintaining sustained competitive advantages. Secondly, SHRD enables the firms to make the best use of existing firm-specific competencies and through the development of new capabilities and skills enables it to cope with change. Thirdly, the strategic human resource management literatures suggest that any conceptualization of SHRD must focus on evaluating the linkages among organizational strategies, HRD systems, policies and practices, incorporate the multiple perspectives of stakeholders, and focus on contributions at multiple levels of analysis. Fourthly, SHRD must be sensitive to both emergent and planned strategies.

Effective HRD must be aware of missions, goals, and the needs of organizations, i.e. to integrate SHRD with organizational missions and objectives. SHRD should focus on interplay between both HRD practices and the broader contexts which these practices ended. According to Thomas Garavan (2007), there are four levels to understand the contributions of SHRD, which are: (1) Global environment, (2) Strategy, structure, culture and leadership, (3) Job value and uniqueness, and (4) Individual expectations, employability and careers. The model below emphasizes on both horizontal and vertical linkages throughout and also suggests multiplicity of results which are stakeholders focused on.

There are also assumptions for organizational practices on strategic human resource development such as the existing overarching mission statement specifying organizational commitment to learning and the mission statement shapes organizational vision, organizational plans and so on, and what should be done is to linking the mission to planned learning experiences via HRD and ensures the value of both HRD and organization is questioned.

This paper aims to discuss the alignment of HRD activities and organizational goals through a questionnaire survey distributed to civil servants to understand their perception towards HRD system.

RESEARCH METHODOLOGY

The survey was conducted by distributing questionnaires to civil servants who attended training sessions at National Civil Service Institute, Civil Service Development Institute, and Civil Service Training Department of Taipei City. The questionnaire contained two parts. The first part was demographic information about the respondents, and the other was topic issue questions about the perception towards Human resource development activities. In the second part, the respondents were asked to indicate the agreement degree of each HRD activity by using a 5-point scale which ranging from 1 (strongly disagree) to 5 (strongly agree). The respondents were asked to answer the questionnaire following a standard procedure.

Instrument Development

The survey questionnaire was adopted from Linda H. Kunder (1998). There are 26 items to measure seven the effectiveness of SHRD. The framework of SHRD model is shown in Table 19.1.

Sample Characteristics

After data collecting, 286 questionnaires were returned. Discarding 11 invalid responses (incomplete or too consistent), 275 valid responses remained for analysis. As shown in Table 19.2, 39.3 per cent of respondents were male, 44.8 per cent were between age of 30 to 49, 16.3 per cent held master and above degree.

Table 19.1: Strategic Human Resource Development Model

HRD activities	*Item numbers*
Status of the Training and Development System	13
Effectiveness of the Training and Development System	9
Value of Training and Development	4

Source: Linda H. Kunder, 1998.

Table 19.2: Sample Characteristics

Demography		*Frequency*	*Per cent*
Gender	Female	160	58.2
	Male	108	39.3
	Total	268	97.5
	Missing	7	2.5
Education level	High school	13	4.7
	College	44	16.0
	Bachelor	165	60.0
	Master	43	15.6
	Doctor	2	.7
	Total	267	97.1
	Missing	8	2.9
Age	30s	59	21.5
	40s	64	23.3
	50s	33	12.0
	Total	156	56.7
	Missing	119	43.3
Position	Managerial	84	30.5
	Non-managerial	184	66.9
	Total	268	97.5
	Missing	7	2.5
Years of Managerial experiences	None	123	44.7
	Below 3 years	47	17.1
	3 years and more	85	30.9
	Total	255	92.7
	Missing	20	7.3
Work unit	Line	100	36.4
	Staff	167	60.7
	Total	267	97.1
	Missing	8	2.9
Job series	Administrative	222	80.7
	Technical	44	16.0
	Miscellaneous	9	3.3
	Total	275	100.0
Government level	Central	25	9.1
	Local	241	87.6
	Missing	9	3.3
	Total	275	100.0

Validity and Reliability

Factor analysis was conducted for each dimension to explore the construct validity through factor loading. In order to verify the reliability of data collected, a reliability analysis of Cronbach's Alpha was employed. As shown in Table 19.3, the factor loading were between .537 and .854 and Cronbach's alpha of each scales were over .730. It indicates the reliability of the questionnaire for this research can be accepted.

FINDINGS AND DISCUSSION

Descriptive Statistics

In order to understand respondents' general perception towards variables, the method of descriptive statistic was employed. As shown in Table 19.5, all of the mean scores to each scale were higher than the average score of 3.0 which means respondents have positive attitude towards HRD functions (range from 3.43 to 3.75). As what Table 19.4 shows, among the following four dimensions, the part of

Table 3: Validity and Reliability

	Item No.	*Factor loading*	*% of Variance*	*Cronbach's Alpha*
Commitment and support to T&D	5	.591-.854	21.523	.860
T&D activities meet different level of needs	7	.588-.821	20.801	.894
Using feedback to ensure T&D function	8	.537-.742	18.082	.863
Effectiveness of T&D	4	.667-.843	58.312	.737

Table 4: Descriptive Statistics

	N	*Minimum*	*Maximum*	*Mean*	*Std. Deviation*
Commitment and support to T&D	270	1.20	5.00	3.7504	.63320
T&D activities meet different levels of need	269	1.14	5.00	3.5789	.63919
Using feedback to ensure T&D function	257	1.50	5.00	3.4343	.58443
Effectiveness of T&D	265	1.50	5.00	3.6236	.58230

"commitment and support to T&D" scored the highest and on the contrary, the "using feedback to ensure T&D function" got the least scores as the results. This evidence could indicate that respondents have lower performance perception on the feedback of T&D activities.

Structured Equation Analysis

To explore the causal relations of HRD functions, the Structures Equation Mode (SEM) was conducted.

Model Fit Assessment

The model fit describes how well a statistical model fits observations; the degree of consistency between the hypothetical model and the observed data. The model fit indices used in this study are: Chi-square statistics (χ^2), Goodness-of-Fit Index (GFI), Adjusted Goodness-of-Fit Index (AGFI), Standardized Root Mean Square Residual (SRMR), Comparative Fit Index (CFI), and Normative Fit Index (NFI) etc.

The assessment of the overall model fit is compiled in Table 19.5. The resulting chi-square value is 42.02 (the P value is $0.00<0.05$), which shows that the difference between the observed covariance matrix and the model covariance matrix has reached a significant difference. Due to the chi-square is fairly sensitive to the number of samples, i.e. the larger the sample size is, the more likely the null hypothesis of chi-square will be rejected, we used other measures to perform the assessment. The result shows that other fit indices provide support for the model. AGFI is 0.77, close to the critical value of 0.8, which means the model goodness-of-fit is acceptable.

Parameter Estimation and Hypothesis Test

Parameter estimation results using maximum likelihood method are compiled in Table 19.6 and Table 19.7. Based on the assessment results of the parameter tests on the measurement model in Table 19.6, all the measured variables fit well with their corresponding latent variables.

In terms of "X" variable, the standardized values from the three measured variables, "XI" (commitment and support to T&D), "X2" (T&D activities meet different level of needs), "X3" (using feedback to ensure T&D function), are 0.53, 0.54, and 0.46 respectively and

Table 5: Model Fit Assessment

Indicator	*Determination value*	*Value obtained by this model*	*Note*
χ^2 (Chi-Square value)	P-Value > 0.05	42.02 (P = 0.00)	Reject Ho, Because chi-square test tends to reject model easily, further tests are required to confirm the result.
CFI (Goodness-of-Fit Index)	>0.9	0.94	Model goodness-of-fit is acceptable
AGFI (Adjusted Goodness- of-Fit Index)	>0.8	0.77	Close to 0.8, acceptable model goodness-of-fit
SRMR (Standardized Root Mean Square Residual)	>0.05	0.047	Model goodness-of-fit is acceptable
CFI (Comparative Fit Index)	>0.9	0.96	Model goodness-of-fit is acceptable
RMSEA (Root Mean Square Error of Approximation)	>0.05	0.2	Bad goodness-of-fit due to >0.1
NFI (Normed Fit Index)	>0.9	0.96	Model goodness-of-fit is acceptable
NNFI (Non-Normed Fit Index)	>0.9	0.90	Model goodness-of-fit is acceptable
IFI (Incremental Fit Index)	>0.9	0.96	Model goodness-of-fit is acceptable

Table 6: Measurement of latent variables

Latent variable	*Measured variable*	*Standard error*	*Standardized loading*	*t*
X	X1	0.030	0.53	17.49
	X2	0.033	0.54	16.53
	X3	0.033	0.46	13.94
Y	Y1	—	0.48	—
	Y2	0.046	0.53	11.42

Table 7: Model estimation

Latent variable	*Standard error*	*Standardized coefficient*	*t-value*	*test result*
X->Y	0.072	0.83	11.50	support

the t-value of them all reach significant influence, which means these three measured variables all have high degree of influence on the "X" variable. In terms of "Y" (effectiveness of T&D) variable, the standardized values from the two measured variables, "Y1" (worthy of spending time and money), "Y2"(usefulness of T&D), are 0.48, and 0.53 respectively and only the t-value of the "Y2" variable reaches significant influence, which means "Y2" has high degree of influence on the "Y" variable.

According to Table 19.7, the latent variable X has significant positive influence on variable Y ($p<0.05$). Figure 1 shows the model path diagram.

CONCLUSION

This paper tries to explore the perception towards training and development activities among civil servants in Taiwan. The statistical results indicate the respondents have pretty high perception. To some extent, it seems that civil servants in Taiwan are satisfied with the activities they got from the organization. The SEM analysis indicates that the effectiveness of training can be predicted and explained by commitment and support to T&D, T&D activities meet different level of needs, and using feedback to ensure T&D function.

For further study, the survey instrument needs to be verified by factor analysis with more samples to avoid cultural bias. It's also possible that the items of meanings in questionnaire implied the respondents to fill the answer in some certain manner. That means social desirability exists. More samples for establishing construct validity of the SHRD scale will be necessary.

REFERENCES

Bernthal, P. R., Colteryahn, K., Davis, P., *et al.* (2004). *ASTD Competency Study: Mapping the Future.* Baltimore, ML: Victor Graphics.

Bing, J.W., Kehrhahn, M. and Short D.C. (2003). Challenges to the Field of Human Resources Development. *Advances in Developing Human Resources,* 5(3), pp. 42-351.

Garavan, Thomas (2007). A Strategic Perspective on Human Resource Development, *Advances in Developing Human Resources,* 9(1), 11-30.

Garavan, Thomas, N., Gubbins, C., Hogan, C., and Woodlock, M. (2007) Transitioning to A Strategically Aligned HRD Function: The Case of A Health Services Organization, in Sambrook, S. and Stewart, J. (ed.), Human Resource Development in the Public Sector, NY: Routledge.

Goldsmith, S. & Eggers, W. (2004). *Governing by Network: the New Shape of the Public Sector,* Washington. DC: Brookings Institute.

Hockey, J., Kakabadse, A.P. & Kakasbadse, N.K. (2005). Developing A Leadership Cadre for the 21st Century: A Case Study of Management Development in the UK's New Civil Service, *International Review of Administrative Sciences, 71(1)*, pp. 83-98.

Luoma, M. (2000). Investigating the Link Between Strategy and HRD, *Personnel Review,* 20(6), pp. 769-790.

Marquardt, M. & Berger, N. (2003). The Future: Globalization and New Roles for HRD. CA, Sage.

Prahalad, C.K. & Hamel, G. (1990). *The Core-Competence of the Corporation.* HBR, May-June.

Swanson, R. and Holton III, E. (2001). *Foundation of Human Resource Development.* San Francisco: Berrett-Koehler.

Swart, J., Mann, C, Brown, S., and Price, A. (2005). *Human Resource Development: Strategy and Tactics.* N. Y., Elsevier Butterworth-Heinenmann.

20

Global and Cultural Human Resources Management

Michael A. Potter

INTRODUCTION

The world around us is changing with many countries experiencing political, social and economic unrest. Despite the slow and uneven recovery from the global economic downturn and lingering high levels of unemployment in many markets, organizations around the world still report that they cannot find the talent they need when they need it. These difficulties in finding talent have led to changes in global workforce demographics as organizations seek to react to the challenges of finding the right talent. Talent is becoming the key competitive differentiator, and countries and companies with access to the right talent are positioning themselves to succeed in the rapidly changing world of work.

THE CHANGING NATURE OF INTERNATIONAL PEOPLE MANAGEMENT

There are some common issues that are seen as to have high importance in foreseeable future. In Manpower Group Survey 2011 of the 40,000 employees worldwide, one in three (34%) employees reported difficulties filling positions due to lack of available talent. Taiwan is among the countries in the Asia-Pacific region where employers are having the most problems finding suitable employers. Approximately 54 per cent of Taiwanese employers said it was difficult to find people to fill job vacancies, which is a rise from 41 per cent the year before. In comparison, only 24 per cent of employers in China said they felt talent shortage was a problem, the survey stated. Talent shortages in Asia Pacific mirror those of the rest of the world, with 45 per cent of the region's employers indicating they are having difficulty in filling positions due to lack of suitable talent in their markets—a rise by 4 per cent from 2010.

Asia Pacific employers believe that it is candidate-specific factors that are contributing most to their hiring difficulty. Across the region, one in four employers cited lack of experiences as the overriding factor of hiring difficulty. The next most common factor cited was an overall lack of candidates (24%) together with other commonly cited reasons such as lack of technical job skills (16%) and candidates' not possessing the right values and mindset (10%).

The Price Waterhouse Cooper survey conducted on behalf of the World Federation of Personnel Management Associations revealed that the top three areas that represent significant challenges for HR Professionals in the Asia Pacific Region were change management, leadership development, and succession planning. A significant issue for Asia Pacific businesses today is to break their businesses away from the *status quo* and move their focus from products to customers also developing more of a business planning mentality.

Leadership development is a critical issue for on-going success of any corporation. Therefore, HR professionals need to focus on developing supervisors into people managers, not just technical specialists. Plenty of tools exist for leadership development, but it is indeed a challenge to find the most appropriate one. Such challenge can be met by gaining support from executives to develop leaders in the future and engaging senior management in leadership development philosophy and practice.

Succession planning will remain an issue due to difficulties in retaining knowledge held by retiring workers and ensuring sufficient time to train successors for which the aging workforce within the company is a key driver. In fact, the aging workforce was noted by many who chose succession planning as an issue due to the issues in retaining knowledge held by retiring workers, and ensuring sufficient time to train successors. Staffing, including international mobility of employees, continues to be a critical element as is noted in other regions.

ECONOMY OF TAIWAN

Taiwan has developed a capitalist economy that ranks 19th largest in the world in GDP and 23rd in nominal terms with gradually decreasing guidance of investment and foreign trade by the Republic of China government which governs Taiwan. In keeping with this trend, most large government-owned banks and industrial firms have been privatised. Real growth in GDP has averaged about 8 per cent during the past three decades. Exports have grown even faster and since Second World War, have provided primary impetus for industrialisation.

Export composition changed from predominantly agricultural commodities to industrial goods (now 98%). Inflation and unemployment are low; the trade surplus is substantial; and foreign reserves are the world's fourth largest. Agricultural commodities contribute 3 percent to GDP, down from 35 percent in 1952, and the service sector makes up 73 per cent of the economy. Traditional labour-intensive industries are steadily being moved off-shore and replaced with more capital-and-technology-intensive industries, as well as creative industries.

The last decade has seen an increase not only in the number of Asian workers moving between nations, but the type of mobility has become more complex and the movement has become less selective. The forces which are responsible for this increase in movement are associated with globalisation, increased levels of education, proliferation of international media, improved transport systems and the internationalisation of business and labour market. In the last decade there has been an exponential increase in the movement of Asians out of the region but also between Asian countries and there has also been an increased movement of people into the Asian region from outside the region.

In the past two decades, Japan and the Asian NIEs of Taiwan, South Korea, Singapore and Hong Kong experienced rapid economic development and demographic transition. These economic developments have created demand for more migrant workers, both highly skilled and non-skilled. Taiwan now faces many of the same economic issues as other developed economies. With the prospect of continued relocation of labour-intensive industries and economies with cheaper workforce, such as China and Vietnam, Taiwan's future development will have to rely on further transformation to a high technology and service-oriented economy.

Taiwanese investors and businesses have also become major investors in mainland China, Vietnam, Thailand, Indonesia, the Philippines, and Malaysia. The tightening of labour markets has led to an influx of foreign workers, both legal and illegal. Because of its conservative financial approach and its entrepreneurial strengths, Taiwan suffered little from the Asian Financial Crisis of 1997-1999 compared to many of its neighbours. Unlike in neighbouring Japan and South Korea, small and medium-sized businesses make up a large proportion of business in Taiwan.

In recent years, Taiwan has successfully diversified its trade markets, cutting its share of exports to the United States from 49 per cent in 1984 to 20 per cent in 2002. Taiwan's dependence on the United States could decrease as its exports to South East Asia and China grow and its efforts develop European markets produce results.

The lack of formal diplomatic relations between the Republic of China with Taiwan's trading partners appears not to have seriously hindered Taiwan's rapidly expanding commerce. The Republic of China maintains cultural and trade offices in more than 60 countries with which it does not have official relations to represent Taiwanese interest. In addition to the WTO, Taiwan is a member of Asian Development Banks as "Taipei China" and the Asia-Pacific Economic Cooperation forum as "Chinese Taipei". These developments reflect Taiwan's economic importance and its desire to become further integrated into global economy.

The following issues are common for an organisation to experience when entering a Taiwanese market:

- *Lack of language skills*. In many countries, language training is provided, however, in many organisations, capacity is lacking or procedures are too complex.
- *Lack of professional skills and education skills*. Many migrant workers face difficulties in being placed in correct positions in the organisation due to lack of understanding of their level of qualification from their home country.
- *Limited knowledge of labour market*. Migrant workers experience a lack of understanding of the organisations and countries' culture and therefore, organisational processes for promotion leading to them not being able to progress.

- *Limited social and professional networks*. Linked to the above point can lead to stinted motivation, productivity and progression within the organisation.
- *Limited flexibility* of the organisation due to a lack of understanding of the culture migrant workers.

Indeed all the above can be related to a lack of 'cultural awareness' and this is key to successful/unsuccessful cultural integration.

THREE LEVELS OF CULTURE

It is, therefore, extremely important that HR professionals and the organisation as a whole have a firm understanding of nature of culture. In Michael A. Potter's view there are 3 key levels of culture to be aware of—country culture, corporate culture and individual culture.

Country Culture

Effective intercultural communication is a "must have" in today's global economy. Business success has always been built on understanding and nurturing strong intercultural relationships. International differences can affect small businesses as well, but more commonly it is an issue for larger organisations. A company might have international staff working within an organisation and different sets of beliefs can make working together difficult. Some cultures take offence of certain comments and actions. For example, a Christmas party might not be seen too keen by non-Christian religions. Therefore, an organisation has to always make sure that it understands what offends others and within reasonable limits act upon it.

In cases where organisations have businesses in different countries getting everyone to work together might become a challenge. Apart from language issues, different countries have different approaches to work. For example, it is common for German employees to often say what they think which may offend English employees. On the other hand, the English are very subtle and the real message may completely get lost on the German. Therefore, multi-cultural organisation can only be successful of all the employees understand each other—both in terms of language and culture. Furthermore, it is important to remember cultural differences with dealing with international customers. A customer from Taiwan or Japan may have completely different expectations from those in Sweden for example. Therefore, an international knowledge must always be possessed in order to create successful relationships with multicultural colleagues, customers and clients.

Corporate Culture

A basic definition of corporate culture is 'the collective way we do things around here'. Culture forms an essential part of any organisational strategy and consists of collective beliefs, value systems, and processes that provide a company with its own unique flavour and attitude. When working towards company goals or when trying to effect change in your organisation, corporate culture can be the very thing that tips you up. If insufficient effort is put towards identifying aspects of the culture that may impact on what an organisation is trying to achieve, then insufficient actions will be taken to circumvent obstacles in a timely manner or harness the way things are done in an opportune direction.

At the core of any corporate culture lie the standards that govern the operation of the business. These standards are usually expressed in terms of the policies and procedures that define how the company will operate. This will include how different departments of functions relate to one another in the production process, the line of communication established between management and the departmental employees, and rile governing acceptable conduct of everyone who is part of that company.

Above and beyond organisational and procedural factors, corporate culture is further informed by the attitudes of everyone involved with the organisation. When executives, managers, and rank and file employees are all on the same page as far as basic corporate values, it becomes possible to have general agreement on the relationships that must be in place to accurately reflect the desired corporate culture.

As with many types of cultures, corporate culture usually involves the inclusion of some rites or rituals. This can be something as simple as annual holiday bonus, a week in the summer when the entire company shuts down, or even the naming of an employee of the month. These rites help to bond people together and provide some sense of collective identity, which is very important to the creation of a positive corporate culture.

The importance of corporate culture is growing as a result of several recent developments. Companies are encouraging employees to be more responsible and act and think like owners. In exchange for more flexible working schedules, employees are expected to always be "on-call". With the demise of more traditional communities, companies are filling employees' needs to belong to a community and at the same time also encouraging teamwork and the formation of teams.

Individual Culture

Every individual lives his life according to his beliefs, values, attitudes and behaviours. These beliefs, values, attitudes and behaviours develop according to peoples' backgrounds, the way in which they were brought up, level of education they have received and their general type personality. However, in multi-cultural organisation personal beliefs and values can often clash. An employee from one background may have totally different views on ethical behaviour at work to another. For example, there may be disagreements on issues such as "borrowing" office supplies for personal use.

Therefore, top management must establish the organisation's culture and define what is and what is not counted as acceptable behaviour in a certain organisation. Sufficient training should be provided to assist with understanding of handling different ethical dilemmas. A formal, written code of ethics can help in stating the exact values and ethical standards that guide a firm's actions.

CASE STUDY

Taiwan Semiconductor Manu-facturing Company (TSMC) is the world's largest dedicated independent semiconductor foundry, with its headquarters and main operations located in the Hsinchu Science Park in Hsinchu, Taiwan. TSMC hires all employees equally based on their job qualifications regardless of gender, religion, race, nationality or political affiliation. Their employment policy is well-defined to ensure candidates and employees are treated equally in recruitment, deployment, development, evaluation and reward, and engagement as well.

Providing continuous training and education opportunities is the cornerstone of TSMC's employee development. It is especially important for the Company's success in this tough economic environment. TSMC provides comprehensive learning opportunities and resources to all employees, and a tailor-made individual development plan is established for each employee based on his or her development and business needs.

As a result of implementing diversity management, more men and women of immigrant background have been recruited and some of them have been appointed to mid-level positions as a result of focused activities related to focus on ethnicity in the company. Provisions for international workers has been integrated into the HRM and aligned closely with the business plan, especially by the marketing department. Moreover, employees are aware of diversity matters and directors and management commitment to it.

At a time when TSMC and many other companies are competing with increasingly difficult global economic markets, diversity in the workforce is not any more prioritized. However, the business case for effective integration of migrants into workforces is becoming more important than ever, because it has a strong resonance for companies as they compete in turbulent world.

FUTURE OF HRM AND GLOBAL PEOPLE MANAGEMENT

The key strategies for the next 2-5 years in regard to Human Resource Management based on the results of surveys and research considered in this paper are:

- *Globally*: two of the key issues currently being experienced by HR professionally are: change management and leadership development.
  - *Change Management* has generally not been a consistent area of focus for training and development of HR professionals. As HR professionals are being required more and more to help in the future strategy of organisations it seems essentials that there should be an intensified focus on training in this area to develop added competencies to deal with issues of change management.
  - *Leadership Development* was also identified as major challenge as again HR professionals are increasingly

being recognised as becoming strategic business partners within their organisations. Across the globe leadership development has been identified as a critical strategic initiative and HR professionals are increasingly going to be required to develop skills and services in terms of ensuring that the right employees are retained.

- *Talent Management and Retention:*
  - The culture of an organisation supports performance from within to gain market position.
  - Managers are equipped to take on leadership roles of the future so that the organisation is viable in the long term.
  - The role of the HR professional in these initiatives will be crucial.

Looking ahead on a more regional level, the key strategies for HR professionals across the Asia Pacific region will include change management and succession planning.

In terms of international migration of workers, the key strategy that HR professionals and organisations should be focusing on in 2011 and beyond has to focus on employee understanding, both of the foreign worker and also of the current employees working in the organisation. This is not just education in terms of the job role and organisational processes, but of the culture of the organisation and importantly an understanding of the culture and values that the foreign workers will be bringing and so what can HR managers be doing to make sure that an organisational culture is one that has an international perspective.

As discussed in a case study, a good diversity management system can really help to create the correct culture for an organisation. The lack of networking opportunities can also cause migrant workers to become despondent, therefore, provision of networking with other colleagues and professionals must be the key. Finally, there has to be a recognition and understanding of foreign qualifications to prevent migrant workers skills and knowledge not being used to their full potential.

21

The Political Economy of Human Capital Outflow

A Case Study of Malaysia

Toh Kin Woon

INTRODUCTION

Alarm has been raised in recent years over the issue of brain drain and what it means to the competitiveness of Malaysia. Brain drain or the flight of human capital is the large scale emigration or outflow of individuals with human skills, knowledge, experiences, creativity and innovativeness from one country to other countries. Many of them leave permanently to settle in other countries, while the rest choose to work abroad, returning to spend their retirement in the country. Their move to settle permanently or work in other countries is likely to bring about high economic costs, such as an erosion of economic competitiveness, to their respective countries of origin. These countries also lose by way of emigrants taking away with them a fraction, often considerable, of the value of their education and training that has been funded and sponsored by their governments and peoples. Conversely, the recipient countries, that is, countries to which these people of talent and skills move and settle down in, gain by way of seeing a considerable enhancement in their creative, innovative and economically productive capacities. This paper will focus only on Malaysia. Several questions with regard to this issue of brain drain or human capital loss will be raised and answers sought.

Specifically, we want to know how serious is this issue of brain drain that has afflicted the country? What is the profile, such as the age, race and skills mix, of those who have migrated? Where have they gone to work or settle down? Why did they leave? What are the implications to the nation's economic health as a result of their out-migration? How have the state responded by way of policies to stop this flight of human capital? How effective have those policy responses been? If they have not been effective, why have they been ineffective? What should the appropriate policy responses then be? To be honest, we are not sure that we have the answers to all these questions. Among the reasons for this is the paucity of statistical data. Be that as it may, an attempt will still be made to provide answers, in order to throw some light on these key questions.

How serious is the problem?

Anecdotal evidence seems to suggest that brain drain or the flight of human capital from Malaysia is serious and widespread. This was acknowledged as much by the New Economic Model (NEM) that was launched by the Prime Minister on March 30th last year. Statistical evidence to back up this assertion is, however, weak and fragmented. Still, some aggregate and crude numbers have been bandied around to provide limited backing to the common perception that the outflow of human capital is serious. But quantum is one thing. Equally of concern is the quality of those who have left. Even when the numbers are not large, the problem of brain drain can still be serious, especially if those who have left bring with them lots of skills, knowledge, creativeness, innovativeness and enterprise that could potentially have contributed towards the expansion of productive capacity of the country. We will discuss more of this later, but first let us look at what data there are on human capital flight abroad. In reply to a question raised in Parliament on Monday, 30 November, 2009, and as reported by Bernama, the Deputy Foreign Minister Senator A. Kohilan Pillay claimed that 304,358 Malaysians migrated to other countries from March 2008 till August 2009. Of these, around 200,000 left during the first eight months of 2009. This implies that the figure that emigrated more than double between 2008 and 2009. The figure for 2007 was 139,696 Malaysians. There was no breakdown of these emigrants by race, skills profile and the destination countries in the answer given by the Deputy Minister. A study done by Winters *et al.*

(2007), which was initially quoted by the Ministry of Science, Technology and Innovation at a Brain Gain Workshop organized by the United Nations Development Programme in 2009, and again in a cover feature article in the *Star Business Week* (Saturday, 6 February, 2010) by Cecilia Kok and Tee Lin Say, estimated that in the year 2000, there were already 785,000 Malaysians residing overseas.1 However, according to the World Bank, the number of emigrants from Malaysia rose from 9,576 in 1960 to 1,489,168 in 2005, an almost 100-fold increase over the 45 year period (as quoted by Dr. Fong Chan Onn, 2010)2. The latest World Bank Report released in April this year estimated the total number of migrants to be around 1 million, of which around one-third or approximately 335,000 were Malaysians with skills and knowledge3. Apart from the large numbers of skilled workers who have migrated, another issue of concern is the rate of increase of brain drain. If outflows to Singapore is anything to go by, it is clear that skilled migration continues to outpace unskilled migration by a significant margin. It went up, for example, from 10 per cent in 1990 to 23 per cent in 2000 to 35 per cent in 20104.

Where have they all gone?

Where have these Malaysians gone? The study by Winters *el al.* (2007), and as quoted by Cecilia and Tee, claimed that of the total Malaysian emigrants, around 40 per cent have settled in Singapore; 30 per cent in member countries of the Organisation for Economic Cooperation and Development (OECD), in particular the United States of America, Canada, Australia, New Zealand and United Kingdom; 20 per cent in other Asean countries, including Brunei, Indonesia and the Philippines, and 10 per cent in other regions of the world. Based on this percentage distribution, there were around 314,000 Malaysians residing in Singapore in the year 2000. Another study estimated the number of Malaysians, who have either become citizens or permanent residents of Singapore, at 306,998 in 2005.5 This figure does not, however, include those who are non-residents, that is, those who are not citizens or permanent residents but hold an employment pass or work permit. These are issued to workers at both the low and high ends of the skills spectrum. Quoting from the United Nations Global Migration Database, 2010, Dr. Fong found the number of Malaysians who have moved abroad by selected countries to be 92,337 in Australia; 14,547 in New Zealand; 54,321 in the United States of America and 61,000 in the United Kingdom in 2007. The World Bank Report maintains that human capital outflows have been to a few countries only, with the heaviest concentration in Singapore, which attracted 54 per cent of the skilled and knowledge workers from Malaysia.6 This was followed by Australia with 15 per cent; USA 10 per cent, UK 5 per cent and Canada 4 per cent.

Who are these emigrants?

The statistics on the number of Malaysians who have left for other countries seem alarmingly large. Of even greater concern, however, is the skills profile of those who have chosen to settle abroad. Already in the year 2000, the number of Malaysian migrants with tertiary education in the OECD countries was 102,321, which represents a 40.8 per cent increase over the figure of 72,649 in 1990.7 In the same year, there were 7431 nurses, 4129 doctors, 652 dentists and 798 pharmacists working in these countries. In 2003, there were 7,955 researchers employed in science and technology in the USA. This was not far from the 10,419 that were engaged in such work in Malaysia. Quoting foreign sources, Cecilia Kok and Tee Lin Say (Star, February 6, 2010) claimed that the total number of Malaysian origin researchers, scientists and engineers working overseas currently could probably have exceeded 20,000, with about 40 per cent of them in the USA and 10 per cent in Australia. Singapore perhaps has the heaviest concentration of Malaysian talent and skills. Anecdotal evidence gathered from friends and relatives suggests a large pool of skilled and knowledgeable Malaysian professionals such as doctors, lawyers, scientists, and academics who have settled there. Although those who have migrated overseas are mainly Malaysians of Chinese origin, there are Malays and Indians who have emigrated abroad as well. But more important than the magnitude of the flight of skills and knowledge is the intensity of the brain drain. This is measured by the ratio of skilled people leaving to the initial skills base of the sending country8. For Malaysia, this intensity is high due to both high human capital outflows and the slow pace of domestic skills formation. The negative economic impact that follows therefrom can be particularly severe, particularly at a time when the government wants to transform the nation from a middle income to a high income country.

No Compensatory Inflows

This negative impact has not been mitigated by compensatory inflows of skilled and knowledge workers. Quoting from the report of the World Bank yet again, Malaysia's in-migration of foreign workers is estimated to be around 2.4 million in 2011. This could in principle alleviate thc outflow of skilled workers if a significant proportion of the immigrants are skilled. Unfortunately, however, these immigrants are mostly poorly educated and are hence hired in low skilled occupations in households, manufacturing, low end services and plantation agriculture.9 Thc result is a work force whose skills base is still low. What further exacerbates matters is the fact that a large number of immigrants are undocumented. Most of these are obviously unskilled and this further adds on to the large pool of unskilled rather than skilled workers in the country.

Why did they leave?

Many factors have contributed to the considerable flight of human capital from Malaysia. These may be categorized into two – the push and pull factors.

Push Factors

(i) Among these is the loss of hope in those who have migrated that there ever will be fair and just treatment for all Malaysian citizens, irrespective of race and religion. This sense of hopelessness has been induced in large part by the state's promulgation and practice of a whole host of policies and legislations ostensibly aimed at restructuring society, but that in effect favours the Bumiputeras and discriminates against the non-Bumiputeras. Nowhere is this more blatant than in the practice of recruitment and promotions within the public sector; the giving of scholarships for overseas education; the recruitment and promotions of academic staff and the enrolment of students into public universities. The feeling is strong that racism has been deeply embedded and institutionalized in all our state institutions. Such racism no doubt influences the nature and implementation of policies of all these institutions. The outcome is, of course, an erosion of confidence among those who are victims of racial discrimination.

(ii) Another major push factor is the declining quality of education in Malaysia. Education is generally acknowledged to be a vehicle for social advancement for the poor across generations. When opportunities for education at all levels are democratized, life chances of the poor will be considerably improved, with earnings across the productive life span enhanced and social justice attained. Education, through imparting knowledge and providing training, is also a vehicle for expanding the productive capacity of both individuals and society. This is, however, conditional upon its quality and standard being maintained at, what many international peer reviewers would regard, as respectably high levels. Unfortunately for Malaysia, the quality and standard of our education has dropped precipitously over the years. A shift in emphasis from meritocracy and academic excellence to race-based affirmative action in staff recruitment and promotions as well as student enrolment has in part contributed to this fall. This has been further exacerbated by a policy to equalize academic outcomes as practiced by the predominantly Bumiputera academic and educational community. The overall end result of all these policy actions is to create race, but not merit-based, barriers that deny educational and training opportunities to many non-Bumiputera Malaysians, especially at the tertiary level. The declining quality of education has led many who have both the academic and financial capacities to seek higher education opportunities abroad. For those less financially able, but are academically very competent, there is always neighbouring Singapore that they can turn to. Once overseas, many of these young and bright Malaysians rarely return but often stay on to live and work there.

(iii) An increasing lack of intellectual, civil and human liberties that continuously restrict the space for intellectual discourse may be another factor that causes some of the brains to leave. This has been further exacerbated by religious intolerance on the part of a faction of state elites, as seen in approvals of permits for entertainment and enforcement of Islamic laws on the general public. In contrast, most of the countries

Malaysians emigrate to have a culturally and religiously liberal and tolerant milieu.

(iv) Bureaucratic inefficiency and the embracing of jingoism have led to much talents and skills being either left abroad or unutilized. Stories have been told of academically high achieving Malaysian students on scholarships granted by the Public Services Department being discharged from their bonds upon successful completion, often with flying colours, of their undergraduate studies in oversea countries. These scholars either stay back to pursue their post-graduate studies or migrate to Singapore, which gleefully welcomes them. Another category of Malaysians forced to migrate are those who marry foreigners. Malaysian women are particularly unhappy and frustrated that their foreign husbands and children cannot settle in Malaysia as permanent residents. Many of them earlier studied overseas. This gender biased ruling has led most of them to stay back overseas or to move back after a short stint here. Malaysian men who are married to foreign wives have their problems too. Often these wives have difficulty getting permanent residency status and hence work permits. And many of them are well qualified too. Their talents are left idle when potentially these could have been utilized to expand productive capacity. Frustrated, these Malaysian men and their wives often choose to migrate overseas, where the productive potential of both can be better and more fully utilized.

Pull Factors

In addition to the push factors, there are forces that attract and draw many Malaysians abroad.

(i) The first is the aggressive approach taken by many countries to draw in high economic value adding intellectuals and professionals. Packages have been drawn up to lure foreigners, including Malaysians, to migrate there. These include employer-sponsored visas (H-iB) in the USA; the Skilled Migration Programme in Australia and the very liberal granting of permanent residency and citizenship to skilled Malaysians in Singapore.

(ii) Many of these countries offer intellectually stimulating and highly rewarding jobs that allow many well qualified Malaysians to utilize their productive potential to the full. When meritocracy and academic excellence are acknowledged as the main criteria for promotion, the result is an academically and intellectually stimulating and challenging environment that will bring out the best in them. There will at the same time be an absence of disappointments and frustrations arising out of unfair race based discriminatory practices. Many Malaysians who are highly qualified want to work in these environments.

(iii) Some countries even attract talent from as young as students in Form 3 to their countries. Singapore has instituted since a long time ago the Asean scholarship to draw in very academically bright Malaysian students to study in secondary schools and later universities there. Even those who do not get scholarships but are from financially able families are sent there by their parents to study from Form 1 on, as Singapore, dubbed the "Global Schoolhouse", offers high standard education that has a more rigorous and demanding curriculum. Often, many of them do not return, preferring to stay on and work thereafter graduating with university degrees. Under this scheme, much Malaysian talent has been lost to neighbouring Singapore. I dare say that Singapore is today a high income country in part because of the huge pool of skills and knowledge drawn there from other countries. Among these, Malaysia must count as one of the largest contributors to this talent pool.

(iv) The giving of incentives such as company grant schemes to ease the costs of employing foreign skilled labour and the rebranding of cities as culturally vibrant cities aimed at attracting foreign skilled workers are among the pull factors that have drawn Malaysians overseas to cities such as Shanghai and Singapore.

Negative effects of out-migration

The large scale flight of human capital overseas can be costly in economic terms to Malaysia.

(i) For a start, the high intensity of brain drain acts as a major drain on Malaysia's produc-tive capacity. For some time now, Malaysia has been trapped in the middle income level. It is increasingly unable to compete in the low value-added, high volume and labour intensive manu-facturing activities. It wants to move into high value-added, low volume and knowledge intensive manu-facturing operations such as research and development (R&D) and design engineering in the key electronics and electrical machinery (E&E) sub-sector; new high technology industries such as green technology, renewable energy, oil and gas, biotech-no-logy, pharma-ceuti-cals; large scale commercial plantation agriculture and agro-based industries and services such as Islamic financing and tourism. While there is a long wish list, the country has been unable, with a few exceptions, to move into most of these. This is because all these require a huge pool of skills and knowledge, as well as a big class of creative and innovative entrepreneurs that we lack. As if this is not bad enough, the country faces a hemorrhage of talent. Besides losing much precious Malaysian talent overseas, Malaysia has been unable to draw in highly skilled expatriates. The New Economic Model has admitted as much to this talent crunch and the country's inability to affect a brain transplant, where brains lost are replaced by brains gained.

(ii) The country's competitive-ness and productivity have been eroded as a result of this massive brain drain. This is because innovation, which is one of the key driving factors of sustained productivity improvement, rests on a solid base of human capital which Malaysia currently lacks.

(iii) Malaysia also suffers from a direct economic cost, since Malaysians who have migrated overseas take with them a fraction, often a large one, of the value of their training sponsored by the government. The higher the levels of education attained in the country by those who have left, the greater is this cost.

(iv) Reinforcing these negative effects is the fact that the large scale flight of human capital may raise productivity growth in destination countries, which will in turn provide more incentives for people at source to leave. This may lead to widening technology gap and income differentials between receiving and sending countries. This applies to the case of Malaysia and Singapore.

How do we Arrest the Brain Drain?

To be fair, the Malaysian Government is aware of the considerable economic loss and cost to the nation resulting from this massive human capital flight abroad. It has in fact earlier responded to the problem through promulgating several programmes, all of which were aimed at drawing Malaysian talents back from overseas. Among these were the Returning Scientists Programme (1995); the Returning Expert Programme (2001) and the Brain Gain Programme (2006). However, all of these failed to achieve the aim intended. Very few Malaysians abroad took up the offers. Given that a large inflow back of our talent will help successfully effect the Economic Transformation Programme (ETP), which is one of the key pillars of the NEM, it is obvious that a rational approach would be to continue efforts to lure these talents back. This is what the NEM says it wants to do, by way of the setting up of the Talent Corporation. Meanwhile, this paper offers some suggestions, for whatever they are worth:

(i) The Malaysian Government should immediately do away with its race based affirmative action and replace it with a needs-based approach. Again, the NEM claims it wants to do precisely this over the next decade through the implementation of the Tenth (2011-2015) and Eleventh Malaysia Plans (2016-2020). However, there is a contradiction when it also says that such needs-based affirmative action will be market friendly. We are of the view that one of the failures of the market mechanism is its inability to provide a level playing field. As a result, the poor and marginalized are grossly disadvantaged, while the rich and powerful, with their abundant access to economic, social, cultural and political capital, stand to gain disproportionately from the operations of free markets. We urge the government to continue to intervene to correct market failures, but such intervention should be based on class and needs and not race. In the process, not only will there be greater social egalitarianism but the frustrations that come from racial discrimination will also be eliminated. This will remove one of the causes of human capital flight abroad.

(ii) It is also time for the Malaysian Government to acknowledge merit and excellence as the basis and criteria for recruitment and promotions and the allocation of resources, particularly within the institutions in the public sector. When the behaviour of Malaysians is driven by these criteria, the result will be hard work, creativity and innovativeness. These are the very factors that are much needed to transform Malaysia's economy from a middle income to a high income country. They will also lessen the motivation of Malaysians to move abroad.

(iii) A liberal ecosystem must also be created to stimulate creativity. As a start, the Malaysian Government must abolish all acts and legislations that curb and restrict basic freedoms such as the Internal Security Act (ISA); the University and University Colleges Act; the Printing Presses and Publications Act, etc. These draconian laws restrict intellectual discourses and disallow dissent, especially against official positions, when in fact dissent, when institutionalized, is an important source of knowledge. Intellectuals with brains want a liberal and democratic system that can provide the space for research and discourses without fear of being penalized or incarcerated. Failure to provide such a space will lead them to move to countries that can provide it. At this juncture, I need to point out that the Federal Government has announced its intention to abolish the ISA and emergency laws. This was, however, quickly accompanied by another announcement that two more laws to replace the ISA and emergency laws will be promulgated soon.

(iv) Major reforms to our institutions such as the police, the Malaysian Anti-Corruption Commission, the judiciary, and the bureaucracy must be instituted so that the abuses that some of them have committed in recent years and that have caused a great deal of anxiety to the larger public can be eliminated. When the professionalism of key state institutions is in doubt and under threat, Malaysians' confidence in these institutions' ability to provide security, protection and justice to them will be considerably eroded. A sense of hopelessness and deprivation will set in, leading to many of them, especially the more mobile ones, to migrate. However, once their independence and competence have been restored, Malaysians will feel secure and protected. This at once removes one more source of frustration that can lead to an exodus of talent. At the same time, Malaysia will also be able to attract highly skilled knowledge workers from abroad, further enriching the talent pool so much needed for the ETP.

(v) One of the key institutions that needs overhauling and revamping is our country's educational system. Essentially, there must be a return to meritocracy and academic excellence, which must be embedded in place of racism, in the governance of all levels of education. At the same time, non-academic barriers to entry, such as financial, must be removed in order for access to be further democratised and life chances, especially of the poor, further improved. If these reforms are carried out, we are confident that one of the causes of the massive outflow of talent from here to overseas will be removed.

(vi) Malaysian experts currently working abroad should be appointed to appropriate senior positions in scientific and technology-based organizations owned by the government. Generous grants should be given to them to conduct their research, while venture capital should be provided them to commercialise their creative and innovative ideas.

(vii) Permanent residencies (PRs) or even citizenship should be given generously to spouses of Malaysians married to foreigners. This will remove one of the reasons, which is the failure to obtain PRs or citizenship for their spouses, as to why these Malaysians choose to remain overseas. At the same time, these spouses, especially the very qualified ones, will be able to work and contribute to expanding Malaysia's productive capacity.

(viii) The Immigration Department must also grant speedy approvals to applications from employers for foreign skilled and knowledge workers. They should be liberal in granting at least PRs to these skilled personnel and their family members from abroad. Our Malaysian civil servants must be reminded that the market for talents is now not just regional but global. The competition to hire these talents is thus extremely intense. Their speedy response is key to enhancing Malaysia's competitiveness.

(ix) The Public Services Department (PSD) must find appropriate positions within the public sector to productively employ all PSD scholarship holders who have been sent abroad. These scholars should not be discharged so readily from their scholarship bonds.

CONCLUSION

Malaysia currently is caught in the middle income trap. It is unable to compete in the low end of the value chain but neither has it the technical and scientific capability to move into the high end of the value chain or move into high technology and knowledge intensive industries. Recently, Prime Minister Dato Seri Najib bin Tun Razak has expressed the government's desire to move out of this trap and transform our country into a high income country, through launching the NEM. This objective is indeed noble. However, it faces, among others, the key human resource constraint, which if not overcome, can frustrate the government's economic transformation programme. This constraint is manifested in two ways. One is a shortage of scientific, creative and innovative skills. The other is the flight of what scarce human capital we have, overseas. While large scale human resource development is important, equally vital is to draw back home the many skilled and experienced talents we have abroad. How successful we are in transforming our economy depends vitally on our success in carrying out these two key tasks. One essential ingredient for this success, in our view, is the dismantling of racism from our core institutional structures; an improvement in the quality of our education and a return to merit and excellence in governance.

ENDNOTES

1. Cecilia Kok and Tee Lin Say, 'Stemming the tide and keeping our talent', *Star Business Week*, 6 February, 2010.
2. Dr. Fong Chan Onn. 'Tracing the brain drain trend', *Sunday Star*, 16 May 2010, F24.
3. World Bank, 'Malaysia Economic Monitor – Brain Drain', April 2011.
4. World Bank 2011.
5. Brenda S.A.Yeoh, Singapore: Hungry for Foreign Workers at All Skill Levels

(Migration Information Source), National University of Singapore, January 2007.
6. World Bank, 2011.
7. Fong, 2010.
8. World Bank 2011.
9. World Bank 2011.

REFERENCES

Brenda, S.A. Yeoh, (2007). *Singapore: Hungry for Foreign Workers at All Skill Levels,* (Migration Information Source), National University of Singapore, Singapore, January.

Cecilia Kok and Tee Lin Say, (2010). 'Stemming the tide and keeping our talent', *Star Business Week,* Kuala Lumpur, 6 February.

Fong Chan Onn, (2010). 'Tracing the brain drain trend', *Sunday Star,* Kuala Lumpur, 16 May.

World Bank, (2011). *Malaysia Economic Monitor – Brain Drain,* Washington, April.

Annexure 1
Annual ARTDO International Conferences and their Theme

Year	*Venue*	*Theme*
2013	Melbourne, Australia	40th ARTDO International & HRD Conference
2012	Cebu, Philippines	Enriching Borderless *Learnvironments*
2011	Taipei, Taiwan	Strategic Talent Management in the Era of Globalization
2010	Kuala Lumpur, Malaysia	Leadership Focus: People Development for Peak Performance
2009	Penang, Malaysia	Developing Human Capital & Talent: The Key to Growth and Prosperity
2008	Cairo, Egypt	Human Capital: Training & Development for the Knowledge Society
2007	Bali, Indonesia	HRM, People and the Environment
2006	Bahrain	The Power Within—Strategies for Maximizing Human Potential
2005	Manila, Philippines	Unified Global HRD: Breaking Boundaries
2004	Penang, Malaysia	Management & HRD Focus on People, Performance & Progress
2003	Macao	One People – One World – The Vision for Improving Human Resources Performance
2002	Taipei, Taiwan	New Era, New Paradigm, New Strategy for Human Resources Development
2001	Melbourne, Australia	Challenging Convention
2000	Penang, Malaysia	Leadership Leap into the 21st Century: Creating Management & HRD Strategic Challenges for Performance, Results & Prosperity
1999	Bali, Indonesia	Entering the Third Millennium: Building a Dynamic Human Resources Development Architecture in the Asia-Pacific Region

(*Contd.*)

Year	*Venue*	*Theme*
1998	New Delhi, India	Comparative Management Practices in Asia & Challenges of The 21st Century
1997	Sarawak, Malaysia	HRD Challenge in the Information Age: Transforming HR with Information Technology
1996	Manila, Philippines	The HROD Professionals: Entrepreneurs of the New Millennium
1995	Melbourne, Australia	Human Resource Development in a Changing World
1994	Penang, Malaysia	Creating the 21st Century, Towards Vision 2020 HRD: Challenges, Responses and Opportunities for Growth and Prosperity in Asia-Pacific
1993	Jakarta, Indonesia	The Challenge of Human Resource Development in Asia and the Pacific Region in the 2000's
1992	Taipei, ROC	HRD Responds to Challenges and Opportunities
1991	Manila, Philippines	Asia-Pacific: A Smaller World, A Global Role and the HRD Difference
1990	Penang, Malaysia	Tomorrow Is Built Today—Meeting the Challenges of the '90's through People, Technology and Change
1989	Bangkok, Thailand	Human Resource Development in a Changing World
1988	Macao	Training for the Future: Objectives, Planning, Effectiveness
1987	Singapore	HRD: Results, Not Promises
1986	Indonesia	HRD Scenarios for the Year 2000: Preparing for the Future
1985	Petaling Jaya, Malaysia	People, Performance, Productivity
1984	Sydney, Australia	1984: The Future Is Now
1983	Taipei, Taiwan	The Role of HRD in a Changing Economy
1982	Hong Kong	Developing Human Resources—

(*Contd.*)

Year	*Venue*	*Theme*
1981	Kuala Lumpur, Malaysia	People Power—Meeting the Development Challenges of the Eighties
1980	Palmerston North New Zealand	The Training Dollar 80's and Beyond
1979	Manila, Philippines	Human Resources Development Horizons in the
1978	Ranchi, India	Training for Economic Development
1977	Suva, Fiji	Human Resources Development in the Asia-Pacific Region
1976	Canberra, Australia	Central Committee Meeting
1975	New Delhi, India	Human Resources Development—Experiences and Experiments
1974	Manila, Philippines	Organizational Meeting

Annexure 2
Name of Presidents of ARTDO International and Photographs from ARTDO International; Bahrain Society for Training and Development

Year	*Name*	*Country*
2013	Jeanne Marshall	Australia
2012	Arthur Luis P. Florentin	Philippines
2011	Samson Lee Sung-Hsien	Rep. of China
2010	Dr. Peter L.H. Chee	Malayisia
2009	Dato' Dr. Toh Kin Woon	Malaysia
2008	Dr. Helmi Sallam	Egypt
2007	Muliana Sukardi	Indonesia
2006	Ahmed M. Al Banna	Bahrain
2005	Evelyn P. Lozada	Philippines
2004	Dr. Peter L.H. Chee	Malaysia
2003	Victor Manuel Kuan	Macau
2002	Dr. Chi-Yuan Lin	Rep. China
2001	Les Pickett	Australia
2000	Dato' Dr. Thomas Chee	Malaysia
1999	Muliana Sukardi	Indonesia
1998	Prof. Dr. Vinayshil Gautam	India
1997	Datuk Haji Abdil Aziz Bin Hj. Hussain	Malaysia
1996	Mojie Ramos-Aquino	Philippines
1995	Les Pickett	Australia
1994	Dato' Dr. Thomas Chee	Malaysia
1993	Dr. Komaruddin M.K.	Indonesia
1992	Gordon L.S. Wan	Rep. of China
1991	Tomas T. de Leon	Philippines
1990	Dato' Dr. Thomas Chee	Malaysia
1989	Dr. Chira Hongladarom	Thailand
1988	Liu Chak Wan	Macau
1987	Adrian K.H. Teo	Singapore
1986	R. Heroetomo Tjokrosubroto	Indonesia
1985	Tan Sri Datuk Dr. Arshad Ayub	Malaysia
1984	Robin Roots	Australia

(*Contd.*)

Year	*Name*	*Country*
1983	Robin Roots	Australia
1982	Tan Sri Datuk Dr. Arshad Ayub	Malaysia
1981	Haji Khalid Mohd. Sidek	Malaysia
1980	Dr. Paterno V. Viloria	Philippines
1979	Dr. V. Ramchandran	India
1978	Dr. V. Ramchandran	India
1977	Jamal-ud Din	Fiji
1976	George Hines	New Zealand
1975	Dr. V. Ramchandran	India
1974	Dr. Paterno V. Viloria	Philippines

Some members of the current Executive Board of ARTDO International

Some leaders of the sponsors of this project i.e. Bahrain Society for Training and Development

Annexures

Annexure 3
A Brief on ARTDO International

ARTDO was founded on November 9, 1974 by representatives of professional training and development organizations from 12 Asian and Pacific countries who gathered in Manila for the *First Asian Regional Training and Dvelopment Conference.*

In the Silver Jubilee Conference of the Organisation held in, Delhi, November, 1998 it was agreed to change from Asian Region Training and Development Organisation to ARTDO International.

Role of ARTDO International

The Asian Regional Training and Development Organization, now known as ARTDO International, is a private non-profit organization which seeks to promote human resource development. It attempts a global reach and operation keeping in mind the Asian perspective. Its specific objectives are:

1. To assist in the formation and growth of training and development organizations.
2. To foster closer relations among these organizations.
3. To cooperate with international organizations and with private and government institutions working in the field of human resource development.
4. To encourage and sponsor researchers and publications designed to meet training and development needs.
5. To upgrade the standards of the HRD profession through a planned programme of education and skills development.
6. To serve as a resource center for training and development.

Strengthening the HRD Profession

ARTDO's main task includes support in the formation and growth of training and development organizations which cover thousands of human resource development professionals.

Amongst other efforts, ARTDO provides educational materials, information and services to its member organizations as one way of encouraging international cooperation in the areas of training and development.

ARTDO International Management & HRD Awards

Institutional Category

State Service Authority (Australia)	(2013)
Deaprtment of Civil Servant Development of Taipei City	(2012)
Meralco Management and Leadership Development Center (MMLDC)	(2011)
Atma Jaya Catholic University (Indonesia)	(2010)
Institut Bank-Bank Malaysia (IBBM)	(2009)
National Civil Service Institute (Taiwan)	(2008)
ITD Group	(2007)
Aluminum Bahrain Alba	(2006)
Saudi Aramco Oil Company	(2005)
Macau Productivity & Technology Transfer Center	(2004)
Civil Service Development Institute	(2003)
United Nations Staff College	(2002)
Asian Development Bank	(2001)
Chunghwa Telecom Co.	(2000)
United Nations Industrial Development Organization	(1999)
Singapore Institute of Management	(1998)
No. Winner	(1997)
Power Grid Corporation of India Limited	(1996)
China Productivity Centre	(1995)
Motorola Malaysia	(1994)
Sarawak Shell Berhad	(1993)
Development Training & Communication Planning (DTCP)	(1992)
UP Institute for Small Scale Industries (Philippines)	(1991)
Intel, Malaysia	(1990)
ILO Regional Office for Asia and the Pacific	(1989)
Asian Institute of Technology	(1988)
National Productivity Board (Singapore)	(1987)
Japan Productivity Center	(1986)
Training Division (Government of India)	(1985)
Asian Institute of Management	(1984)

Individual Category

Dr. Peter L.H. Chee	(2013)
Prof. Dr. Irving Yi-Feng Huang	(2012)
Mr. Samson Lee Sung Hsien	(2011)
Mr. Muliana Sukardi (Indonesia)	(2010)
Mr. Ahmed M. Al Banna (Bahrain)	(2009)
Mr. Ebrahim K. Al Dossary(Kingdom of Bahrain	(2008)
Dr. Lyndon H. Jones (UK)	(2007)
Mr. Ali M. Dialdin (Saudi Arabia/Middle East)	(2006)
Dato' Dr. Toh Kin Woon (Malaysia)	(2005)
Dr. Chi-Yuan Lin (Taiwan, ROC)	(2004)
Prof. Dr. Vinayshil Gautam (India)	(2003)
Dato' Dr. Thomas Chee (Malaysia)	(2002)
Kofi Annan (United Nations)	(2001)
Dato' Dr. Kang Chin Seng (Malaysia)	(2000)
Mr. Binay Umar (India)	(1999)
Mr. Masaaki Imai (Japan)	(1998)
Mr. Felipe B. Alfonso (Philippines)	(1987)
Mr. Bernardo F. Ople (Philippines)	(1986)
Sen. Blas F. Ople (Philippines)	(1985)
Mr. Les Pickett (Australia)	(1994)

The following countries have been represented in the organization:

- Australia
- Bangladesh
- Bahrain
- Brunei Darussalam
- Canada
- Cambodia
- Denmark
- Egypt
- Fiji
- Indonesia
- Japan
- Malaysia

- Mauritius
- Nepal
- New Zealand
- Philippines
- Papua New Guinea
- People's Republic of China
- Saudi Arabia
- Singapore
- Sri lanka
- Sudan
- Taiwan (ROC)
- Thailand
- United Kingdom
- United State of America
- Vietnam

Since member organizations are made up of individuals and/or institutions, ARTDO International effectively represents thousands of HRD practitioners actively working in such fields as industrial training, organization and management development, personnel management, vocational and technical training, non-formal education, productivity improvement, agricultural training and entrepreneurial development.

Index

Abstract subjective constructs, 23
Academic institutions, 112
Action learning, 21
Action Power Consulting Model (APCM), 13, 32–33, 36
Action research
  environment, 25
  general characteristics of, 30
  group, 29
  spiral, 35
Active export promotion, 47
Active learning attitudes, 211
Adjusted Goodness-of-Fit Index (AGFI), 231
Administrative reforms, 155, 170
Aerodynamic technology, 138
Africa Competitiveness report, 62, 64
Agricultural industry, 45
Agricultural revolution, 139
Agro-based industries, 252
Anglo-Saxon activity, 15
Arab Administrative Development Organization, 164, 168
Arms-length transactions, 184
Army Research Institute, 101
ARTDO International Management & HRD Awards, 265
Asian Development Banks, 238
Asia-Pacific Economic Cooperation, 238
Association of British Insurers, 86
Atmajaya University CHRP Programme, 175, 177, 183
Atmajaya University Continuing Education (AUCE), 181, 183

Backward integration, 125
Backward production stages, 198
Bahrain Society for Training and Development, 261, 263
Bankable projects, 196
Boston Consulting Group, 92
Brain drain acts, 252
Brain Gain Programme, 253
Broad-based departmental activity, 87
Business associations, 198
Business Development and Performance Monitoring, 124
Business Intelligence (BI), 212

Capital-and-technology-intensive industries, 237
Career development, 90, 179
Case Study of Malaysia, 244
Case study sessions, 182
Catholic University of Atmajaya in Jakarta, 175
Cause Analysis and Intervention Selection, 5
Certificate of Primary Education (CPE), 66, 73
Certified Human Resources Professional (CHRP), 175–76
Certified Management Consultant (CMC), 37
Charts/Graphs Devotion Charisma Values, 128
Civil Service Development Institute, 228
Civil Service Modernization Project, 157
Classic comparative advantage theory, 186
Codified mechanisms, 223
Collective Labour Agreement, 180
Commercial banking, 193
Commercial elements, 33
Communication revolution, 138–39
Communication Technology, 139
Community development, 28
Company grant schemes, 251
Comparative Fit Index (CFI), 231
Competition rules, 156
Competitiveness development, 40, 42
Competitiveness Policy Council, 42
Computer industry clusters, 185

Conflict resolution, 196
Consultancy activities, 106
Consulting industries, 21
Consumer price index, 45–46
Contextual factors, 117–18, 126
Continuing Education Programme, 114, 175
Continuity factors, 118
Continuous quality improvement practices, 181
Contracted industries, 46
Converging factors, 17
Coordination mechanisms, 186
Core industries, 191
Corporate Social Responsibility (CSR), 51
Cost-benefits analysis, 209
Council of Ministers, 163–64
Covariance matrix, 231
Creative industries, 237
Critical element, 61, 77, 236
Critical factors, 4
Cultural awareness, 239
Cutting Edge Practices, 1

Debt agreements, 196
Decision-Making Group, 33
Deforestation, 152
Deming, Edwards, 77
Democratic practices, 158
Departmentalizing creativity, 148
Determinant factors, 65
Development
- community, 61
- framework, 56
- institution, 61
- market, 109
- of advanced knowledge, 108, 113
- of special programmes, 110

Digital Equipment Corporation, 136
Distance education institutions, 66
Dominant industries, 83
Downstream industries, 45–47
Downstream-industry products, 45
Dynamism, 76

Early Childhood Education, 68
Economic activities, coordinated, 193
Economic conflicts, 58
Economic Transformation Programme (ETP), 253, 255–56
Education opportunities, 241
Education skills, 238
Educational community, 249
E-learning activities, 205, 207, 209, 213
E-learning Centre, 206–9, 211–12
E-learning competition practices, 209
E-learning programme, 205–6, 213
E-learning System, 204–5, 209, 211
Elite Internet Forum, 208
Employment and Collective Labour Agreement, 180
Employment contract, 214
Energy industries, 181
English employees, 239
Entrepreneurial institutions, 106, 113
Environmental factors, 86
Environmentalism, 58
Ethnic conflicts, 57
EU Multi-Stakeholder Forum, 87
European Commission, 87
European Union, 115
Export industry, 44–47
Export Processing Zone, 63

Factor analysis, 230, 233
Factor loading, 230
Fair employment practices, 87
Fellowship schemes, 106
Fixed contract, 218
Forest tracking, 97
Free market capitalism, 57
Fund managers, 190, 199

Global Value Chain (GVC), 185–87, 189, 191, 193, 199
Goal Setting Theory, 8
Goodness-of-Fit Index (GFI), 231
Green technology, 252
Group synergy, 148
Gulf Cooperation Council-GCC, 184
Gulf Institute of Management, 130
Guru Theory, 19

Healthcare company tracks, 223
Higher Education Institutions, 66, 68
Higher education, 103–4, 108–9, 111
Higher education policies, 107
HR Group, 61
Human activity systems, 19, 22–23
Human conflicts, 131
Human Development Index, 64
- international, 62
- trends, 66

Human resource (HR), 23, 54, 63–66, 72–74, 83–86, 88–90, 160–61, 168, 174–77, 179–80, 222–23, 226–28, 235, 242–43, 256

Human Resource Development Council (HRDC), 74
Human resource development, 63, 65–66, 73–74
Human resource practitioner, 100
Human resources activities, 175
Human Resources development, 176–77, 179
Human resources practitioners, 176
Incentive mechanism, 207
Industrial activities, 140
Industrial and Vocational Training Board (IVTB), 66, 70–71, 73–74
Industrial cluster formation, 196
Industrial cluster membership, 188
Industrial clusters, 184–87, 190–93, 197–98
Industrial companies, 191
Industrial development policy tools, 199
Industrial economies, 15
Industrial era, 3
Industrial firms, 237
Industrial goods, 237
Industrial innovation systems, 108
Industrial organizations, 193
Industrial R&D, 108
Industrial Relation Court, 180
Industrial Relation Dispute, 180
Industrial Relations, 175–77, 179
Industrial research, 109
Industrial revolution, 137
Industrial structure, 200
Industrial Technology, 68
Industrialisation, 237
Industry collaboration, 116
Industry-friendly universities, 109
Information and Communication Technology (ICT), 62, 64, 74–75
Information revolution, 139
Institute of Training and Development (ITD), 37
Institutional category, 265
Institutional learning capacity, 61
Institutional reforms, 160
Institutionalize continual improvement, 8
Instrument development, 228
Intellectual analysis, 129
Intelligent acting, 75
Intensive industrics, 115, 256
Inter-firm cooperation, 194
Internal Security Act (ISA), 254
International co-operation, 107
International curriculum development programmes, 109
International development, 171
International research agreements, 109
Internationalisation activities, 108
IVTB training centres, 71

Job description card, 163, 166–67, 169
Joint research centres, 110

Key driving factors, 252
Key elements, 78, 188
Key institutions, 255
Key success factors, 174
K-leaders, characteristics of, 77
Knowledge development, 102
Knowledge institution, 116
Knowledge management (KM), 9, 54–55, 60, 75–77, 80–81, 114, 179, 205, 211–12
Knowledge token mechanism, 208
  experienced-based, 112, 114
  flow of, 75, 79
  organizational common, 205
  specialized, 81, 192
  technological, 2
  theoretical, 59

Labour Management Cooperation, 180
Labour-intensive
  activities, 62
  industries, 237
Lancaster University, 25
Latin American company, 216
Leadership development, 78–79, 179, 236, 242
  philosophy, 236
Leadership dynamism, 77
Leadership education, 110–11
Leaping Forward, 1
Learning mechanism, 223
Legacy factors, 117
Longitudinal thinking, 117–19, 126
Low-wage industries, 187

Mahatma Gandhi Institute, 68
Malaysian Anti-Corruption Commission, 254
Management action, 118
Management education, 17, 24
Management faddism, 21
Managing Organizational Development, 179

Manpower Group Survey, 235
Manufacturing sector, 63, 70, 137, 197
Market mechanism, 253
Marketing department, 242
Matrix organizations, 124
Mauritius Institute of Education, 68
Mauritius Qualifications Authority (MQA), 73
Merchant bankers, 190
Minimal activities, 26
Ministry of Economic Planning and Development, 70
Mujawar, Ali Mohammed, 165
Multi-direction dynamism, 155
Mutual trust, 106

National Civil Service Institute, 228
National competitiveness development, 41–42
National Productivity and Competitiveness Council (NPCC), 73
Native tribes, 153
Needs-based affirmative actions, 253
Negative economic impact, 247
New Economic Model (NEM), 245, 252–53, 256
Normative Fit Index (NFI), 231

Open systems theory, 27
Operating Financial Review (OFR), 86
Operational logistics, 124
Operational marketing function, 125
Organisation for Economic Cooperation and Development (OECD), 103, 105, 195, 246
Organization Development approach, 10
Organization for Economic Co-operation and Development, 103
Organizational Development Research, 165
Organizational thinking, 136
Organizational values, 133
Organizational vision, 227
Outsourcing industries, 218
Overnight factories, 137
Overseas education, 248

Pension funds, 85
Permanent residencies (PRs), 255
Personal moral agency, 145
Physical element, 138
Planning activity, 35
Policies Research Development Group, 169
Policy formulation, 19
Political pluralism, 155
Porter's theory, 187
Practical Entrepreneurship Finance, 128
Private institutions, 183
Private manufacturers, 212
Private training institutions, 66
Problem Based Learning Mechanism (PBLM), 212
Procedural factors, 240
Process groups, 125
Professional associations, 181
Professional practices, 108, 113–14
Professionalism, 64, 175, 183, 254
Project Negotiation, 33
Psychosynthesis Typology theory, 133
Public administration reform, 171
Public Services Department (PSD), 250, 256
Pull factors, 248, 250–51
Push factors, 248, 250

Quality Management System, 7
Quota factors, 63

Racism, 248, 255–56
Reciprocal exchange mechanism, 208
Reductionism, 18
Regional Civil Service Development Institute, 204
Reliability analysis, 230
Reputation-Based Business Cultural Practices, 196
Research centres, 107
Research institutes, 112
Returning Expert Programme, 253
Returning Scientists Programme, 253
Reward collaboration, 60
Reward incentive mechanism, 205
Rewarding Employee Performance, 179

School of Industrial Technology, 68
Scientific analysis, 118
Scientific management theory, 3
Scientific research systems, 161
Screening mechanism, 143
Second World War, 104, 237
SEM analysis, 233
Shareable Content Object (SCO), 212
Shell Annual Report, 84
Sized Enterprises (SMEs), 107, 184–95, 197–99

Skilled Migration Programme in Australia, 250
Skills Development, 60, 73–74, 175
Social egalitarianism, 253
Social era, 156
Social responsibility index, 85
Socially responsible investment (SRI), 85
Societal institutions, 112
Socio-economic development, 160
Soft Systems Methodology (SSM), 24–28, 32, 34, 36
Software
  clusters, 198
  designers, 59
  development engineers, 72
  tools, 143
Sound warnings, 19
Special training programme, 74
Square Residual (SRMR), 231
Standardized values, 231, 233
Strategic Human Resource Development, 226–27
Strategic industries, 39–40
Strategic industry protectionism, 199
Streamlining co-promotion activity, 126
Structured Equation Analysis, 231
Structures Equation Mode (SEM), 231
Student-oriented training programmes, 109
Sugar industries, 63
Survival mechanisms, 144
Sustainable development, 41, 102

Taiwan Semiconductor Manufacturing Company (TSMC), 241–42
Talent Corporation, 253
Talent war, 221
Talent warfare, 84
Tax incentives, 63
Technical School Management Trust Fund (TSMTF), 70
Technology utilization, 223
Tertiary institutions, 68
Textile industries, 64, 68
Thailand's Export Industries, 41, 47
Top management, 117, 124, 155–56, 165, 169, 221, 241
Total Quality Management (TQM), 19–20
Tourism, 62, 71, 74, 206, 252
Trade associations, 185
  regional, 56
Traditional centres, 16
Traditional labour-intensive industries, 237
Training centres, 71
Transforming Institutional Knowledge, 53
Transitional pilot case, 157
Transparency, 160, 162–63
Trust fund mentality approach, 199
Trustworthiness, 91
T-value, 233
Types Personality Profile, 128, 133

Universal free education, 65
Universal practices, 85
University Colleges Act, 254
University of Atmajaya, 175–76, 180
University of Mauritius, 65, 67–68
Unmanageable activities, 105
Unregulated industry, 36
Upstream industries, 45–47
Upstream-industry products, 45
Upward mobility, 11

Value chains (VCs), 184, 188, 190–91, 193–95, 197–200, 256
Value creation process, 61
Value proposition, 217

Wal-Mart, 136
Warning signals, 152
Wave industrialization, 139
Wireless Learning, Mechanism for, 212
Women participation, 163
Workers
  aging, 236
  contractual, 215
  diversified, 217, 220
  global, 216, 220–21
  migrant, 237–38
  multi-cultural, 217
  retiring, 236
  traditional, 60, 218
  transient, 219, 223
  transitory, 218, 224
World Bank, 62–63, 103, 193, 246–48
World Development Report, 193
World Economic Forum, 42
World Federation of Personnel Management Associations, 236

Yoghurt industries, 199

Zero-sum game, 41